Other Books by
the Author

*For brief synopses of Mark's other books, an author profile,
as well as an engaging conversation with Mark about the
writing of* BOLDLY GOING ON YOUR INNER VOYAGE *,
please go to the Extras section at the end of this book
or visit our website at www.IFMedia.org/IFBooks.*

BOLDLY GOING
ON YOUR
INNER VOYAGE:

DAILY
MEDITATION
MANUAL

Mark S Haskett

IF BOOKS

MODESTO, CALIFORNIA

First Publication, November, 1996.
Revised Second Printing, April, 1997.
Updated/Third Edition, November, 1999.
First eBook Edition, April, 2016.
Fourth Print Edition, December, 2017.

Copyright © 2017 by Mark S. Haskett.
Published by IF Books.

ISBN 978-9971259-9-3 (print)
ISBN 978-9971259-1-7 (ebook)

Produced in the United States of America.

Table of Contents

What's New in this Edition

The format, for one thing.

While previous print editions of *Boldly Going on Your Inner Voyage* were published in a "handbook" size featuring only one daily meditation per page, this new edition offers two on each (larger) page, or four meditations per "page spread."

According to feedback the publisher has received over the years, most of the book's readers weren't using their handbooks like other "daily devotionals" that were popular when *Boldly Going* first came off the press. They were taking in several meditations at one sitting, or even a month's worth. Or they were using the new Topic/Character Index to read all the entries related to a single issue, or that were inspired by quotations from one specific character. This was especially true for readers who could use the ebook edition's touch-screen technology to instantly transport them to every meditation related to "Living in the Present" or "Self-Acceptance," say, or to those inspired by quotes from Spock or Data or Captain Janeway.

The ebook was also first to incorporate meditations based on lines from Star Trek's spate of movie "prequels" as well as the short-lived *Star Trek: Enterprise* TV series. Moreover, it introduced an Appendix that brought back all of the meditations that had been successively "retired" to make room in the 366-day annual cycle for new entries. This edition not only includes these popular updates, but additional meditations drawn from the characters and most quotable lines in 2017's spring blockbuster, *Star Trek: Beyond,* and now in the latest TV incarnation that premiered in the fall, *Star Trek: Discovery.*

Ever-improving print and ebook technologies now hold the promise of continuous updates of *Boldly Going* for as long as Star Trek's newly-introduced characters continue saying things worth meditation on! In the meantime, we hope you enjoy the current edition.

Be inspired. Again.

IF Books
Modesto, California
December, 2017

Preface

After all this time, it's still an issue. Ever since the first print edition was published in 1996 under its original title, *The Unauthorized Starfleet Daily Meditation Manual* – and now, in both an updated eBook and print-on-demand edition – many would-be readers automatically assume this is just another "Star Trek book."

It wasn't meant to be. And for the majority of people who have purchased a copy, it still isn't. Because the voyages of the starship Enterprise were never primarily about frontiers in space. They were about the frontiers within our*selves.*

Nor were all those fanciful aliens merely the inhabitants of distant planets. In reality they represented members of our own species and our own communities whom we see as "different," or who continue to challenge us in some way. Or maybe they stand for aspects of our own personalities with which we are still struggling.

Even for the serious Trekker, boldly going "where no one has gone before" was only a ruse, a gimmick to make our Inner Voyages seem more dramatic and compelling. "Space" made a convenient symbol not only for going within, but for forging ahead – into the future.

Two decades into our Third Millennium, the words spoken by Star Trek's diverse characters continue to give voice to our ongoing efforts at self-discovery and self-understanding. But as profound as those words may be, there is nothing really new in them. They simply bring the wisdom from centuries of human experience into the futuristic setting of starships and space stations, alien civilizations and "the undiscovered country."

As it turns out, Spock and Picard are only repeating lines spoken by earlier prophets and sages. Guinan and Kes merely echo the timeless voice of Mother Earth. Kirk and Dax, Worf and Burnham are simply reprising the role of scriptural hero. And the clues to our own salvation – or "self-realization" or "self-improvement" or "personal fulfillment," if those terms seem less loaded – are only translated for us, not essentially changed.

Of course, those of us who continue to enjoy an occasional late-night episode of *Star Trek: The Next Generation,* or the latest big-screen release, don't watch with all this symbolism in mind. In fact, as with any good film or novel, moral and spiritual messages often have a much greater impact if they reach us at a subconscious level. That's why, in order to get the most from this Manual, we're going to transport ourselves several centuries ahead in time, into Star Trek's vision of the future.

In other words, we're going to, well... *pretend.*

Using This Manual

To begin with, we are no longer Americans or Europeans, Africans or Asians. We're Starfleet personnel whose homeworlds are scattered all across the galaxy. And now we're embarking on a year-long mission of exploration into even more distant regions of our universe.

To optimize our mental and spiritual well-being during what might be a long and potentially dangerous Voyage, we will start each new day with a thought-provoking meditation. And who better to provoke those thoughts than "past" Starfleet officers, crewmembers and other colorful characters whose words have been recorded in the starlogs of Federation archives?

The period immediately after awakening, but before reporting for duty ("work" or "school") makes an ideal time for personal reflection. So too is the hour before we settle into our bunks at the end of our day. A quiet break in the midst of our work routine might also be effective. But what's most important, as most spiritual disciplines have confirmed through centuries of practice, is that a daily (or at least *regular*) regimen has the most lasting impact.

Of course, readers of an ebook version of the Manual may be less likely to follow this once-a-day ritual, if only because there are no separate pages to "isolate" each meditation as there were in the original handbook. Likewise this latest print version, where four consecutive day's readings are spread before you, making it harder to quit after just one. Regardless of your reading regimen, it's best to allow time to ponder each meditation, to reflect on how it might relate to your daily life, and to repeat the "affirmations" at the end of each one. If a different affirmation or action would be more appropriate to your specific circumstances, feel free to create another for yourself, and be sure to recite it aloud. Either way, *applying* it at the first available opportunity – to "learn by doing," as Captain Kirk would say – is the most efficient way to turn each daily lesson into genuine personal growth.

Since the numeral preceding each quotation/meditation/affirmation corresponds to Earth's solar calendar, you may want to begin the book by turning to whatever today's date happens to be. Or you can simply let the meditation on page "01.01" represent the first day you start reading the Manual, whether the current day is June 8th or November 23rd. After all, *some*where in the galaxy, a brand new year is beginning right now.

As you commence your voyage, keep in mind that the quotations that inspire each meditation were spoken in the context of "previous" voyages of exploration. For this reason alone they should have historical significance for those of us who follow. But there are also deeper meanings hidden within them... meanings that transcend the boundaries separating past, present and future... that blur the distinction between Star Trek's warp-speed space adventures and our own, more deliberate voyages into our selves.

And it doesn't matter whether you're a seasoned Trekker, or you have only a passing familiarity with the franchise. The stories of The Enterprise, Voyager, U.S.S. Discovery and all the rest are *our* stories. The challenges and obstacles their crewmembers faced are the same ones *we* face every day. And the inner resources they learned to call upon, that gave them strength to overcome all those challenges and obstacles, are the same resources now available to us.

Inevitably, by the end of this year's Inner Voyage, we will all be different people. By next year, chances are we won't simply be "going along for the ride." We may even find ourselves in the proverbial Captain's Chair.

Make it so.

CORRESPONDING TO THE MONTH OF

January

01.01

A person's life — a future — hinges on each of a thousand choices. Living is making choices.

— CAPTAIN PICARD : A MATTER OF TIME : 45349.1

Some decisions feel like they're "forced on us." Some events occur that seem beyond our control. And yet our lives are still basically in our own hands, if only because we can control our reactions to those "uncontrollable" events. We can choose to feel angry or helpless… or we can choose to learn from the experience and move on.

More importantly, we can also take the initiative. Because all around us are keys to our own future. These are the choices we make hundreds of times a day, that accumulate slowly, over time, to make us what we are. They're the opportunities to stop and listen to another person – or hurry off again because we're "late for an appointment." They're the frequent occasions we have to break old habits, to exert a little self-discipline; to say a kind word rather than an angry one; to forgive and release rather than hold on to the past.

We often fail to acknowledge how crucial these little choices can be. For they not only express Who We Are, they literally *re*-create us with each new moment. They take us along the same familiar path, or they point us in new, more promising directions – perhaps to where no one has gone before.

I am ready to go where I have never gone before, into the future I will create through my choices, by first accepting that I alone am responsible.

01.02

The greatest danger facing us is… our irrational fear of the unknown. But there is no such thing as the unknown. There are only things temporarily hidden, temporarily not understood.

— CAPTAIN KIRK : CORBOMITE MANEUVER : 1512.2

A similar refrain is repeated not only in Earth's history, but throughout most other planetary societies: We have nothing to fear but fear itself.

Biologically speaking, fear is a completely natural survival response. It tells us not to react hastily, not to get involved until we know what we're up against. We need to better understand the situation, to consider our options – assuming there's time. That's only logical. Fear is what "the need to know more" *feels like* emotionally.

But when we concentrate on the "fear itself" instead of the situation our fear is urging us to investigate, that emotion can paralyze us. And then it no longer serves its biological purpose.

Fear is the emotional trumpet blast that calls us to advance, not retreat. It's our sense of inner resources gathering themselves for The Mission, to go out in search of what is temporarily hidden and not yet understood.

And when we find it, we'll understand.

Courage – boldness – is not the opposite of fear, not an "antidote." These qualities are its offspring. I will acknowledge and embrace my fears, and look beyond them to the wonderful opportunities The Universe is now arranging for me.

01.03

One can begin to reshape the landscape with a single flower.

— SPOCK : UNIFICATION, PART II : 45245.8

As the ancient holy books say, Creation will always remain unfinished – if only because sentient beings like ourselves are essential to the "finishing" process.

But when we look around at what's yet to be done, we can easily lose heart: Poverty, ignorance and destruction still exist on a large scale, despite education and technological "progress." Physical and spiritual wastelands still occupy much of the galaxy, as well as the recesses of our own hearts. What difference can one person make?

Which is exactly the excuse reeled out by those who prefer to avoid any responsibility.

Fortunately, the ancient holy books also say that we're not required to finish our various tasks, only to contribute to their completion. Or sometimes, if The Universe so honors us, to begin a *new* task and thereby inspire others to contribute to its completion.

A single flower, symbolically speaking, can be enough. In fact, planting and nurturing that one tender shoot may be far more important in the scheme of things than the wholesale transformation of the landscape. Overcoming inertia, going ahead regardless of the odds – these are the hallmarks of redemption, not the final outcome.

I refuse to let the magnitude of the task prevent me from getting started. If I am sincere, and the goal worthy, The Universe will provide help.

01.04

I can't sacrifice the present waiting for a future that may never happen.

— COMMANDER CHAKOTAY : RESOLUTIONS : 49690.1

As responsible Starfleet personnel we often think our goals should be about our next assignment, about career advancement, about future honors and achievements. Most of what we're striving for is "out there." We expect our efforts to be rewarded at some future date – when we've paid our dues, put in our time; when we've finally earned it.

But if this attitude controls our thinking, we've made a fundamental mistake about what goals are *for*. Because planning for the future is not primarily about improving our conditions at some later time. The value of a goal is less in giving us something to "achieve" than something to guide our thoughts and actions in the present.

In short, we shouldn't select our goals based on the difference they might make in the distant future. We should choose a goal for the difference it makes in our lives *now*.

Ask yourself: Is the discipline and effort of working toward your goal fulfilling in itself, even if "someday" never arrives? Does your goal inspire you to look more closely at the world around you, and enable you to experience your life and your *self* more fully? Can you feel your outlook and attitudes being transformed by your steady progress toward your goal into a less isolated, more spiritually-connected, more joyful individual?

Let the future you seek make your present come alive!

The right future for me is the one that helps me draw more growth and fulfillment – and more lasting joy – from each new moment.

01.05

The more difficult the task, the sweeter the victory.

— COMMANDER RIKER : CAPTAIN'S HOLIDAY : 43745.2

It's a cliché in a thousand different languages, on a hundred different planets. But no less true.

It's also a good thing to remember – and to repeat as often as necessary – when frustrations pile up, when our best efforts fail, when defeat follows us like a plague.

We should be thankful there are no medals given for mediocrity. No one deserves cheers for doing "the minimum required," or for taking "the easiest route." Difficulty is necessary for excellence. And for a bigger payoff.

Then again, sometimes the payoff isn't what we think. Sometimes the real victory is one more hurdle away.

Which is why so many of the rewards of all our hard work turn out to be so unsatisfying. Our trophies and Certificates of Merit only end up gathering dust. Even the long-awaited benefits of "the good life" can turn sour.

Because the sweeter victories come from the difficult work we do *within*. Like overcoming our own anger and negativity. Like learning how to be a genuine friend. Like knowing that what you did was the right thing to do, even if it wasn't the most popular. Or like discovering that there's goodness and meaning in everything that happens to us.

Even in the events we once considered "defeat."

I neither seek difficulty nor shrink from it. The choice is not whether the task is difficult, or how big the reward, but whether it is right.

01.06

Sometimes you have to go in blind. That's the exciting part.

— CAPTAIN JANEWAY : INNOCENCE : Stardate Not Given

Naturally, we're more comfortable when we know what to expect. We feel more confident, more "in control." But sometimes we *can't* know what to expect; we don't have enough data. Or *any* data. Yet we're forced to act.

At times like this we must remember that we're never really "blind." We may use that term to describe how we feel at the moment. We may call ourselves "blind" because we're not conscious of the resources that are there to help us. But that doesn't mean we *have* no resources.

In fact the resources that often help us most are the very ones we are not conscious of, that work below the level of our awareness. For example, in critical situations where lightning-fast decisions must be made, it's often better to trust our instincts, to not think things through logically. If we're meditating regularly, if we've begun linking ourselves to others and to The Universe in our daily thoughts and actions – those "instincts" will come from our spiritual network, not just us.

And the "exciting part" is simply the anticipation of finding out that we weren't blind after all; that a higher Power was seeing *for* us; and that sometimes it's not a matter of knowing what to expect, but simply expecting to know... when the time comes.

The Inner Voyage opens me to the inflowing of Universal Wisdom. Guidance comes as I ask for it.

01.07

A little suffering's good for the soul.

— DR. McCOY : STAR TREK / PREQUEL : CIRCA 2258

The Inner Voyage does not demand that we suffer in order to grow spiritually. But some of our most important spiritual growth comes from *having* suffered.

Many ancient disciplines inflicted suffering on adherents for that very reason. Some Earth-centered traditions still require physical ordeals of various kinds, from self-denial to self-flagellation, from afternoons spent in sweat-houses to weeks of meandering "walk-abouts." And while these ordeals are in a sense "artificial," they often teach valuable lessons.

But the trials of everyday life continue to be our most profound teachers: Facing the death of a loved one; recovering from a broken relationship; dealing with failure, (especially when others were counting on us). After our inevitable periods of suffering have passed – and they *do* pass – we can begin to make sense of them, place them into the larger context of our lives… we can "be philosophical" about it all.

On the other hand, trying to be philosophical about our suffering while still undergoing it is not just "hard," as Dr. Crusher would later observe. It's one of the worst things we can do. Because we need to *feel* the pain of our losses, not just analyze them. We need to fully experience our experiences before we start theorizing about their meaning. For only then do we have the raw data – sometimes very raw – from which true wisdom may come.

I do not seek suffering, but I will not close my heart to it. Nor will I rush to "understand" my suffering, but allow any lessons to emerge in their own time.

01.08

The things I do for money!

— QUARK : MERIDIAN : Stardate Not Given

Most of us have expressed the same surprise – or even horror – at what we sometimes give in trade for our standard of living.

Actually, our surprise is a healthy sign. It shows that we not only have a standard of living, but standards for *making* a living. And every now and then we find ourselves bumping up against them.

We shouldn't pass off these occasions too lightly. They are opportunities to further refine our standards, to ask ourselves what we would – and *wouldn't* – do for money. The answer can help us define Who We Are and what we believe.

Our beliefs, after all, are not mere theological "speculations." They're what we do. They're the priorities we establish, the values we demonstrate by our willingness to sacrifice our time and possessions on some things, less so for others.

What often surprises us is how easily we sacrifice what are presumably "higher" values – honesty, friendship, peace of mind – in pursuit of money. Which means we value money more, we "believe" in money more. We end up "serving" money in ways not unlike many ancient cultures served their idols.

But what happened to them need not happen to us.

My first priority is to learn and do what The Universe calls me to do. The money will follow.

01.09

Confidence is faith in oneself. It can't easily be given by another.

— COUNSELOR TROI : LOUD AS A WHISPER : 42477.2

Most of us have less than we'd like. A few of us operate on very little. And all of us, sooner or later, will face that terrifying moment where our personal supply of it seems to have evaporated entirely.

We often talk about "confidence" in this way — as if it's some kind of commodity we can measure and use and sometimes "run out of" like the fuel in the combustion-powered vehicles of past centuries. And yet most of us also recognize that confidence is an inner quality. A *faith.*

The problem is, faith in oneself doesn't come out of the blue. We usually "earn" it by attempting new things and generally succeeding at them. And if, instead, we experience mostly failure in those attempts, then maybe it's just as well we're *not* confident since, that way, we're less likely to go out and fail again.

On the other hand, maybe the problem is our mistaken assumption that "faith in oneself" means relying solely on one's own resources. Or on needing to succeed.

Genuine confidence flows from our sense of being connected to resources beyond our own — or beyond anyone else's. It's the realization that the power which created the universe lies within us… that it nurtures us still, even when we "fail." And sometimes *because* we do.

My strength lies in being aware of my connectedness to The Universe – and through it, to others.

01.10

Are we there yet?

— LIEUTENANT CHEKOV : STAR TREK BEYOND : CIRCA 2263.3

Mothers and fathers across the galaxy have no doubt heard this simple question from their children, probably as many times as there are stars above the dome enclosing Yorktown. And children aren't the only ones asking, even if (unlike Chekov) they use more words.

Because all of us have a tendency to be impatient. We all want to *be there.* We want the waiting to be over, the job completed, the goal attained. It's the curse of modernity: There's always so much to do, and so little time. Just get it done already!

The antidote to this, and to the debilitating stress it causes both to our bodies and our psyches, is not to become more "efficient" with our time, to learn how to manage it more wisely. It is to accept the lesson taught to us by the Ancients for countless generations: Take pleasure in the journey itself, not only the destination.

Getting there quickly is sometimes crucial, of course. It would be counter-productive for the Olympic athlete to distract herself by taking notice of the way her track shoes grab the abrasive surface as they push from the starting blocks, to survey the roaring crowd as she rounds the final turn toward the finish line, to admire the sheen of perspiration on her opponents' faces as they all lunge for the tape. But even in this example, the victory isn't so much about winning the race. It's about the training beforehand, the gradual gain in one's strength and endurance, the satisfaction in small improvements, about overcoming one's fear of failure. It's the serene, inner conviction that even if one finishes in second place — or last place — all the effort was worth it. *Well* worth it.

Being there, or being first, is not why I strive. To make the effort is to win.

01.11

The real secret is, turn disadvantage into advantage.

— RIVA : LOUD AS A WHISPER : 42477.2

It's nice to be handed things on a silver platter. To have our accomplishments come easily. To enjoy the benefits provided by birth or position. Or plain, dumb luck.

But it's a far greater "gift" to have *earned* those benefits through planning and hard work; through successfully overcoming the interior and exterior obstacles that hold us back; through turning what seemed like a disadvantage into the very thing that leads to our salvation.

Exactly *how* to do that is one of life's enduring questions. Because the answer is different for everybody. But everyone who succeeds *does* begin in the same place.

The starting point is a change in attitude. It is our decision to stop calling the world "unfair" if it doesn't lay its riches at our feet (like it seems to do for many other people). It's the recognition that the obstacles in our lives are really the urgings of a loving Universe to learn something essential to our spiritual progress, to win our fight against the flaws and weaknesses that impede us. It's our realization that the person we can become after we've fought that battle will be far wiser, far stronger, and far more fulfilled than we could ever be without having fought it.

I accept my "disadvantages" as opportunities for growth. I recognize the obstacles in my Path as the secret gateways to a higher, stronger Self.

01.12

We learn by doing.

— ADMIRAL KIRK : THE WRATH OF KHAN : 8130.3

The opposite used to be called, in colloquial terms, "book larnin'." In most planetary cultures, learning from books – or from computer files or video – has at times achieved a status far in excess of its true educational value. Amazing as it now seems, university degrees and special honors were once conferred on individuals not for demonstrated abilities or real life skills, but merely for absorbing and regurgitating the contents of certain prescribed repositories of information.

The fallacy of this approach became evident late in Earth's twenty-first century, when methods were developed to electronically transfer vast amounts of information and "book knowledge" directly into the human brain. What once took years of "study" could be accomplished in a few sessions of cortical data transmission (CDT).

Books, however, can still serve a purpose. *This* book has value – at least potentially – because it's what we can learn by applying it that makes a difference. It's the information we absorb and then refine by *living* it that empowers us. It's the knowledge that is eventually reflected in our behavior, that has seeped into our very muscles and nerves, that alone can transform our lives and our world.

Of course, in doing anything, we're bound to make mistakes. Fortunately, that's often how we learn best.

I welcome opportunities to turn mere "information" into genuine knowledge by applying it in my daily life and relationships. I do, therefore I know.

01.13

Curious how often you humans manage to obtain that which you do not want.

Insightful as ever, Spock has put his finger on it: It's almost as if we have some magnetic power to attract the very things we don't want. Or the things we fear most.

And it's not just humans. Any sentient being will attract what it thinks about often enough. Or with enough emotion. And since our psychic (or spiritual) energy can't be a negative force, *not* wanting something sends energy to that "something" just as much as if we wanted it!

Which simply means we'd better spend our time thinking about what we *do* want, not what we don't. But even when we get what we want, it's "curious" how often we act as if we don't really want it. Many people with high-ranking positions, fancy shuttlecraft and luxurious domiciles are still as joyless and unfulfilled as ever. Why?

The answer is, what we truly "want" cannot be found in the world of objects and events. Though we can generate the energy to help bring these things about, genuine fulfillment comes from *inner* riches. Like developing an attitude of love and acceptance. Or learning to value relationships and experiences over material possessions.

Ironically, if we've been getting a lot of what we don't want lately, at least it shows that we *can* affect reality. And besides, maybe what we *do* want is a little clearer to us now.

Starting today, I will devote less time to "wanting," and more time to thinking about what I really need.

01.14

You gotta get in the spirit of things. Learn to be spontaneous... live in the moment.

— DR. CRUSHER : GENERATIONS : 48650.1

There's something delightfully liberating about allowing oneself to embrace the moment, to "go with the flow." But true spontaneity isn't blanket permission to do whatever "feels right." It's not about saying "yes" to every opportunity that pops up, to follow emotion over reason, to stop planning things and just let them "happen." Spontaneity *requires* planning. Or at least preparation.

An ancient wisdom tradition talks about a process that underlies all existence, a Way, a Tao that seeks to express itself through nature as a whole, and through the actions of individual beings. Known as "Spirit" in other traditions, the Way works quietly, inevitably, toward wholeness and harmony. It blends the needs of each individual with every other, so that all things work for the greatest good.

In order to participate in this process, however, we must first acknowledge that we're part of it. We must also accept that our way is subservient to *its* Way – if only because its "consciousness" embraces the entire universe and ours doesn't. Finally, we must learn to tell the difference between its still, small voice, and the noisy shouting of our own limited perceptions.

To be prepared to listen, and then act, is to be spontaneous.

I open myself to increasingly more opportunities for The Universe to act through me, by learning increasingly more about The Universe.

01.15

Only fools have no fear.

— LIEUTENANT WORF : COMING OF AGE : 41416.2

The goal of spiritual growth is not to deny physical emotions, or somehow banish them from one's life – even if that were possible. Fear, for example, is one of the most universal emotions among physical beings. And one of the most fortunate.

In the evolution of autonomous life forms, those forms which could "feel" fear had a decisive advantage over those who could not. Fear, after all, heightens the senses; it pumps energy into the system. Surprisingly, it can also galvanize "community" because fear seeks safety in numbers, and a communal response is usually the most thoughtful and effective over the long haul.

To completely lose one's fear, therefore, means to cut oneself off from a valuable personal and communal resource. And if a "fool" is defined as an individual who acts without a genuine connection to self and community – what some people might call a "loose phaser" – then to act with no fear is indeed foolish.

Not that we should let our fears run rampant. Our Inner Voyage (or Spiritual Path) encourages us to acknowledge their existence, to honor them for the positive role they've played in bringing our species to this point. For only then can we enlist their energy in a higher service.

My fears are natural. But they do not control me. By facing them I will transform them. By accepting them, I can assign them a new role in my life.

01.16

To function in any human activity, you must learn to form relationships.

— DATA : DEJA Q : 43539.1

All across the universe, the most successful species are those who balance personal independence with some form of "social contract." We live in groups of interacting individuals because we are thereby able to benefit from each others' strengths. We trade on what one person can produce for another. Our own knowledge and experience are multiplied by everyone else's in the community. Not to mention that the community provides mutual protection.

In exchange for all these group benefits, we agree to interact according to certain rules and patterns. And in putting these rules and patterns into daily practice, we learn to "form relationships."

It seems less a question of "spirituality" than what's practical. Relationships help us live; sometimes our very survival depends on it. Still, in relating to one another we are doing more than exchanging goods and services. Our relationships provide the clearest mirror of what we think and feel, what we value, what we believe. In fact, we learn more about who we are by "relating" to others than by any other method of self-discovery.

And if we aren't satisfied by what we see, we can work to improve ourselves – by improving our relationships.

My relationships with others are extensions of Who I Am. I grow by nurturing those relationships, by learning from them, by celebrating them.

01.17

I seem to be the last to know just about everything around here!

— THE DOCTOR : TIME AND AGAIN : Stardate Not Given

Voyager's holographic medical man often puts into words the frustrations we all feel. And one of the worst frustrations is living *re*actively rather than *pro*actively.

So much of our life is spent reacting to events instead of shaping them, in handling the latest crisis rather than carrying out a preconceived plan. That's why things can feel "out of control." Half the time we have no idea what's headed our way until it arrives. And by then it's too late.

The Doctor had an excuse: He was often "turned off" between medical emergencies. We, on the other hand, have the ability to remain "on" if we choose. And we do so not by trying to plan our lives down to the last detail, or by inventing some scheme that somehow eliminates all the surprises in our lives. (Not that we'd succeed, anyway. As one of Earth's most beloved troubadours wrote, "Life is what happens while you're busy making other plans.") Rather, we leave ourselves "on" by being more present to the world around us, by connecting with the world at deeper levels than the merely physical.

Meditation can help. Because by connecting with our selves we connect with The Universe. And The Universe already knows what's headed our way.

True "knowing" comes from within. I will look to my inner Source for help in guiding my actions, and my reactions will take care of themselves.

01.18

Give yourself some credit!

— KES : PHAGE : 48532.4

Most recent converts to the practice of meditation probably know a lot about stress. Many are high achievers – both professionally and personally – and are usually more critical of themselves than any Starfleet officer.

Meditation is often begun as a necessary antidote to this kind of pressure-cooker lifestyle. But as Kes reminds us, there's another exercise that can also work wonders.

Everyone knows that emotionally healthy children are more often rewarded for good behavior than punished for the bad. Yet how often do we apply this simple strategy to our own development? How many times have we achieved some personal goal, or successfully overcome some inner flaw, and really rewarded ourselves for it?

Too often we think that, because we're adults, our achievements should be enough of a reward "in themselves." Or at least that doing the right thing will "eventually pay us back." Intellectually, we may know this to be true. The trouble is, our emotional lives thrive on immediate feedback. Our bodies need to *feel* it . . . now.

We can re-educate our bodies to enjoy learning and growing by giving ourselves the emotional equivalent of a warm hug or pat on the back. If this seems too childish, remember that new patterns and directions are *like* children. And we know how to produce healthy ones.

I deserve to celebrate my successes. I will reward myself as an incentive to continue growing.

01.19

You were a good officer... until you weren't.

— FIRST OFFICER SARU : CONTEXT IS FOR KINGS : Stardate 1389.5

Some of our wrong turns in life, our personal failures, our moral downfalls, are so sudden and dramatic that they can easily catch everyone off-guard. Everything seems fine... until it isn't.

Most people harbor secrets from the past and hidden corners in their private lives of which others are unaware. So it should come as no surprise when someone else's scandalous behavior or appalling actions strike us as "out of character," leaving us wondering what clues we might've missed. But when our *own* actions likewise baffle us, it's time for some genuine soul-searching.

Because it's obvious we *did* miss something. Maybe an unseen wound has been festering. Or we're supressing anger or hurt. And either we stopped running the regular "self-diagnostics" that all operating systems require to prevent a meltdown, or we've never instituted the weekly sabbaths or other ritual observances designed to provide an environment for self-reflection and healing.

When we hide behind false fronts or mindless entertainment that leaves no time for spiritual housekeeping, we're only asking for trouble. And just as good government demands transparency to prevent corruption, so it is with our personal lives. We must find a community where we can be fully open to others, and to ourselves, so we can root out corruption... *before* a meltdown occurs.

I will seek full transparency in myself, so I'll have nothing to hide from others.

01.20

You can settle for less in ordinary life. Or do you feel like you were meant for something better? Something special...?

— CAPTAIN PIKE : STAR TREK / PREQUEL : CIRCA 2255

Many of our frustrations in life — the seemingly out-of-the-blue outbursts of anger that characterized Kirk's early life, for example — are actually messages from our own subconscious. And one of the most common messages is: "You are meant for more. You can *be* more."

But that's only half of it. The other half is the question, "What are you doing to achieve it?" And what really frustrates us is our secret suspicion that the answer is, well, "Not so much."

Whenever we feel this way The Universe is basically asking us to stop, and think... to define our dreams. And then to decide what price we're willing to pay to achieve them.

It may take a while, but most of us will finally realize that "something better" isn't about amassing material things, or even the accolades our achievements might earn. It's about the treasures *within,* the spiritual work that brings balance and purpose, connection and service to others.

At the same time, we shouldn't underestimate the simple satisfactions of an "ordinary life": The process of getting an education, building job skills, raising a family, putting money away for a down payment and a two-week vacation and a comfortable retirement. Even so-called "ordinary" lives are filled with a beauty, with awe, with satisfactions many "special" people will never know.

And let's not forget that Captain Pike was doing a "sales job" when he spoke these words to an aimless and impetuous Kirk. In the end, defining our dreams isn't meant to drive us toward fame and fortune, but to start us down the path of refining our souls.

I am special not because of my dreams, but because of the opportunity The Universe has given me to better my Self.

01.21

Do not fear your negative thoughts. They are part of you. They are part of every living thing.

— LIEUTENANT TUVOK : COLD FIRE : Stardate Not Given

Even Vulcans have been known to harbor low opinions of themselves or others. Or to be seized by the idea of doing something contrary to their own high standards.

Actually, negative thoughts are a natural by-product of a healthy imagination. The same mental process that makes us aware of our options does not also censor them for us. In response to the events in our lives, several possibilities for action will inevitably spring to mind. It's not unusual when one or more of these thoughts are judged by our conscience as immoral. Even repulsive.

The fact that we have these thoughts does not require us to act on them. In a sense, by giving us a wide range of choices, including negative ones, our subconscious is affirming its "trust" that we'll make the *right* one. In fact, the right choice is often all the more obvious and compelling precisely because we *can* imagine the negative possibilities. The mind is only doing its job.

Our job is to take the energy of those thoughts – the anger, the impulse to lash out, the thrill of a secret fantasy – and transform it. Having had the negative thought, we are now empowered to be even more positive.

My negative thoughts arise from the same source as my positive ones. They are necessary building blocks that support my positive goals and actions.

01.22

The ride's going to get a little bumpy. Things are going to happen fast. Just keep alert, stay calm. Let's focus on what we're doing.

— ENGINEER LA FORGE : ARSENAL OF FREEDOM : 41798.2

Sounds a lot like our lives, doesn't it?

The ride can be bumpy at times. Things happen fast. And the physical sensations can easily distract us from what we're doing – or what we're *supposed* to be doing.

Sometimes we get carried away with all the thrills and turn the trip into a pointless joy ride. Or, what's more likely, all those bumps frighten and disturb us, and getting rid of them becomes more important than getting to where we're going.

The Inner Voyage helps us, first of all, by preparing us for the fact that the ride *is* bumpy. And if we *expect* all those bumps, maybe we'll be less likely to over-react when they occur.

More importantly, the Voyage reassures us that it's "we" who are going somewhere, not just "me." La Forge says "Let's focus on what we're doing" as if to remind us that we're all on this ride together; that we depend on one another; that if we concentrate on our own assigned duties we may not even notice the bumps anymore.

And the mission – our lives – will be a success.

Today I will be alert, yet calm, focusing on my duties rather than my comfort, and thereby allow others to focus on theirs.

01.23

The stars are not just up in the sky. They're all around us.

— COMMANDER SISKO : EXPLORERS : Stardate Not Given

Stars have played a symbolic role in almost every culture the Federation has encountered. Most often, stars represent other-worldly forces that somehow seem to affect – and even control – our lives. Or else they symbolize the hidden patterns in seemingly random events. Or the bright spots in our otherwise dark existence. Or the individuals who illumine our lives in some special way.

In the fables of several planets, stars are the "windows of heaven," portals in some celestial veil through which we glimpse the glories of a dimension beyond this one.

Each interpretation, in its own way, represents a truth. But what all of them seem to suggest is that these other powers and personalities are distant and distinct from us. They are inaccessible, above and beyond our ordinary experience or ability. We cannot understand or become like them, much less control them. Different rules apply.

Benjamin Sisko wisely reminds us that this view is flatly wrong. The forces that shape our lives *can* be known. The lights that brighten our lives and illumine our paths need not be limited to pinpoints in the night. If we open our spiritual eyes, they are everywhere, bathing us in their power. And we are made of the very same star-stuff!

The power of the Universe surrounds me, sustains me, energizes me. I can reach "up," or go within. I am a luminous body no less than the stars.

01.24

Feelin' philosophical, huh? A massive blood loss will do that to you.

— DR. McCOY : STAR TREK BEYOND : CIRCA 2263.3

Sleep is nature's demand that we take time out of every day to restore our bodies and reconfigure our subconscious minds. The sabbaths and worship services of earlier times were mandates to undertake the same process on a conscious and regular basis.

Sometimes, however, we ignore these opportunities for restoring and reconfiguring… that is, until life reminds us with some sort of crisis during which our very survival may be at stake.

Assuming we *do* survive, we must take these life-threatening events as not-so-subtle hints to contemplate (as Spock says just prior to McCoy's observation) "the nature of mortality." And the result of those contemplations needn't be a decision to avoid any further risk or the possibility of losing more plasma in the pursuit of one's goals. In fact, sometimes we need to double-down on those goals, to head straight back to the battlefield once our wounds are healed, to accept that life may be testing us.

McCoy's use of the word "philosophical" wasn't for nothing. The word "philosophy," after all, means "love of wisdom" or "love of knowledge." That's what our battles in life are about – gaining wisdom, going back into the fray with a little more knowledge, a greater appreciation for life's challenges, greater respect for what we're up against.

And why we're up against it.

I will react to the crises in my life as occasions to become "philosophical," to ask myself what lessons may be learned, and to remind myself that life's most important lessons often come at great price.

01.25

I'm not bothered by what people think of me!

— LIEUTENANT TORRES : PARALLAX : 48439.7

It's an affirmation we would all do well to repeat.

Because what others think is no substitute for one's own internal guidance system. To let other people's view of us determine our thinking is dangerous not merely because they can't always be there every time we need guidance. What's worse is that we learn to distrust our own inner resources, our own innate ability to decide for ourselves, our own direct com-link with The Universe.

Which is not to say we should ignore what others think. Other people frequently have insights and experiences that can complement our own. Not to mention that seeing ourselves through others' eyes is a useful way to objectively assess our talents and flaws. Other people's opinions can also act as a check against "privatizing" reality, against our pretense that the world revolves solely around what we happen to think at any given moment.

In the end it's not a question of whether to ignore or to consider the views other people have of us. Or even whether we finally agree or disagree with those views.

It's simply a matter of not being *bothered* by them.

Other people may form opinions about me. But it's what I think about myself that determines my course of action... and my happiness.

01.26

On Earth, there is a cautionary tale about the dangers of releasing a magical creature called a genie from a bottle. Once it's out, it's extremely difficult to put back in.

— DR. PHLOX : THE FORGOTTEN : CIRCA ECE2154

Like genies waiting impatiently for their release, there are hidden resources and powerful energies within nature that are ripe for discovery. The Arabian fable about the Magic Lamp expresses our shared sentiment that the Universe is an awesome, wondrous place, full of powers we can somehow harness, that might even work miracles if and when we release them.

But there are rules. And all-too-often unforeseen consequences. Nuclear power can fuel an entire planet's energy needs, but it can also turn whole cities to rubble. Technology and artificial intelligence have replaced manual labor and helped to manage the affairs of nations all across the galaxy… but in some cases these have gone on to enslave and finally eliminate their creators.

Understood on an deeper level, the Magic Lamp represents not the physical world, but the incredible power of consciousness, and especially our subconscious, to bring us spiritual and material riches. But here again there are rules, and unforeseen consequences. That's why there are gurus and rabbis and psychologists to offer guidance, not only for discovering these unseen powers, but for controlling them.

Knowing the "spell" to release them is the easy part. Knowing how to keep from falling under their spell is much more difficult. And if, as the story goes, the genie within us will grant just three "wishes," hopefully we'll know what we really want – or rather, what we *need* – by the third one.

My first wish is to know myself. My second is to find my path. My third is to share my discoveries, and myself, with others.

01.27

If we can help, we should.

— CAPTAIN JANEWAY : STATE OF FLUX : 48658.2

As we grow into a relationship with The Universe, as we become more and more aware of our connection to everything around us, the idea of "luck" becomes less meaningful, less operative. We realize that events never truly happen "by chance."

We find new information and knowledge being given to us at the precise moment we're ready to absorb it. Events conspire to send us on new voyages of discovery soon after the urge to explore new vistas excites our imagination. And if we get into trouble along the way, help seems to come to us just when we need it.

The Universe, somehow, seems to be shepherding our lives, actively leading us along the paths of our becoming. And it's not just "events" that play a decisive role in our growth. More often it's *people.*

So it should not surprise us when we are asked to become the agents for growth or assistance in other people's lives. Whenever we find ourselves in a position to help someone who needs it, we ought to assume that this event, too, is no mere "coincidence."

In fact, whether or not we accept the opportunity to help becomes part of our own ongoing development. For as we help others grow, we help ourselves grow.

I gratefully accept the help that The Universe continually arranges for me. And I open myself to the opportunities It provides for helping others.

01.28

Running away solves nothing.

— CAPTAIN PICARD : COMING OF AGE : 41416.2

It's one of the hardest lessons to learn — and among the two or three most essential: Our relationships and our external conditions are primarily a reflection of our *internal* conditions. Our spiritual understanding and attitudes inevitably create the physical reality we live with. Our "world" mirrors our "self."

Running away therefore can't solve anything because we can never escape ourselves. The same problems that plague us in our present surroundings or relationships will haunt us in the next, and the next — until we finally deal with the inner turmoil or spiritual defects that continue to generate those problems.

Not that "running away" is always a mistake. Sometimes the temporary respite we get from changing our physical environment gives us the mental distance we need to objectively face our problems. That's why there are spiritual retreat centers. That's why a regular "sabbath" is still practiced by many planetary cultures.

That's also why recreation is so important. Because to change our world, we must engage in re-creation. We must re-create our world from the inside out. And if we run anywhere, it must be to that sacred place within each of us where true transformation begins.

I'm finished with running. So that I may live fully with others, I will learn to live with myself. So that I can love others, I will learn to love myself. Starting now.

01.29

There are a million ways to the Captain's Chair. Find your own.

— SCIENCE SPECIALIST BURNHAM : LETHE : Stardate 1412.3

Having a mentor or guru who can offer wisdom and reassurance, who can help us navigate life's most treacherous waters, can be important to realizing our ultimate goals and inherent power (i.e. the "Captain's Chair"). But we have a right to be skeptical of any counselor who charts a too-detailed course, who dictates the exact steps we must take to follow our dreams.

Those steps may only retrace the path our mentor took to find his own way, or the route prescribed by an organization to earn a certain rank or level of expertise. It may be how a friend might accomplish a specific task if it were assigned to her, or how a fellow alcoholic (or workaholic) managed to overcome his addiction. Maybe that's how *they* would do it. It's not necessarily *your* way.

Because all of us are different, with unique personalities and talents that may work for some but not others. Because there are too many variables on our journeys for anyone to foresee – from random events to unexpected opportunities. We must be ready to take advantage of them, to be willing to let go of our best-laid plans, to leave the prescribed path if The Universe shows us a shortcut, or perhaps a side trip that may take longer but adds to our experience and confidence.

Yes, we should definitely listen to others who are already ahead of us on the trek we too have embarked upon. But let's remember that their success isn't guaranteed; their journeys aren't over yet. And that the best advice is about being *on* the journey, not what's waiting at the end.

I will consider others' advice, but pay greater heed to the Spirit moving within me, and to the messages The Universe is writing on my soul.

01.30

You know what they say: Be careful what you wish for; you may get it!

— COMMANDER UHURA : THE SEARCH FOR SPOCK : 8210.3

Long before it became a proverb on Earth, the truth behind Uhura's words was already well known. Centuries earlier, in fact, visitors' wishes were being routinely transformed into reality on the so-called "Amusement Park Planet." Frequently with less-than-desirable results.

Even under ordinary conditions, our consciousness has numerous mechanisms for bringing about the fulfillment of our dreams. Unfortunately, we often block these mechanisms with feelings of unworthiness or negativity. And because we therefore assume that our wishes will "never come true," we tend to let them run wild. We fail to consider what consequences they might have if they ever *did* become real. Why not wish for unlimited power and pleasure if it'll never happen anyway?

And then suddenly it happens: A dream comes true. Perhaps it's because we finally throw off the shackles of self-doubt. Or because we finally accept the miraculous power of our own minds. The problem is, if our dream is a holdover from that earlier stage when we couldn't care less about "consequences," we may be in for a shock.

Which is simply to say that we must "be careful" even with our fantasies. Could we really live with them? Would they truly add meaning and purpose to our existence?

Let my dreams be in harmony with the longings of my highest Self. I wish for no more... and no less.

01.31

Change doesn't come easily. Change will come by itself if you're open to it.

— ALIXUS : PARADISE : 47573.1

Such creatures of habit we are! Our bodies and nerves are literally imprinted with the patterns we've established over the years; and it becomes harder and harder to affect them, even when we're convinced change is needed.

The conflict often deteriorates into a battle between body and soul. All our "bad habits" or "primitive desires" are seen as products of evil forces we personify as demons, The Devil, or our own, inherent "sinful nature." After all, something else – not us! – must be holding us back, right?

Feeling this conflict is actually part of the growth process. It's the price we pay for being conscious – for realizing that we are more than our physical bodies, that we can transcend our previous limitations if we'd only work at it.

And fortunately, it's not as much work as we might think. We can see it as a battle if we insist. But we can also simply envision the kind of person we want to be, doing the things that type of person would be doing. As if by magic our transformation begins to unfold. And as long as we keep this "model" in our awareness, we inevitably become more and more like it. A new person slowly but surely emerges.

Not really "by itself," but because that's how transformation works. That's how The Universe works *in us.*

I will meditate daily on the stronger, more blissful, more spiritual person I have decided to be, thereby allowing The Universe to change me from within.

CORRESPONDING TO THE MONTH OF

February

02.01

For everything there is a first time.

— SPOCK : THE WRATH OF KHAN : 8130.3

"Are you serious? No one's ever done that before!"

"Me—? I could never do that!"

I could never… No one's ever… These litanies of negativity act as reverse affirmations. Because if we tell ourselves we can't do something, we usually can't. If we keep pointing out that a certain goal has never been achieved, we build barriers against achieving it. Or at least *our* achieving it.

And yet, everything good that was ever done had once never been done. If we let that stop us, there would be no new achievements, no breakthroughs. Our barriers are often less a problem of difficulty than of attitude.

Then again, sometimes not. Many of the things we haven't yet accomplished – whether as a species, or in our personal lives – are genuinely difficult. Achieving them requires stretching our abilities, taking risks, making sacrifices… perhaps even changing certain aspects of ourselves. But that's why "firsts" get into record books. That's why firsts are such a major cause for celebration. They are hard won. And they deserve to be celebrated, if only to encourage us to achieve many more of them.

A continuing succession of these firsts is another definition for "growth."

I will search my life for opportunities to do for the first time the things I know I must do eventually. I will act boldly and celebrate my successes.

02.02

A little less analysis and a little more action… that's what we need.

— DR. McCOY : THE GALILEO SEVEN : 2821.5

Sometimes we must act before there's time to think. We can learn much about ourselves – about our strengths and weaknesses – from watching our own behavior in these situations. "Gut reactions" reveal current programming.

But sometimes we have the luxury of analyzing the situation before we act. We can consider the variables, the possible outcomes, potential plans for action. And we can learn much about ourselves here, too.

Because in our need to "be right," we all-too-often *over*-analyze. We consider so many possibilities that we lose perspective. The law of diminishing returns kicks in. What's worse, we end up surrendering our responsibility. We let the Ship's Computer decide, or we seek the safety of decision-by-committee. We create a convenient excuse for failure, since we can always blame others for giving us faulty data or "insufficient information." Or we simply put off doing anything at all.

Except that we *can't* put it off. We grow not by "thinking about it," but by acting. And if we're mindful, the very action we undertake contains the clues to its own "rightness." The Way becomes clear only as we begin to move.

And mid-course corrections are always possible.

I acknowledge that I am Captain of the voyager that is my Self. I accept responsibility, and look for the lessons my own actions teach me.

02.03

We're not gods and prophets. We're people. We make mistakes.

— COUNSELOR EZRI DAX : STRANGE BEDFELLOWS : Stardate Not Given

The description that we're only "people" bears repeating. Not to excuse our flaws or our laziness. Not to free us to act out our worst impulses, but to act out our *best.*

In our quest for excellence and self-realization, we need to know that we'll often miss the mark. There will be long seasons of failure. Mistakes may haunt us for years.

…Unless we accept that we are imperfect, that life is about learning from our mistakes and then moving on.

But that's just half of it. Ezri's words aren't meant only to make us feel better. "We're not gods or prophets" is also the principle which should guide our relationships with others. For just as *we* must be free to fail (or else we can't grow), so must they. Forgiving others for their inevitable mistakes is inseparable from forgiving our*selves.*

A Bajoran prophet echoed this universal sentiment when she said: "Be compassionate toward your neighbors, and to the strangers among you. Know that they are searching for self-understanding just as you are. Do not think their struggles easier, nor their mistakes more grievous. In truth you are all on the same journey, and the comfort you offer them along the way becomes your own."

Sometimes comfort is all we need to keep moving.

I accept myself exactly as I am now, just as I accept others. Admitting my imperfections removes the obstacles between me and my ideal Self.

02.04

You may not care about you. But I do.

— DR. CULBER : CHOOSE YOUR PAIN: Stardate 1408.7

Sometimes we take chances that can't possibly yield benefits equal to their potentially negative consequences, like risking our lives for some temporary thrill, say. Sometimes we simply ignore whatever consequences there might be – negative or not – and we act on impulse, on a hunch, out of duty, or because somebody dares us, to the point that others become convinced that we must not give a damn about ourselves.

And that's because there are times in our lives when we really *don't* give a damn about ourselves. Maybe someone has rejected our affections, turned down a business proposal, or given us a failing grade, leaving us feeling unloved, unappreciated, or simply stupid. Maybe we haven't been able to achieve some sought-after goal, or we've committed an act that betrays our own sense of Who We Are (or ought to be), and now we feel disgusted and deserving of punishment. For these and countless other reasons, our wounded egos can react like reckless children, without thinking, as if we just don't care anymore.

But someone, somewhere, *does* care. A relative or friend. A member of our support group or wider community of whom we may not even be aware. Not to mention the Universe that created us.

We have a responsibility to remember those who care for us, to allow their presence in our lives to buoy us up when we're down… until, again, we're able to handle the job for ourselves.

My life inevitably affects those around me. It is enough, in moments of crisis and self-doubt, to care for myself if only because others care for me.

02.05

What the hell... nobody said life was safe!

— COMMANDER RIKER : PEAK PERFORMANCE : 42923.4

There are two distinct components to the Commander's statement. The second contains the obvious truth.

Obvious, because experience has shown that our lives can't be both satisfying and totally safe. Growth can be dangerous. To fulfill our potential, we must often journey through the "badlands." Or even uncharted space.

But the first part of Riker's statement is problematic. Too often we interpret "What the hell" to mean "It doesn't matter." It implies a tendency to do things carelessly or impulsively, without thinking about the consequences.

That's hardly the case here. Ryker knows what the consequences are. He's thought about it. He simply accepts the danger and prepares to go ahead anyway.

Which is exactly the attitude *we* need to succeed. Not that it doesn't matter, but that it *does*. To become the person The Universe calls us to be, we must accept risks. As one holy book put it, we must be ready to "walk through the valley of the shadow of death." A movie classic from Earth's Twentieth Century put it more bluntly. "Damn the torpedoes... full speed ahead!"

It's a line that might just as easily have come from the bridge of the Enterprise. Or, once we understand what's at stake, from our own personal lives.

I accept the risks and challenges of life as the price for becoming the person I want to be. Whatever happens on my journey, I am never alone.

02.06

I'm just following the blueprint.

— COMMANDER SISKO : EXPLORERS : Stardate Not Given

It's always good to have a blueprint. Whether you're working on a specific project or your life's goals, a plan provides guidelines, reinforces the need to proceed one step at a time (i.e. you can't build the penthouse before you've laid the foundation); and helps measure your progress.

Perhaps the biggest benefit is that you make your plan in a calm, objective state of mind. You line up resources in advance. You anticipate problems before they occur. You see things more clearly now than you will during the heat of construction. And later, when you're in the thick of it, when you're tired, distracted, maybe having second thoughts – you can still rely on the calm, clear vision you had earlier. You won't give in to pressure, or yield to temptation. You'll let your Blueprint think for you.

Of course, that strength is also its greatest weakness. Because reality is never so compliant as to follow your plans exactly. Problems will arise that no blueprint could foresee. Unexpected opportunities are just as likely. Both will have the potential to scuttle things entirely, or help them turn out better than you could ever have dreamed!

The best blueprints are therefore not too specific. They are "working plans." Some of the details become clear only after we roll up our sleeves and start building.

My life is a construction zone. My blueprint gives me a specific direction, but enables me to develop and receive new guidelines as conditions change.

02.07

You must trust yourselves.

— DR. CRUSHER : SYMBIOSIS : Stardate Not Given

Sounds too easy, doesn't it? Just *trust* yourselves and everything will magically take care of itself.

And of course it isn't that easy. But not because the doctor's advice is mistaken or simplistic. It's because we seem so unwilling to believe there's a resource within us that we can trust to guide us and give us answers.

Furthermore, some of us have tried "trusting in ourselves" and we know better than to do that again! The results have been disastrous, or at least not encouraging.

The problem is, trusting in that inner guidance is a *learned skill.* It's natural to get "mixed signals," mentally speaking. How do we separate the messages our hormones are sending us from the counsel of our rational mind – and finally from the intuitive urgings of our Higher Self?

But remember: A four-year-old can't just hop on a bicycle and ride it the first time, either.

Remember also that, in trusting "ourselves," we don't rely solely on the limited, fallible resources of our own conscious "ego." The Self we must learn to trust is linked in some subconscious, hyperspace-like way to the wisdom and power of The Universe itself. Through that Self we can access a perspective that harmonizes our own needs with those of others, that guides us through life's obstacle course to our goals… that trusts us even when we don't.

I respect my own guidance. I am learning to trust myself even as The Universe already trusts me.

02.08

No one is expendable.

— DR. BASHIR : THE SEARCH, PART I : 47212.4

It's easier to see on a small scale: In an Away Team exploring a newly-discovered planet; on a Federation outpost in deep space, or a starship two generations from home. Here, every individual has a specific, visible function within the group. The unique talents of any one person can make a critical difference. And the loss of a single crewmember will create a vacuum that impacts everyone else… directly… personally.

How odd to think this kind of personal impact, this visible interconnectedness, no longer applies in larger groups. The sheer numbers fool us. We assume that people can be "replaced." Or at least that's the way most bureaucracies and economic entities treat us.

But we must not let their treatment of us determine our view of ourselves. Because that view is not only ultimately destructive, it's not even accurate. If we could only look more closely, we'd see that every individual added or subtracted from a group changes it. The energy may be spread over a broader area, like a single oboe in a vast concert hall. And when the whole orchestra is playing, we tend to hear the symphony rather than the individual instruments playing it. But take away the oboe and the symphony isn't the same. People notice the difference.

Not the least of whom is the musician beside you.

My presence here makes a difference. Inevitably. I will strive to make that difference a positive one.

02.09

The universe has been my playground.

— Q : DEJA Q : 43539.1

It may seem odd to quote Q, that enigmatic being who is so contemptuous of human weakness. After all, in Q's eyes we are such pathetic creatures – for showing compassion, for forgiving one another, for all those attributes we celebrate as reflections of our deeper divinity.

Then again, Q himself could be compassionate and forgiving; and his contempt was more out of frustration for the high cost of those feelings than a conviction that we shouldn't have them. In fact, it is Q who teaches us that compassion requires the *most* strength.

And there are other things we can learn from Q. One of them is his attitude toward the physical world.

It's a kind of faith, really – a way of viewing one's life. According to Q, the world around us exists precisely to be used, experienced... *enjoyed.* We have far more to gain by treating life as an ongoing game than as some deadly-serious final exam. We'll learn the rules faster, with more lasting effect – and with more assurance – by running out there onto the playing field than by watching from the sidelines. Handbooks and holosuites are boring, anemic substitutes for the real playground.

And anyway, who do you think is out there supervising all the fun?

The Universe gives us our lives to play with as well as to learn from. Playing by the rules is what makes the game more fun, not less.

02.10

It's too easy to turn a blind eye to the suffering of a people you don't know.

— CAPTAIN PICARD : INSURRECTION : Stardate Not Given

How far beyond our immediate circle – family, friends, community, nation, planet – must we go before we're no longer required to respond? Or, put another way, what are the limits of our responsibility to others in need?

Picard reminds us that we are often tempted to draw the line conveniently close. "We don't know those people" is an easy excuse. And there are plenty of others, like "It's complicated." Or "Risking our scarce resources is a cost we can't afford." Or simply, "We have no right to interfere."

Then again, what's right isn't only a matter of "rights," of legalities. We are linked to others even before we may know them. Their sufferings – and their successes – can affect us both materially and spiritually, despite the fact that we're not even aware of their existence.

But when we *do* become aware of them, we can no longer avoid responsibility. Not just because we may discover something that compels us to come to their aid. It's because our failure to act would also harm ourselves.

Karma extends equally to what we *don't* do as to what we do. And if we turn a blind eye to others, the universe will turn a blind eye to us.

Fortunately, the flip side is also true.

I earn help by giving it to others. I free myself from bondage as I work to release others from theirs.

02.11

*You humanoids have a hard time giving up the things you love...
no matter how much they might hurt you.*

— CONSTABLE ODO : HEART OF STONE : 48521.5

What Constable Odo means by "love," Bajoran and Terran gurus would call "attachment." It's not that we love certain objects or foods or activities. It's that we've become *attached* to them. They've become so intertwined in our lives that we simply can't imagine ourselves without them. They seem no less a part of us than our hands and feet and the face in the bathroom mirror.

Trouble is, some of these attachments aren't good for us. Like the Terulian brandy we enjoy but may anesthetize us to our problems. Or the secret, self-indulgent fantasy that may boost our ego but prevents us from seeing the world as it really is. And even when we finally admit the damage they do, we still figure we're stuck with them, like a chronic limp or an untreatable disease.

The solution, ironically, is to *lose* one's attachments. Not just those that hurt us, but *all* of them. We must learn to see ourselves, our core identity, as separate from the habits and personal preferences that outwardly define us. Only then can we make a conscious choice about which ones to eliminate, and which to keep. Only then can we access the power we have to change our lives.

*I am not what I eat, or what I like, or even what I do. I am responsible for these
things, but separate from them. Therefore I can change them as I see fit.*

02.12

Human intuition and instinct are not always right. But they do
make life interesting.

— GUINAN : THE LOSS : 44356.9

Though "intuition" and "instinct" are often used interchangeably, they are as different as thought and feeling.

Instinct refers to the physical drives and survival responses hard-wired into our bodies – almost as if our higher faculties didn't exist. (That's because our higher faculties actually *didn't* exist when our instincts evolved.) Intuition, on the other hand, *is* one of our higher faculties.

In fact, it may even be "higher" than rational thought. Because intuition not only draws on our mental abilities, it draws on our instincts, too. And on other subconscious processes we've only recently begun to understand.

When we "intuit," therefore, our minds are attempting to integrate information that may be intellectual, hormonal, sensory – and perhaps even extra-sensory. Some of these sources of information are not strictly logical, nor are they always compatible. So it should not surprise us that our intuition isn't always right.

But we diminish our capabilities if we simply label our intuition "wrong" and rely on logic alone, or only on what we can put into words. Instead, we must learn to listen even more carefully to our inner wisdom. We must learn to trust ourselves. *That's* what makes life interesting.

*I will not discount my instincts and my inner guidance, even if they are sometimes
wrong. I trust the diverse resources within me to help light my way.*

02.13

There's a million things in this universe you can have and a million things you can't. It's no fun facing that, but that's the way things are.

— CAPTAIN KIRK : CHARLIE X : 1533.6

The popular notion is that we can "be whatever we want" — and *have* whatever we want. After all, when we finally admit to ourselves that the universe is "good," and that its infinite resources supply everything we need, we can easily fall into the trap of thinking that the universe must therefore exist simply to satisfy all our desires.

We forget, in short, that getting everything we want is not always "good." And that, if we want a certain thing, we must often give up something else. We can't have both.

We can't drink the nectar of the gods for long and still keep our sobriety. We can't maintain committed, intimate relationships if we use others merely as tools to get what we want — or to satisfy our glandular needs. We can't reach the destination The Universe calls us toward if we refuse to explore or learn any of the Paths required to get there.

To have the "million things" that truly enrich our lives, we must consciously choose to *not* have the other million that only seem enriching. The Ancient Ones called this process "repenting" — turning away from what can't give us life, so that we might turn back to what *can*.

In the end, the stakes are that high.

I accept the fact that Life has rules, and that "the way things are" is ultimately for my own good.

02.14

Until I saw you, there was nothing in my heart. It sustained my life, but nothing more. Now it sings!

— NATIRA : FOR THE WORLD IS HOLLOW AND I HAVE TOUCHED THE SKY : 5476.3

On Earth there is still a minor holiday that celebrates the joys of love and physical attraction. Its origins are now obscure, as is the source of the figurine which is its mascot — an infant angel, or "cherub," who shoots heart-tipped arrows that turn its "victims" into instant lovers.

The symbolism is not as obscure as the origins. The cherub, for example, signifies that genuine love exhibits a childlike innocence and playfulness. The arrows represent the fact that feelings of love often strike us as if from an outside source, unexpectedly, without our "permission" and without any logical justification. It's as if we have no control.

But in return for our seeming lack of control, there are compensations. The pleasure lovers take simply by being in each other's presence cannot be duplicated. Every sense, every emotion, is heightened. A touch, a smile, a mere glance from one's lover can communicate more information than a Ship's Computer. The heart *does* sing!

Of course there are complications, too. And as sentient beings, we can't always permit the heart to rule our minds. But there are days when we enjoy pretending that it can.

It is good to feel. I give myself permission to enjoy the presence of another person, to practice caring for someone else — as The Universe cares for me.

02.15

Humans don't throw morality out the window when things start getting a little rough.

— CAPTAIN ARCHER : HATCHERY : ECE01.08.2154

Any decent system of ethics isn't just for "everyday use," for those times when our lives seem to be running smoothly, when the economy is good, when peace prevails. It's when we're faced with the really hard choices, when social systems break down, when wars break out between nations and planetary alliances – *that's* when our ethical foundations matter most.

And how quickly we revert to "every man for himself" under those conditions! How disheartening it is when our moral veneer is so easily stripped away. What a tragedy to see followers of the Prince of Peace engage in the same torturous tactics as their enemies. As Archer reminds us, "There are rules… even in war."

But we can't wait for wars to test our morality. We need to ask ourselves, in advance, how we'd react in those extreme situations, what we'd do when confronted by the most difficult decisions. After all, we are Who We Are not merely as a result of choices we've made in the past, but in view of the options we allow ourselves – and the options we rule out – "when things start getting rough." Even if we haven't faced those conditions yet. Even if we never will.

Because it's not our morality we're in danger of throwing out the window. It's our humanity.

Who I am is not merely a result of biology, but of morality. I will strive to insure that my guiding principles cover not only "routine maintenance," but the conflicts and crises I'm sure to face.

02.16

Sometimes people blindly make the same mistakes again and again.

— ENSIGN D'SORA : IN THEORY : 44932.3

Nobody would dispute these words from Data's one-time paramour. Except perhaps to say that many of our mistakes aren't made all that "blindly." We often seem to commit the very same act that got us into trouble once before, now with our eyes wide open.

The question is, *why?* Didn't we get hurt enough? Or do we simply enjoy the punishment?

First, let's give ourselves a little credit. Maybe we had reason to believe things would turn out differently the second time. Perhaps we thought we'd grown enough to know where things went wrong, and we could stop the same disaster from happening again. Besides, an even bigger mistake would be to assume that, just because something didn't work before, we should give up trying.

But when the same failure occurs repeatedly, it means we probably *are* blind. We're not seeing something crucial. We've missed the lesson. Or maybe we *do* feel some "need" to punish ourselves, and we aren't aware of it.

Whatever the case, it's not as if the universe is being cruel. It simply doesn't want us to "get things right" by accident. Or to go on ignoring something that requires our undivided attention. It wants us to understand something important. Let's be grateful for one more chance to learn.

I open my eyes to the messages hidden within my mistakes. If I repeat them, I will look deeper.

02.17

May cultural differences encourage us to build bridges of understanding to all that makes us unique.

— SEVEN OF NINE : SOMEONE TO WATCH OVER ME : Stardate Not Given

To those aware of her background, the "toast" Seven offered on this occasion was the sign of a personal breakthrough. For her to acknowledge the value of diversity, to promote uniqueness as a quality to be preserved, was like a former slave announcing her freedom from bondage.

Many of us likewise need to set ourselves free: From the notion that cultural differences are roadblocks to unity. From the assumption that uniqueness and individuality are a hindrance to harmony. From the dogma that we all need to be "the same" before we can be accepted.

Seven's words call us to celebrate and learn from our differences. But not merely for the purpose of adding new technology to our arsenals, to assimilate what others know so we can use that knowledge for our own benefit.

The fact is, building bridges between our differences creates new opportunities and new ideas neither could generate without the other. By respecting and preserving our "uniquenesses" we become resources for one another, models for looking at things differently, guides to show the way out of the ruts we're in, inspiration for our ongoing Voyages through the universe… and into ourselves.

Diversity is a gift The Universe has given me. Each month for the remainder of this year, I will study another faith or culture, and reaffirm its relationship to my own.

02.18

We prefer permanence… the reward of relationships that endure and grow deeper with the passing of time.

— CAPTAIN JANEWAY : PRIME FACTORS : 48642.5

As convenient as it may be, our brave new world of instant gratification also carries some unfortunate side effects. A tray of food appears at the push of a button. We access libraries of information with a single word to the Ship's Computer. Transporters and holodecks take us to other worlds — both real and imaginary — in moments.

It's no wonder we sometimes treat one another with little more regard than holographic images. We're so busy moving from one experience to another that we tend to forget that another person is involved — a real person not unlike us, with dreams… with feelings.

And while real people may not respond to our whims like some computer-generated fantasy figure, there are rewards: Knowing that the feelings you have are shared by another; imagining what the other person is doing whenever you're apart; anticipating the next time you meet.

It's because life is so full of activity and technology and impermanence that person-to-person relationships are so precious. Enduring friendships provide emotional grounding, constants in a universe of Relativity. They are worth all the effort we put into them. And more.

My relationships are an important gauge of my emotional health… and a tool for improving it. I grow as they grow, and endure as they endure.

02.19

We're big enough to take a few insults.

— CHIEF ENGINEER SCOTT : THE TROUBLE WITH TRIBBLES : 4523.3

How sensitive we are to criticism, or to verbal abuse, is a good indicator of our self-confidence. For example, if someone's cutting remark elicits a strong emotional reaction, it's often because we're not sure of ourselves. Or else we suspect there's some truth to it.

Rather than simply feel hurt by the remark, we need to process it. Instead of lashing back, or immediately constructing arguments to prove how wrong it was, we need to stop and ask "why." *Why* did a certain comment cut so deep? Why did we feel a need to respond so defensively?

There are several possibilities. The criticism may point to a real flaw we've tried to keep secret, and now we've been exposed. Or maybe we're worried that someone important to us will be influenced by the remark — whether it's true or not. Perhaps the insult seems out of character for the person who made it, and now we don't know what to think of them. Or we simply decide the remark is unjustified, in which case we dismiss it and get past it.

Being "big enough," as Scotty puts it, means doing all of this processing before we respond — if a response is even necessary. More importantly, it means we're content with the truth. Because Who We Are — as revealed in our actions — always speaks louder than anybody's words.

Insults say most about the person giving them. Nevertheless, I will look for any kernels of truth they may contain, and learn from what I find.

02.20

For any event, there is an infinite number of possible outcomes. Our choices will determine which outcomes will follow.

— DATA : PARALLELS : 47391.2

Even Data could exaggerate to make a point.

Whether the possibilities really *are* infinite is debatable, if not downright mistaken. But the point is, they might as well be infinite if we truly accept the awesome power we possess to choose our own future.

"I had no choice" is a line we often employ to excuse our actions, or our blindness to other alternatives. Our behavior may even be understandable — when we're unprepared or frightened, or when a certain choice is likely to bring us pain, or when the world seems to be against us. But "I had no choice" is never really true. *Never.*

As people who make thousands of choices in the course of a single day, it is to our advantage to continually expand our awareness of the possibilities. The Inner Voyage increases those possibilities if only because it offers alternatives that do not depend on outer circumstances. We can choose self-control even if we can't control "the world." We can choose inner peace even when those around us are in conflict.

And the irony is, inspired by our choice, the world is more likely to conform itself to *us,* than we to *it.*

My choices determine my future. I always have a choice; and in choosing, I choose the person I am.

02.21

We come in peace. That's why we're here.

— COMMANDER BURNHAM: THE VULCAN HELLO: Stardate 1207.3

The irony with this statement is that it was understood as a threat by most Klingons of that era. Members of that Empire saw peace as a fatal condition in which there were no longer any opportunities to prove oneself, no further quests or character-building battles. No *honor.*

And the Klingons had a perfect right to see it that way, insofar as they interpreted "peace" as the kind of quiet serenity that might describe a graveyard.

From the Starfleet perspective, however, to "come in peace" means to seek a relationship with another person, community or culture, confidently expecting to discover shared values and inter-ests that might fuel commercial ventures and other projects of mutual benefit. The challenge, of course, is to introduce oneself in such a way that the other party understands that the hoped-for relationship will not be one-sided, meant to exploit or even subjugate them — and in consideration of the Klingons' native belligerence, that an alliance isn't being sought out of fear, or from a posi-tion of weakness. Hence the extreme show of force that came to be known as the "Vulcan Hello."

In Earth's Hebrew and Islamic traditions, the words *shalom* and *salaam*, often translated as "peace," are closer in meaning to the concept of "wholeness." It's the condition where everything works together for the greater good, even when there is occasional dissention or dysfunction.

And sometimes, *because* there is.

I will strive for wholeness in every new relationship, seeking to understand others' differences as new perspectives and talents that may complement my own.

02.22

You can't hide from your feelings.

— COUNSELOR TROI : NEW GROUND : 45376.3

The old cliché about "getting in touch with your feelings" still contains some of life's best advice. Not just because feelings convey important (and usually-reliable) information. It's because knowing exactly what those feelings are trying to tell us is an art.

The same feeling might convey an intuitive message that somebody we've just met can't be trusted, or that we're still unsure what to think about an earlier meeting with someone else. Either way, our subconscious is trying to tell us something, using physical cues which, if we were only in touch with our feelings, would be as clear a message as the flashing lights on the Ship's Panels.

One of the most common of these messages is that we still need to resolve some emotional issue from our past. When we suffer humiliation or loss, for example, we often deal with it by simply ignoring or suppressing our memory. But our built-in Mental Management System knows better. Even a suppressed memory can affect our judgment and emotional stability. And our sub-conscious will send a "reminder" — continually — until we face it.

It's not just that "hiding" from these distress signals is futile. It's that we should embrace them. We should be following where they lead us. For our own good, and for others'.

My emotional feelings are messages of love and concern from my deeper Self.
I commit myself to learning how to decipher my own "secret code."

02.23

It is unwise to trivialize that which one simply does not understand.

— SPOCK : STAR TREK BEYOND : CIRCA 2263.3

First, let's remember that ignorance is not the same thing as stupidity. To be "ignorant" is to *not know* something. To be stupid, on the other hand, is to *lack the intelligence* to know something.

The latter can result from genetic factors, of course. But it can also result from one's attitudes, from one's unwillingness to learn. Or from one's fear of discovering the truth.

The most intelligent people can be ignorant; they simply may not have the facts yet. Fortunately, most of those intelligent people are also curious. They *want* to find out what the facts are. That's what being "wise" means. It's not about knowing a lot – although most older, wiser people *do* know more than us average folk – but that you consciously and consistently strive to replace ignorance with knowledge.

Stupid people can't do that, or they don't want to. And they often try to justify their intellectual laziness by saying that the search for truth and understanding takes too much effort, that it's a low priority, a "trivial" matter, that in the end it won't really change anything.

When we catch ourselves making such excuses, or others point this out to us, it's more important than ever to start asking questions.

Not only can I overcome ignorance by striving for understanding, I can overcome my stupidity by no longer making excuses for my lack of it.

02.24

'Tis at the heart of our natures to feel pain and joy. It is an essential part of what makes us what we are.

— CAPTAIN PICARD : THE BONDING : 43198.7

The most crucial component of this quotation is the word "and." Pain *and* joy… Sorrow *and* happiness…

Because we can't have one without the other. It's simply a requirement of our emotional hardware. We can choose to turn off our agony, yes; but the ecstasy circuit will shut down at the same time. Without fail.

One of Earth's premiere poets, Khalil Gibran, framed this relationship in a simple question: "Is not the lute that soothes your spirit the very wood that was hollowed out with knives?" His own answer makes it even clearer. "The deeper that sorrow carves into your being, the more joy you can contain."

Too often we assume that our emotions are independent of one another. We think we can – or *should* – feel happy all the time. (Or at least that we shouldn't feel any pain.) We forget that our capacity to feel one emotion is the direct result of having experienced its opposite.

Not that we should *pursue* pain. It will inevitably find us. But we *can* be grateful for our seasons of sorrow, if only in retrospect, for without them, we could not harvest such profound joy.

I will accept and embrace my pain so that I may deepen my capacity for happiness.

02.25

We're lost... but we're making good time!

— COMMANDER SULU : THE FINAL FRONTIER : 8454.1

How often we repeat Sulu's observation — and what we're really talking about is our own lives!

After all, we seem to be going somewhere in a hurry, don't we? — our engines at warp speed, our daily lives filled with all sorts of activities (and maybe even a taste of personal satisfaction). And all that activity is sometimes a good sign that we know what our lives are about.

Then again, it can also be a good sign that we *don't* know.

Because being busy often results from our lack of direction. We rush breathlessly through our lives, hardly stopping, often taking on new projects in a desperate search — though usually an unconscious one — for something that might give our lives meaning and focus. Or we simply keep ourselves so preoccupied and "rushed" that we don't have time to reflect on how lost we really are.

But we must stop; we must give ourselves time to breathe, to reflect, to ask the important questions: What does The Universe uniquely want to say through me? What is the Prime Directive in my own life?

Without an answer — even a tentative, changing one — "making good time" is only the joke Sulu meant it to be.

I hereby commit myself to regular opportunities for reflection. The busier I am, the more I will stop to review where I'm going, and whether I'm getting there.

02.26

Never judge a fruit by its skin.

— NEELIX : CARETAKER : 48315.6

...Or, as humans used to say, "a book by its cover."

Some of the sweetest fruits have the thickest husks. And, alternatively, many of the least enriching works of literature have had the most attractive covers.

In fact, by the end of Earth's Second Millennium, the ability to make all sorts of products appear wholesome and enriching — despite the fact that they were not — had become a major art form. From petroleum to politicians, "image" became more important than substance. And the bottom line was, people fell for it left and right.

Things are not so different today. We are still easily deceived by appearances. That may help explain why we often compensate — consciously or not — by learning to deceive others. Or at least by concentrating more on looks than character. Which amounts to deceiving our*selves*.

To "never judge a fruit by its skin" is certainly one way to guard against deception. But the statement also reminds us that opportunities and treasures sometimes lie hidden in the most unexpected places and relationships. If we expect the worst, if we react only to outward appearances or first impressions, we will probably get what we expect. But if we search deeper, we may discover more beauty — and sweeter fruit — than we ever thought possible.

I will not equate appearance with substance — not merely because I might be deceived, but because I might miss something truly wonderful!

02.27

Maybe we weren't meant for paradise. Maybe we were meant to fight our way through... struggle, claw our way up... scratch for every inch of the way.

— CAPTAIN KIRK : THIS SIDE OF PARADISE : 3417.3

Life ain't easy. No one promised you a rose garden. Welcome to the School of Hard Knox.

There are thousands of ways to say it. And the underlying message is not merely that our lives can be tough and we'd better get used to it. The message is, *That's the way it's supposed to be.*

After all, our biggest triumphs never come from the victories handed us on a silver platter. We draw our greatest satisfaction from taking on a new challenge, perhaps risking something of value in the process, pushing ourselves beyond previous limits. And the prize has less to do with the outcome than the struggle itself.

It would be tempting to ascribe that "satisfaction in the struggle" to our roots in the Animal Kingdom – nature's emotional enticement to keep our survival skills in working condition. But it's more than biological. It's *spiritual.* It's the realization that there's always more for us to learn; a reminder that "perfection" is an action verb, not an adjective; a lesson that heaven isn't so much a place where all our needs are fulfilled and provided for, but a lifestyle in which we're all fulfilled by providing for our needs.

I will face whatever Life sends my way, knowing that the rewards are in the effort, not in the outcome.

02.28

You are making a statement about the sanctity of life, and it will be heard!

— LWAXANA TROI : HALF A LIFE : 44805.3

Talk is cheap. Which is why a good argument or a well-polished speech might move us temporarily, but it will rarely transform our thinking in the long run.

It's the statement people make by *doing* something that has power to change the world. It's the eloquence of action that cuts through public apathy, that brings home an otherwise remote issue, that reaches into our hearts and minds with images that compel us to respond.

Think of the human rights movement of the late Twentieth Century – from Mahatma Ghandi's March to the Sea to Martin Luther King's March on Washington. Consider the war protester who loses his legs on the railroad tracks outside an ammo dump, trying to stop a freight train carrying bullets and bombs. Recall the courage of a single Chinese student blocking a tank in Tienamen Square as he demonstrates for democracy.

Such "statements" do more than raise our consciousness about an issue, or mobilize us to join hands – although that would be enough. They also teach us that life is sacred, that our lives must have meaning to be worth living, that some common chord connects us all at a level that runs much deeper than speech, beyond race, that outlasts time.

They teach us that our *lives* are our loudest voices.

I will meditate on what I truly believe in, and what actions would visibly demonstrate those beliefs.

02.29

It's so easy to become jaded... to treat the extraordinary like just another day at the office. But sometimes there are experiences that transcend all of that.

— CAPTAIN JANEWAY : EMANATIONS : 48623.5

There are hidden layers, deeper dimensions, in everything that happens. Like exploring the miniature worlds that surround us – the thriving community in a single plant leaf, or the dance of DNA in our own cells, or the electromagnetic energies filling the space between and inside us. We have only to shift our point of view to discover how much more life offers.

For most of us, unfortunately, it's "business as usual." We draw lines around the experiences we'll permit ourselves, or the feelings we'll allow. We enforce our own "tunnel vision." After all, we have jobs to do. Sometimes it's critical to our very survival that we stay focused and not get distracted. And if we've developed an ability to concentrate on the work we're doing, we've learned an important life skill, haven't we?

Perhaps. But if we continually tune out the deeper dimensions that underlie our existence, we pay dearly for that "skill." We lose the capacity for awe, for surprise, for the ability to imagine that things can be different... _better._

And without these skills, we lose the power to change.

It is only my own tunnel vision that hides the deeper layers of existence from me. I will open myself to new ways of seeing, and see my life anew.

03

CORRESPONDING TO THE MONTH OF

March

03.01

Our function is to contribute in a positive way to the world in which we live.

— DATA : THE OFFSPRING : 43657.0

You'd think it would be obvious. But even with the best intentions, short-term self-interest can cloud our vision. After all, we can see the results of selfish efforts. We try to do something to benefit ourselves — and either it works for us or it doesn't. Even if it fails, at least we know.

Long-term self-interest is harder to track. We often lose the connection between what we did, and the benefit we finally receive. We may not feel rewarded, even if we are.

Contributing "to the world" is even more obscure. We can rarely see the slow, cumulative effects of our altruistic efforts. The positive influence we've had on certain people, the difference we've made in the wider scheme of things — these are very difficult to identify, much less take credit for. So we fall back on the behaviors that give us immediate reinforcement: Being selfish.

What we don't realize is that our contributions to the wider world *are* selfish. Computer scenarios have proven it: Members of a theoretical society who work toward the "greater good" actually produce more benefits to the individual than if each member worked only for himself.

But computers don't help us *feel* that fact. It comes down to having faith. And acting on it.

Each day for the next month, I will do at least one nice thing for someone else — a different person every day — without thought of my own benefit.

03.02

There's a human expression… "Follow your heart."

— SUBCOMMANDER T'POL : E-SQUARED : CIRCA ECE2154

As much as humans revere logic — as does the race T'Pol belongs to — the left side of our brain is simply not sufficient for setting goals or finding one's life purpose. "Follow your heart" — or, in Eastern tradition, "Follow your bliss" — captures the notion that our most important decisions and directions in life are products of a much wider network. This all-encompassing network includes not only logic but feelings and intuition, and what the Ancients called our "still, small voice."

Whether our ancestors actually heard voices, as religious fanatics and schizophrenics still claim today, is a matter of some debate. Either way, external voices came to be seen as deceitful or at least dubious. Or as a sign of mental illness.

Instead, the "heart" came to symbolize one's guiding principle, the inner source that infused body and spirit with vitality and meaning. You might, for example, think accounting or engineering is a perfectly rational career choice, and no doubt lucrative; but working with people instead of numbers is what inspires you. Brain surgery saves lives, but so does teaching children at an inner city preschool. A prospective suitor might be rich and good-looking, but it's someone else who makes you feel happy and loved.

So the real question is, which vision of your future gets to the core — *cara,* heart — of what you're about? What really gets your blood pumping? What, or *who,* makes you feel most alive?

Chances are you'll know soon enough. Maybe you already know.

My heart helps me to choose my goals. My mind helps me plan the ways I can achieve them.

03.03

Indulging in fantasy keeps the mind creative.

— GARAK : OUR MAN BASHIR : Stardate Not Given

Fantasy is to the mind as sports are for the body.

A game like Karo-Net (Odo's favorite), or the recently-revived pastime of "baseball," not only provides a physical workout but fine-tunes our concentration while channeling our energies. Even as they masquerade as "fun," these sports actually serve to enhance our physical fitness for the rigors of our jobs and our daily lives.

Our minds, too, can be enhanced by a similar kind of workout. While also masquerading as fun, fantasy provides an arena in which we can experience new situations, take on challenges and invent solutions – and thereby practice the same mental skills we need in our jobs and daily activities. Psychologists have long known that the richer our fantasy lives, the better our creative skills in our "real lives." The more we indulge our imaginations, the more likely we'll explore reality and extend the boundaries of factual knowledge. The more we dream, the more intently we pursue our goals.

Our fantasies are like prayers. "Universe, let my life be this way," our fantasies say. And more often than not, The Universe answers. We must remember the power of that.

And the responsibility.

My fantasies are "practice" for the life I want to lead, not a substitute for it. The person I imagine and continually meditate on, is person I will become.

03.04

You need to run a self-diagnostic.

— LIEUTENANT PARIS : TIME AND AGAIN : Stardate Not Given

Androids do it. So do Ships' Computers. Even ordinary household appliances are designed to do it.

Whenever performance falls below prescribed levels, or if other warning signs should appear, these "intelligent" machines automatically run a program to uncover possible malfunctions. The more sophisticated systems can take action based on their findings, essentially repairing themselves. Less sophisticated systems will flash lights and sound buzzers to summon outside help.

We could all take a lesson.

Trouble is, most of us aren't sensitive to the warning signs our own systems send us. Or else we're so busy rushing though our daily routines that we don't even realize we're malfunctioning until the lights and buzzers are going off all around us. And by that time the damage may be difficult or impossible to repair.

Our Inner Voyage provides regular opportunities for self-diagnosis – either in supportive groups and relationships, or in private meditation. Through its disciplines we are re-sensitized to our psyche's subtle messages, helping us re-connect with our own higher Self. And with the deeper Source from which solutions come.

In fact, proper diagnosis is already half the solution.

I cannot be whole if I lose touch with myself. I will make my spiritual discipline my top priority.

03.05

Like all humans, you depend on feelings and instincts to guide you, and they invariably let you down.

— LIEUTENANT TUVOK : STATE OF FLUX : 48658.2

No one is suggesting that we ignore our feelings. The damage caused by dissociating ourselves from our emotions can't be overstated. An ability to repress feelings without any damage would require genetically re-engineering our entire nervous systems. Or else transforming ourselves through thousands of years of evolutionary change.

As a matter of fact, our systems have *already* been transformed by thousands of years of evolution. And the result is precisely that we now possess feelings and instincts – because they serve a purpose. We feel, therefore we act.

But evolution has also provided us with sentience. And that too was purposeful. Because being aware of our feelings and instincts allows us to recognize when they are inappropriate guides for action, and to transcend them.

The Vulcan disdain for emotion isn't because feelings are always inappropriate. Or because they mislead us half the time, or a tenth of the time. It's because the situation will arise, inevitably, when they simply aren't able to clearly point the way. Or they point the *wrong* way. And if we rely on feelings alone, if we don't back them up with Mind and Spirit, they *will* invariably let us down.

I'm grateful for the counsel of my feelings, but I do not depend solely on them.
I will balance my emotional life with reason and spiritual discipline.

03.06

You won't last long bangin' into walls. I'll be there for you... believe me.

— ENGINEER LA FORGE : Q WHO? : 42761.3

Even by ourselves we are powerful. Even when we are alone, we can still stand up to the forces of negativity and destruction.

Because we're *not* alone if we're aligned with The Universe. As one tradition put it, "God plus one is a majority."

Unfortunately, the Divine Presence can be difficult to feel. In the thick of our daily struggles – and especially during the tough times – nothing is quite so reassuring as the physical presence of a sympathetic friend. Having another person around to "be there for us" can be a lifeline.

But not to *rely* on. Not to become dependent upon every time we face a crisis. The true friend is "there" not so much to save us, but to help us save ourselves.

In fact, we may still end up banging into a few walls. A friend isn't doing his job by protecting us from the harsh realities of life. "Being there" is about comforting us when we do get banged up, cheering us up when our spirits sag, reminding us we'll survive when we're not so sure.

Mostly, a friend is someone who reconnects us with our own resources. By seeing love and strength in our friend, we remember those same qualities in ourselves.

Find yourself a friend. More important, *be* one.

I am not alone. Whenever I need help, there is at least one special friend who can remind me of the deeper resources I already possess.

03.07

Fencing tones the muscle, sharpens the eye, improves the posture.

— LIEUTENANT SULU : THE NAKED TIME : 1704.2

You're catching on. This isn't really about fencing. It's about doing something to keep our physical machinery in good working order, fencing or otherwise. It's about our realization that The Inner Voyage includes both mental and *physical* disciplines.

Among the gifts The Universe provides in this life, our material, biological form is primary. Though we are in a sense "separate" from that form, our body is our most useful tool for knowing and refining our spiritual identity. It's not simply that our bodies are the vehicles by which we act in the world, thus revealing Who We Are — to ourselves as well as others. The fact is, how we deal with our bodies is the training ground for the way we treat others.

Which means that a balanced exercise program does more than improve our posture. It becomes our stance toward life. By toning our muscles, we learn the discipline to keep our relationships healthy. By using our body wisely, we learn to use *all* of our possessions wisely. (Of course, if our body monopolizes our time, chances are we've become self-centered in many other ways, too.)

Through our body, we affirm the goodness of physical existence, and our gratitude to The Universe.

My body is a tool, not an idol. I will be mindful of its needs, but also of its limits. Without comparing my body to others' bodies, I affirm and give thanks for it.

03.08

In a crunch, I wouldn't like to be caught without a back-up system.

— CHIEF O'BRIEN : DESTINY : 48543.2

DS9's plain-talking engineer reminds us of a question we all must answer — if only because our lives may depend on it: What is *our* back-up system?

What can we rely on in a crunch? What can we turn to when our usual coping mechanisms fail… when all our hopes and dreams seem to be crumbling down around us?

From computers to Starships, our technologies have incorporated fail-safe features and back-up systems almost from their inceptions. How ironic that many of the people who designed these life-enhancing (and life-saving) systems haven't taken the lesson to heart.

But we still can. Before it's needed. Or needed again.

We can start by building a network of others who will care for us, and for whom *we* will care, when crunch-time comes. People who have lived through their own personal crises, who can point to resources they've already used successfully, can be especially valuable.

Chances are those resources will involve the kinds of spiritual disciplines that help people transcend their pain; that allow them to take the longer view; that can connect them to the power which turns even loss into learning. That's the Back-Up System behind *all* back-up systems.

Knowing what my ultimate resources are gives me strength and confidence. Through my spiritual community, I will come to know those resources better.

03.09

It was logical to cultivate multiple options.

— SPOCK : STAR TREK / PREQUEL : CIRCA 2258

It's admirable to pursue one course of action, one dream, with single-minded focus and fierce dedication. And if that course, that dream, is meant to be, chances are good that other people (not to mention The Universe itself) will join us in our efforts.

But what if other people *don't* join us? What if The Universe seems indifferent — or worse, it "rewards" our best efforts with constant roadblocks and continual failure?

Early on, it's common for our progress toward self-realization to meet resistance. Our old Self may not be convinced we're serious. Other people might be uncomfortable with the changes in us, or even jealous that we might actually achieve the new goals we've set for ourselves. And The Universe may indeed be blocking our way, *purposefully...* in order to confirm our commitment, sharpen our skills, perfect our patience. In short, it's possible we're simply being tested.

On the other hand, if our every effort is stymied, if there's no way to get there from here, it may be time to consider other options. In that case, what's our Plan B? Or Plan C, D, or E?

What we often discover at this point is not only that, as Chief O'Brien recommended, we should always have a "back-up," but that the best Plan A includes Plans B, C, D and E from the very start. After all, most people who "succeed" rarely do so on the first try, and usually at something other than what they originally set out to achieve.

Besides, our pursuit of only one dream or our cultivation of multiple options isn't what matters. It's what we learn in the process.

I will dedicate myself to my goals, but not fixate on them. The Voyage is not a straight line, but an ever-changing course.

03.10

You cannot take away what someone does not have.

— LT. COMMANDER WORF : THE WAY OF THE WARRIOR : 49011.4

Through the centuries, dictators and preservers of the status quo have recited a similar statement almost as a portent of doom: "The most dangerous people are those who have nothing to lose."

All over the Quadrant, governments have been toppled by ordinary people who no longer felt any "ownership" in The System — or sometimes ownership in anything. Under such conditions people are quite willing to risk their lives, to work (or fight) for change; to wipe the proverbial slate clean and start over.

The political message here points to a spiritual truth. From Hindu, Sufi, and Native American to Klingon and Bajoran, various traditions have encouraged this same nothing-to-lose attitude through the practice of "non-attachment." By not becoming dependent on the objects they "own" and the materialistic lifestyle that goes with them, people become far more adaptable to change. They also recover from loss more easily, take risks more willingly, and try new paths more readily.

Which means they grow more.

What they've willingly given up already, no one can take away. More importantly, what they gain as a result, no one can take away either.

I hereby make my top priority those "possessions" that cannot be taken away.

03.11

The future contains wonders you can't even imagine. The universe could be your playground.

— Q : TRUE Q : 46192.3

Though he wouldn't be called "religious" in any ordinary sense, Q is nevertheless talking about faith.

Because he's talking about his world-view here. He's referring to the way we all look at what's going on around us, the level of excitement and joy we bring to each new day, the way our vision of the future can affect our lives in the here-and-now.

He's reminding us, in so many words, that too many of us seem to wear blinders through life. We focus on our daily chores, hardly taking notice of other events or other people unless they bump into us. We lose sight of future possibilities. We lose touch with our imagination. It's almost as if, in trying to "fit" into this world, we end up blending into it. Like the Borg, we become "assimilated."

Q suggests a different approach: *Don't* be assimilated. Instead, we must look on this world as if we're tourists from another dimension, scientists on holiday, seeking answers to the riddles of this strange new existence by exploring everything, questioning everything. And the best way to do this is to take on the identity of one of its residents – even as we remember who we really are.

Maybe Q's suggestion is more than it seems.

I've waited long, studied hard, and now I can go out and play! I must play fair, and take care of my playground, but I can do anything else I want!

03.12

Who's trying to break any records? I'm doing this because I enjoy it!

— CAPTAIN KIRK : THE FINAL FRONTIER : 8454.1

It's not so much that we enjoy what we do well. It's that we do well what we enjoy.

One of life's most crucial lessons is that personal fulfillment is ultimately what matters. Money, power, "breaking records" – these are hollow rewards for our labors. That which gives us *joy* is what makes life worthwhile.

But make no mistake: True "enjoyment" is no simple pleasure. We're not talking about the passing satisfactions of a full body massage, or a well-played game of softball, or a stimulating afternoon in the holosuite. Joy is more like the "bliss" of Earth's Hindu or Sufi mystics. It's the abiding sense that something we are doing is connected to the very purpose of our lives – that *this* is what we were meant for. It's the biofeedback system designed by The Universe to guide us along our personal Path.

Too often we turn off that system because it conflicts with what society tells us. Yet if we follow society's advice, we are usually left unfulfilled, even enslaved.

The irony is that if we follow the guidance of our bliss instead – if we seek first what gives us true joy, lasting joy – we end up doing so well that what society values often comes to us as a by-product. And if we don't exactly break any records, at least we've broken some of our chains.

Fulfillment is my first priority. I will look for the signs of true joy that illumine my path through life.

03.13

The game isn't big enough unless it scares you a little.

— COMMANDER RIKER : PEN PALS : 42695.3

Here's one of those truths you can take to the Federation Credit Center: There is no learning without challenge. There is no growth without overcoming some obstacle, without pushing the limits of what you've done before.

If you knew you'd succeed every time out, if there was no doubt you'd return safely – if you weren't scared – the journey would be little more than round-trip transportation back to where you started. It's the voyage into the Unknown that opens up new possibilities.

And opens up our blood vessels.

Because there's an emotional, visceral rush that comes from the prospect of discovery, from knowing that you're about to learn something, but you're not sure *what.* Being a little bit afraid, as Riker points out, isn't your body's warning to cut your potential losses, to fold your hand without playing it out. It's a message from your own psyche that the potential gain is worth the risk, and now you're mobilizing your energies for the effort.

"Big enough" is about growing room – or more specifically, about our need to make room in our lives for personal growth. In this case, if it's too comfortable, it doesn't fit!

I enjoy the "game" of improving myself. I accept the risks; I feel invigorated as my body rises to the challenge; I am fulfilled by having made the effort.

03.14

Live long and prosper.

— SPOCK : AMOK TIME : 3372.7

The traditional Vulcan benediction is now repeated so often, and in so many parts of the galaxy, that it has become one of the most common slogans of our time. So common that we rarely pause to reflect on what it means anymore.

Certainly it means more than the parting words humans uttered for centuries – the lukewarm "Good day" or, later, "Have a nice day." Then again, compared with some of Earth's other benedictions – like "Peace be unto you" or "May the Lord shine his face upon you" – the Vulcan "Live long and prosper" sounds almost... well, commercial.

But the literal meaning is less important than what happens when one person speaks the words to another. Because it's more than mere words. It's what the Ancients called "well-wishing" or, in spiritual terms, a "blessing."

When we bless someone, we are essentially affirming their connection to The Universe. We are reminding them that all the bounty and goodness the universe has to offer can be theirs – in fact it's *already* theirs.

And that reminder is not lost on our own ears, either. Because if we can affirm the goodness of the universe for others – or even "bless them that curse you" – we not only claim it for ourselves, we unleash such a positive flow of energy that lives can be changed overnight.

I will wish others well in both word and thought – especially my so-called "enemies" – and watch as my relationships, and my world, are transformed.

03.15

You weren't stirring up trouble. You were exploring.

— CAPTAIN HERNANDEZ : HOME : CIRCA ECE2154

Clearly, our journeys toward recovery and wholeness, our ongoing explorations of new ideas and new lifestyles, can often upset the status quo. Friends and co-workers may no longer know what to expect of us. Sometimes we don't know what to expect of our*selves* as we peel back the layers of our public and private lives, as we experiment with new rituals, try out new responses, new methods of dealing with the same issues that may have created problems for us in the past.

But it's our relationships with others that seem to stir up the most trouble. Especially those who were invested in the person we were before we sought change: Our drinking buddies, drug connections, members of the crowd we once "ran with," co-conspirators in maintaining the habits we now realize were either unhealthy or holding us back, or both.

We can't let others' expectations short-circuit our explorations. Without ignoring our valid responsibilities, saving our *own* souls must be our primary focus. Yet we must also give others the space to explore, to stir up trouble. We must be ready to adjust our relationships as our friends and co-workers, our lovers and leaders likewise change and grow, knowing that their Inner Voyage is as important to them as ours is to us.

I realize my actions inevitably impact others in ways that may trouble them. But I also know the changes that truly benefit me will ultimately benefit them.

03.16

It is possible to commit no mistakes and still lose. That is not a weakness. That is life.

— CAPTAIN PICARD : PEAK PERFORMANCE : 42923.4

One of the most difficult lessons to learn is that even if we do our best, even if our phasers are charged and ready, success is not guaranteed. We can still be defeated.

There are limits to technology. Unknown factors inevitably come into play. An old proverb from Earth's past (and elsewhere) suggests that if anything can go wrong, something *will* go wrong. But as another of Earth's Ancient Ones said, we are responsible not for the outcome, but for *making the effort.*

Failure, in spite of our best efforts, is a great teacher. It keeps us humble. It reminds us that we're only a finite part of an infinite Whole.

More importantly, failure teaches us to live fully in the present, to do the very best we can now, and then trust that the future will take care of itself… if only we'd let go.

Of course, the expected outcome can motivate us to make the effort, just as a destination can energize us to begin a voyage. But life – and personal growth – lies not in our having "arrived," but in the voyage itself.

I derive satisfaction from making the effort. I will concentrate on doing my best now, and turn over responsibility for the outcome to The Universe.

03.17

Like m' wee grannie use'ta say, "Ye canna' break a stick in a bundle."

— CHIEF ENGINEER SCOTT : STAR TREK BEYOND : CIRCA 2263

"Strength in unity" is not just a meaningless slogan. It is practical, verifiable, and proven by experience through trial and error. No wonder much of our folk wisdom continues to be passed down from one generation to the next, in this case from Scotty's "wee grannie."

A lone twig can be easily snapped. But gather a few dozen fresh ones together and the bound bundle is as strong as steel. Being an engineer, Scotty might have used his own experience to point out that the strongest cable is actually woven from dozens or hundreds of metallic strands twisted together, like the spiraled hemp ropes of earlier times. The outer enclosures of today's starships are less like the sheet metal skins of yester-year's automobiles and jet airplanes than hybrid metal fabrics woven together on a microscopic level.

It's no doubt true that a single person, acting alone, can sometimes make all the difference. That's what heroes are known for. But the greatest heroes aren't celebrated so much for their personal achievements as for inspiring the rest of us to bind ourselves together in common cause, to the point where a unified assemblage of ordinary, otherwise powerless individuals can change the status quo if not the course of history… and in the process change the people within it.

I will search for communities in which I'm free to share both who I am and who I'd like to become. My true strength as an individual lies in linking my unique talents and my self to others.

03.18

We are far from the sacred places of our grandfathers, and from the bones of our people.

— CAPTAIN JANEWAY : THE CLOUD : 48546.2

One of the risks of "boldly going where no one has gone before" is the possibility that we may lose touch with where we've *been*. Unfortunately, where we've been – our past – very much affects who we are now. And if we make a wrong turn, sometimes the only way to get back on course is to retrace our steps.

The "bones of our people" provides a powerful symbol for "where we've been" and "who we are." The ancient practice of setting aside sacred ground for the dead may seem primitive. But burial was never meant primarily to preserve bodies for an afterlife. Its major effect was to keep us connected to those who went before, to preserve their hard-won lessons – to keep their legacy alive *in us.*

It shouldn't be surprising that physical separation from hometowns, much less home planets, will sometimes unsettle us. The evolution of a species in a certain environment can't help but produce psychic patterns which only that environment can satisfy. To remember "sacred places" and honor ancestors is to reaffirm our roots – not for the purpose of living in the past, but to keep our bearings as we venture into uncharted territory.

Where I came from remains part of me now. In learning to accept and celebrate those who went before me, I am better prepared to face the future.

03.19

I have found that humans value their uniqueness – that sense that they are different from everyone else.

— DATA : SECOND CHANCES : 46915.2

Data was correct, of course. But there is a dark side to his observation as well as a brighter side.

The fact is, throughout human history, an individual's sense of being "different" from others has usually been connected with the idea of being *better*. More often than not, "I'm not like you" has been a way of saying "I'm superior." Or "My country/culture/religion is superior to yours."

Which is ironic: When most individuals or countries feel compelled to assert their own superiority, it's usually a sign that, deep in their souls, they suspect they're not.

But even this sentiment hides a piece of the truth. Because what we really suspect, deep in our souls, is that we're all "better" if we maintain and even celebrate our differences. The "brighter side" is that we were never meant to be cookie-cutter copies of one another. And even if we are basically the same, making ourselves "unique" in some way is essential to our own – and our society's – happiness and success.

The advantage of uniqueness is written all over the evolutionary record. Species that maintain diversity survive the inevitable natural disasters and epidemics. So do individuals. So do we.

My differences don't make me better than anyone else. They make us *better... together.*

03.20

Perhaps you know of Russian epic of Cinderella...? If shoe fits, wear it!

— COMMANDER CHEKOV : THE UNDISCOVERED COUNTRY : 9521.6

One of Chekov's more charming traits was his unabashed assumption that every useful invention, every scientific breakthrough, every classic of literature was a product of Russian culture. (Actually, Chekov was playing off his shipmates' assumptions to the contrary – an admission he makes in his memoirs.) But the Cinderella "epic" not only echoes a theme common to every human culture, it can be found all across the galaxy.

Equally charming is Chekov's assumption about what the Cinderella story means. (Or was he playing games here, too?) Surely he isn't suggesting that the message is merely about accepting the personal foibles others help us to see. Cinderella's glass slipper can't simply be a symbol for the personal qualities we must "own" before we can reach an accurate understanding of ourselves.

Or can it?

Because one of the qualities we sometimes have the most trouble accepting is our own inherent goodness. Unlike many of us, Cinderella was true to that "royalty" within her, despite being treated like a slave. And the message is, if only *we* would be true to our higher Self, our royal destiny will come looking for us, too.

The Universe has already outfitted me with the divine image. Today I will remember to put it on; to wear it, act it, become it.

The ways our differences combine to create meaning and beauty!

— SPOCK : IS THERE IN TRUTH NO BEAUTY? : 5630.7

One clear sign of our spiritual progress is our capacity to appreciate differences. True, we may feel more at home in a certain culture. We may find one spiritual tradition more conducive to our personal growth and understanding of reality. But our recognition of the positive role other cultures and traditions play is an essential step along our Path.

Despite all the shared traits that make us essentially alike, each of us is different. Our childhoods shape us in ways that make us more or less sensitive to certain experiences, more or less receptive to various approaches to learning. So, what conveys meaning or beauty to one person may have little impact on someone else.

Which simply means that our spiritual unfolding may happen in very different ways. Ironically, only by using a wide diversity of symbols, disciplines and experiences can The Universe teach all of us the same identical Truth.

But what's amazing is, once we realize this, we begin to see that same Truth behind its multiple expressions. We enable ourselves to gain new insights from a broader spectrum of sources. We can leave the confines of our own racial, social or religious circles and feel no less "at home."

A garden with only red roses soon loses its appeal… unless there are yellow tulips nearby.

I celebrate the diversity of forms beauty and truth can take, and by which The Universe can teach me.

03.22

Chance is irrelevant. We will succeed.

— SEVEN OF NINE : NIGHT : 52081.2

It's a bold, even admirable sentiment. But the fact is, many people who make this statement *don't* succeed. Sometimes they fail… spectacularly.

What's admirable, then, is not so much the outcome, but our determination. Simply to make the attempt – to overcome inertia and decide to act – is already a kind of success. One that's equally spectacular.

In a parallel universe, a great sage taught his students, "Do, or do not. There is no try." His point was well taken. For if our aim is merely to "try," we often take our eyes off the goal. We focus on the effort alone. Or worse, we're distracted by it, worrying so much about the energy and the cost that we forget what we're trying to achieve. We soon forget the very relationship between trying and achieving until, at last, we see no reason to try at all.

But even this great sage would admit that, without trying, there is no doing. Doing is what trying turns into, if we keep working at it.

To say "Chance is irrelevant" isn't to deny the role of luck – or at least the role of unknown and unforeseen forces luck represents. But, as Captain Sisko says elsewhere in the record, "Fortune favors the bold." And what fortune and luck often turn out to be, if only we have the determination to try, is The Universe itself rallying around us.

To try is to succeed. To make the effort is to give others, and The Universe, an opportunity to help.

03.23

It's not a crime to believe in yourself.

— LT. COMMANDER DAX : THE QUICKENING : Stardate Not Given

For many of us, the past is little more than a case study in self-disappointment. We can hardly count the number of times we've failed to accomplish what we set out to do, or we end up accomplishing exactly the opposite. It's no wonder we've stopped believing in ourselves!

Trouble is, our resulting lack of confidence only makes matters worse. We stop trying – or at least trying anything *new* – for fear of failing again. We defer too easily to what others think, or what others want, or what others say we should do. We give up responsibility for our lives.

And that's the real crime here: Giving up.

For one thing, we'll never regain our confidence if we won't even give ourselves the opportunity to succeed. More importantly, each of us has a mandate from The Universe to keep trying. No matter how many mistakes we've made in the past, no matter how many more times we may fail, every one of us is divinely authorized to continue believing in ourselves.

And if it's admittedly difficult to believe in the person we've been, we can still believe in the person we *can be.*

That person exists within us even now, calling us out, challenging us to live up to our potential. If we sit quietly, we can hear that voice. And in hearing, we become.

I affirm the Self blossoming within me, the Self I will become, and therefore the Self I am already.

03.24

Personally? I'd rather go down fighting!

— LIEUTENANT TORRES : TWISTED : Stardate Not Given

Looking beyond the specific situation in which she spoke these lines, B'Elanna's statement reflects her entire attitude toward life. One we'd do well to emulate.

Because, like all warriors, we too must ask ourselves if there are some things more valuable than life itself; what we'd do everything in our power to get or keep, and without which our spirits might as well be dead. And then, symbolically at least, we must *fight* for those things.

In fact we must *go down* fighting. And if that language sounds rather extreme, it's simply to emphasize how high the stakes are. The truth is, our daily lives put us in just as much physical jeopardy as a warrior going into battle, since what we stand for and believe in can have immediate, tangible consequences on how we live. Or whether we ever truly "live" at all.

B'Elanna's words also remind us that fighting for our beliefs is a struggle to which we must commit the rest of our lives – whether we have five more years or fifty. It's not like our jobs; we do not "retire" after putting in a prescribed number. In fact, remaining committed until the very end, until the final moment of our "going down," may be what the struggle is ultimately about.

I value the life given me, not by trying to preserve it, but by using it up. I will know my true purpose in life because it will keep me "fighting" to the end.

03.25

The Borg... party poopers of the galaxy!

— THE DOCTOR : DRONE : Stardate Not Given

"The Borg" has always served as a useful metaphor for the forces that rob us of our individuality, that reduce us to interchangeable parts in an impersonal, mechanized whole. To be a Borg, symbolically speaking, is to let some exterior framework or ethos determine Who You Are, to allow it to substitute its thoughts for yours. The Borg can stand for the clique we belong to, or a culture or religion whose precepts and customs we unthinkingly follow.

In a more literal sense, The Borg represent the temptations of technology, whose "progress" and products we blindly embrace whether we truly need them or not — and that insidiously transform us over time until we're no longer aware how much of ourselves we've lost, and we no longer care anyway.

To call The Borg "party poopers" is simply to inject a little humor into an otherwise serious situation: The loss of our own identity and autonomy. Ironically, many spiritual traditions would also have us lose our identity, by finally merging with the universe... or, as The Borg might say, to assimilate with the Ultimate Collective.

But that kind of assimilation takes place only when each individual has been fully developed. And thankfully, the process of unfolding our individuality never ends.

I celebrate my quest for autonomy. I am grateful for the freedom to make choices that are considerate of others, without being determined by them.

03.26

That's the thing about faith. If you don't have it, you can't understand it. And if you do, no explanation is necessary.

— MAJOR KIRA : ACCESSION : Stardate Not Given

We've all heard this argument used by people to justify actions they can't defend otherwise. "It was a matter of personal faith," they'll say. "You wouldn't understand because you're not..." And then they fill in the blank with whatever religion (or political party) they belong to, and you *don't*.

But just because the argument is misused doesn't mean it's not true. Faith truly *isn't* something you can readily understand without having experienced it directly, without having lived it. And trying to explain an action motivated by faith is rarely satisfying, because there's so much more involved than logic.

For example, try to logically justify your love for someone else, and why that love motivates you to do all the things you do. Try to explain why we should have compassion for a total stranger, freely give them our food or clothing or hard-earned latinum even though we may never see them again. We can't explain it. We just *do* it.

The concepts and disciplines that give direction and meaning to our lives are, in a sense, indefensible. They justify themselves only by their effects on us — how we feel about ourselves, how we treat others, and whether they inspire us to strive for our highest potential.

I need not justify my beliefs to others. But I can affirm their truth for me by the positive effects they are having on my life, and on my relationships.

03.27

We all have our assigned duties.

— ADMIRAL KIRK : THE WRATH OF KHAN : 8130.3

It's as if The Universe is calling us to do something, to perform some important task for which our lives have uniquely prepared us. Some of us are lucky enough to discover our mission early in life, others only later. If at all.

Many of us think we know what it is. We may even get offended if anyone should question us about it. "Mind your own business," we might reply, bluntly suggesting that they focus on *their* assigned duties and leave us to ours.

Which is usually a clue that we may not know what our mission is, because few of us can work completely on our own, without input (and sometimes hard questioning) from others. In fact, others can often help us discover our mission and continually refine it as we go through life.

But once we *do* discover it, nothing can distract us. Our "assigned duty" takes precedence over everything else.

An ancient tradition tells the story of a man whose duty was to plant fruit trees for the next generation to enjoy. As he was planting one such tree, a neighbor rushed up to tell him that the long-awaited Messiah had finally arrived, and that they should immediately go to greet him. "Later," the man replied, "after I finish planting my tree."

He was right to wait until he'd finished. That, after all, was *his* life's mission. And who's to say the man's dedication – and that of others like him – isn't precisely what brought the Messiah?

I have an essential role to play. If I meditate and open myself, The Universe will teach me what it is.

03.28

You may eliminate the symbols, but that does not mean death to the issue those symbols represent.

— COMMANDER RIKER : ANGEL ONE : 41636.9

During Earth's Nineteenth and Twentieth Centuries, certain reactionary groups often held "book-burnings." Publications deemed heretical or unwholesome were thrown into a huge pile and torched. The bonfire would supposedly rid the community of their evil influence.

The practice is hardly isolated. Hundreds of planetary societies have sought to suppress unwelcome messages by destroying the vehicles that carried them. And not just the words and symbols. The writers and prophets themselves have also been torched or otherwise put to death.

But trying to eliminate the "vehicle" without dealing directly with the message has always failed. In fact it's likely to draw even more attention to the message.

So it is with our personal lives. We can't heal our moral or spiritual illnesses by applying "band-aids." We can't finally rid ourselves of emotional pain by anesthetizing our minds with drugs or endless "entertainment." If anything, our problems will only become worse.

We must confront the deeper issues which our behavior and our feelings represent. Our lives are an open message to others, and to ourselves. Stop and listen.

I am learning to see through my life's experiences to the messages they hold for me. If I don't like what they tell me, I know that help is available.

03.29

Somewhere along this journey we'll find a way back.

— CAPTAIN JANEWAY : CARETAKER : 48315.6

For many of us — and for many religions — this statement is a concise summary of the very Purpose of Life: To find our way back home. Whether conceived as "Heaven" or "Nirvana" or "walking with the Prophets," some final reunion with our Creator or Supreme Source is the ultimate goal.

The irony is that, according to these same traditions, we've never really left to begin with. We are, deep within us, in contact with our Source even now. But in the course of our lives we've built up layers of crust and corrosion; we've bound ourselves with chains of karma or sin. We've not so much lost our way as lost our connection.

"Finding our way back" makes a powerful symbol for re-connection and recovery. The "journey" reminds us that we can expect many wrong turns, many side trips, and many ongoing adventures designed to teach us important lessons. For most of us, returning will take years, or even a lifetime.

In fact, we will finally come to realize that "getting back" is less important than the journey itself. To repeat, the final destination is not so much a goal as an excuse to undertake the voyage in the first place. And our patient expectation of returning *some*day, regardless of how long it may take or what trials we must endure along the way, is the Faith that sustains us.

"Somewhere" is here. My "way back" is within. I welcome and celebrate this voyage of spiritual reunion as it expresses itself in my physical life.

03.30

The best way to know yourself is to know others.

— CAPTAIN GEORGIOU : THE BUTCHER'S KNIFE CARES NOT FOR THE LAMB'S CRY : Stardate 1403.4

A line from her holographic Last Will and Testament, this gentle reminder for Commander Burnham — whom Georgiou expected to earn her own starship one day — applies equally to *all* of us.

The Stoic philosopher Zeno, Earth's own version of a Vulcan sage, is perhaps most famous for the axiom Georgiou recalls here, to "Know thyself." Which calls for another adage: "Easier said than done!" Because *how* we come to know ourselves is the real issue. And our greatest challenge.

The hard truth is, many of us are still only remotely aware of what makes us tick. Our own motivations frequently baffle us as much as they do others. In our inherent lack of discipline. In our inability to get started, to stay focused, to get outside of our own selfish point of view. We fall into negative habits without much thought, and over which we seem to have little control.

One proven method for gaining more control is to study ourselves as if we were an "outside observer," noting our own weaknesses and strengths without judgment like a psychologist might analyze her client. We can hone this technique by first practicing it on others — preferably *not* our family or friends! — looking at what they do and what they say, what appears to work for them and what doesn't. And then, knowing that our "subjects" face the same challenges as we do, comparing our actions and words to theirs in hopes of learning any lessons that might benefit us.

And the biggest benefit is that what we learn becomes our Testament for those who follow.

I will not judge others or measure my spiritual progress against theirs, but reflect on others' experience to find the clues that might help unlock my own mystery.

Thy will be done.

— CHIEF ENGINEER SCOTT : THE VOYAGE HOME : 8390

It's probably the most common meditation, the most common prayer, in the universe. It is also the most deeply religious, for it symbolizes what amounts to our own salvation.

The fact is, sooner or later we realize who – or *what* – is truly in command of this Voyage. After trying to live as if we were the center of the universe, something comes along to turn our world upside down. The "precipitating event" is as different and unique as we are. But all of us learn, at last, that our lives are in the grasp of the same Power that fashioned the stars and the planets; and that, under its direction, we are like so much soft clay.

We also figure out that *other* lives are likewise being shaped and sustained by that Power. And we realize that our very survival – both together and individually – depends not on trying to carry out our own separate wills, but in aligning ourselves with *its* Universal Will.

Ironically, this life-changing realization can't come through meditation. Even as "Thy will be done" becomes our meditative mantra, we can't learn its truth except through life experience. We must hit the streets, interact with other people, perhaps even live as if we *are* the center of the universe until, inevitably, Reality catches up with us.

Or sometimes pounds us into pancakes. And the saving grace is, it turns out to be the best thing that could've happened.

By surrendering my will to The Universe, I won't lose it. I'll find it – transformed and newly empowered.

CORRESPONDING TO THE MONTH OF

04.01

You are fully capable of deciding your own destiny. The question you face is: Which path will you choose?

— SAREK : STAR TREK / PREQUEL : CIRCA 2249

That's The Big Question, isn't it? And whether you realize it or not, the answer is already within you.

After all, you have the necessary tools. You know where the resources are, both in the lessons and the wisdom you've gained from your experiences, and in the vast treasury of spiritual traditions that connect you to an even deeper wellspring of wisdom. And while you may not feel particularly connected, or you don't exactly consider yourself "wise" at this point, your life *is* in your own hands.

Admittedly, it may seem a bit simplistic to repeat the old adage that, even if you can't control the events around you, the way you handle them *is*. But that's the simple truth: Your attitudes, your *reactions* to those events, are fully within your capability to "decide."

The path you choose, therefore, isn't really about career choices or your life's mission, as important as those may be. It's a matter of deciding whether money and possessions should motivate your actions instead of relationships and knowledge; whether self-interest overrides others' needs; whether getting to the destination is what counts, or the journey itself is enough for now.

In short, your "destiny" is to live as a material creature caught up in a material world, or as a visitor exploring and mining the material world for its spiritual riches. Sarak is only reminding us that the path is neither predetermined nor permanent. And you're already well on your way.

I determine my destiny by the choices I make, not just once, but with every new moment. That is my responsibility... and my saving grace.

04.02

A man does not own land. He doesn't own anything but the courage and loyalty in his heart.

— COMMANDER CHAKOTAY : INITIATIONS : 49005.3

Most societies throughout the galaxy still retain some notion of "ownership." In a positive light, the concept embodies the notion of "personal responsibility." Because I own this, I'd better take care of it; I alone am responsible.

Of course, certain things *can't* be owned by anyone — at least, not as some societies see it. The indigenous peoples of Earth's North America were one such society. In their view, people could no more own land than they could possess the sunset or the seasons. They could take from the land what they needed to live — that's why the Great Spirit had provided it. But even those "necessities" were meant to be used and recycled, just as our bodies grow and age and revert to the elements.

As another society put it, "You can't take it with you."

But what *can* be taken, what you *do* own — and are therefore solely responsible for — is Who You Are. The "courage" Chakotay mentions really stands for all our personal qualities. "Loyalty" represents our sense of inter-connectedness with others, with the network of Life, with The Universe. This is what truly matters. And as Chakotay went on to say, "That's where my power comes from."

My strength comes not from things, but from character. I do not seek possessions or honors — or even knowledge — so much as a brave heart.

04.03

The only person you are truly competing against is yourself.

— CAPTAIN PICARD : COMING OF AGE : 41416.2

It's not that we shouldn't look to other people as role models – for examples of how to live our lives, or perhaps how *not* to. It's just that, in the end, those other people don't live in our shoes. They can't fully appreciate the challenges we're up against. Or the possibilities this life offers that theirs doesn't.

In short, there is no ideal role model, no concrete standard to measure yourself against, except…

Except for *you.*

Which doesn't mean there are no standards. The Universe, in its mysterious way, "knows" the person each of us is capable of becoming at any particular stage in our lives. Deep down, we do too. And we can allow previous habits and external circumstances to continue their hold on us, or we can work diligently toward our higher vision.

But first we must get in touch with that highest and best vision of ourselves – the person only we can be, despite the challenges we face, and because of the unique possibilities our life offers. We must measure ourselves by *that* standard and, in a sense, compete with it like an athlete striving to beat his own "personal best."

If we're lucky, the competition never ends.

I will measure my failures and successes not by what other people think, but by my own highest aspirations – mine, together with the Universe's.

04.04

Words are here, on top. What's under them – their meaning, is what's important.

— RIVA : LOUD AS A WHISPER : 42477.2

There's no avoiding the fact that the right words can be crucial. The ground-breaking Treaty of Alliance between the Federation and the Klingon Empire would've been useless without wording that offered no chance for misinterpretation. Ordinary business contracts, too, require careful selection of words to define obligations and relationships, not only for the parties directly involved, but for those who may inherit their provisions.

Interpersonal relationships, however, often rely on meanings that can't be captured by words. In fact, what is *not* said can be more important that what is. Sometimes the real meaning may flatly contradict the words. Even strong criticism can communicate love if delivered with compassion, or with an arm gently encircling another's shoulders. The most bumbling, clumsily-worded apology – or compliment, or proposal of marriage – can sound like poetry if one's heart is in it.

Words, after all, are only tools. We must practice listening "through" the words we hear to what lies "under them." And we must measure our own words in the same way – not by the mere sounds our vocal chords make, but by what resonates within us, and by what we do.

Genuine meaning lies deeper than words. Without discounting what people say, I will look into their eyes and listen to their hearts. And to my own.

04.05

When you're under conditions of extreme stress, the mind manufactures all kinds of things.

— DR. CRUSHER : FRAME OF MIND : 46778.1

The effects of extreme or chronic stress are well documented. The heightened energy levels designed to galvanize us for action can end up eating away at our own bodies. And our psyches.

Because without any clearly-defined problem to focus on, to analyze and to solve, our minds literally invent a substitute. We imagine problems that don't exist. We project our frustrations and fears onto others, and onto the world. Those projections sometimes manifest as hallucinations, but more often they are experienced as a vague uneasiness, or even the feeling that everything and everybody is "out to get us."

The fact that we have such feelings so much of the time should give us pause. More importantly, it should remind us that we need to pause more often in our daily routines — to close our eyes and mentally remove ourselves from the moment; to regain our objectivity; to seek guidance.

One of Earth's sacred traditions would have us stop for meditation and prayer five times each day. Another tradition counsels us to "Pray unceasingly." Whatever our Path, finding some way to regularly reconnect with a Higher Reality is essential. Because when we are connected, the mind stops "manufacturing." It's too busy... *receiving.*

I will be sensitive to the signs of my own stress, and take a "time out" whenever my body/mind needs it.

04.06

They don't arrest people for having feelings.

— DR. McCOY : THE UNDISCOVERED COUNTRY : 9521.6

Not now, maybe. But there have been times when the opposite was the case. On some planets, it's *still* the case.

Because feelings can be dangerous. After all, they're so "irrational." Not to mention compelling. They often make us do things we never intended.

What's worse, they're *communicable.* One person's public display of emotion will often infect another with the very same feelings. Group passions can be aroused. More than one rebellion has been sparked when a single person expressed deep feelings of discontent. The broken dam starts with a small crack.

Then again, it's the holding back of those emotions — the building up of churning waters behind the dam — that allows a single crack to have such a devastating effect. If only we could release our natural feelings as they arise, the damage would be reduced, if not eliminated.

Not that they would no longer be "communicable." The fact is, feelings have been designed by the universe for communication. They link us at the level where we all "live" — where all of us are equal despite differing I.Q.'s and languages and cultures. To feel is to be connected.

We are meant to share one another's joy and sadness. Because only through others are we made whole.

My feelings are not only natural, but empowering. I will neither hide my feelings from others, nor hide from the feelings of others.

04.07

Unity is not your strength. It is your weakness.

— KRALL : STAR TREK BEYOND : CIRCA 2263.3

This dispirited claim from a former (and deeply disillusioned) Starfleet officer is a direct response to Lt. Uhura's earlier assertion that "There is strength in unity." And the equally dispiriting truth is, Krall's claim is frequently borne out by the facts.

For one thing, "unity" is too often claimed when it does not exist. After all, it sounds so enlightened; advanced societies *should* be unified, right? Trouble is, genuine unity demands vigilance. It requires that people tolerate differences in order to concentrate on similarities, to continually focus their efforts on projects that reflect common principles and shared goals. Which is why it's our job, as crewmembers, to guard against the conditions that exacerbate differences and disagreements. It takes real commitment. It demands *work.*

But the other thing is, claiming "unity" can also be an excuse for some people to let others do the heavy lifting, to slack off while others carry them along. If I can convince you to sign onto one of my pet projects whose goals you happen to share, that means I needn't work as hard — which can ultimately undermine the very relationship we're giving lip service to. And if our claimed unity is to become anything more than an empty slogan, we must all do our part. Even the weakest members can contribute something.

Krall is right to remind us: Unity must never be taken for granted. Or the result *is* weakness.

By affirming strength in unity, I commit myself to the hard work of building it, maintaining it, and living as if my own good is inextricably linked to everyone else's.

04.08

I hardly believe that insults are within your prerogative.

— SPOCK : THE CITY ON THE EDGE OF FOREVER : 3134.0

One of Earth's great Spiritual Teachers tells the story of a man who is always quick to point out the "motes" in other people's eyes. Yet this same man can't see the chunks of debris in his own eye that make him all but blind.

Psychologists tell a similar story. Just as most people who are genuinely insane don't recognize their insanity, the people who are most in need of an ethical overhaul rarely realize their immoral behavior. And the people who continually point fingers, who are especially critical of others, are usually the ones most in need of help.

The Magic Mirror strikes again. It works like this:

The negative traits our fragile egos won't permit us to see in ourselves, we project onto others. The character flaws, the moral failures, the "sins" we find in everyone else are really reflections of our *own* flaws, failures and sins. Our subconscious mind is trying to show us what we can't see — or won't see — using other people as mirrors.

So if we notice ourselves being critical of others, it's time to ask ourselves what it is about *us* we need to change. And if we've actually insulted somebody, it's a pretty good sign that things are getting desperate. We need to change our ways… now.

I will concentrate first on changing myself. And I will be more understanding of others who face the same uphill battle in their own lives.

04.09

There will always be those who mean to do us harm. To stop them, we risk awakening the same evil within ourselves.

— CAPTAIN KIRK : STAR TREK / INTO DARKNESS : CIRCA 2259

Fighting an enemy by using the same evil tactics *he* uses has always been risky. To make the same point, Captain Picard would later warn that "the seed of violence remains within each of us." Meeting violence with more violence usually ends up harming *us* at least as much as those we fight.

And violence isn't the only "seed" that remains. Every ancient instinct, every primordial drive, lies buried in our biology, subject to a sudden resurgence under just the right conditions.

Some of us may characterize these latent instincts as "inner demons." Others believe our demons are quite real. Both are ways of acknowledging the legacy of our past while trying to rise above it. In other words, the seeds may still be there, but we don't need to fertilize them!

Vigilance against our primitive tendencies, however, is only part of our challenge. The fact is, we may have struggled with other inner demons — more modern "evils," like an obsession with money or material things, or a case of low self-esteem, or a serious addiction. And having finally overcome them, we assume our struggle is behind us.

Not necessarily. Because the seeds of these problems also remain within us, subject to resurgence. Look at it as The Universe's way of keeping us from becoming too confident. Or for keeping us connected to others who are now having the same struggle… and who need our help.

I will guard against my lowest inclinations by striving to achieve my highest. I grow even stronger by striving to bring out the highest in others.

04.10

I don't have a life. I have a program!

— THE DOCTOR : TATTOO : Stardate Not Given

For many of us, our lives have become programs, too. Our reluctance to try anything new; our fear of falling behind if we pause now and then to review where we're going; our willingness to let our jobs take priority over everything else… these are signs that we are no longer controlling our lives so much as being controlled.

Not that we can avoid responsibility. Things could've been different. But we made choices. And now we've accepted our routines as if they were installed by our manufacturer, and any tampering might crash our system!

Ironically, our personal programs are very much like the "software" of the early Computer Age. They are easily frozen by conflicting commands, highly sensitive to hidden viruses. And when we develop a program which seems to work for us, we are very reluctant to change.

Pre-computerized societies called it "habit." Or being "stuck in a rut." But life is about getting unstuck, about setting off on new paths. Because one of the programs our manufacturer did install is the ability to rewrite those programs. Beginning with the "Pause" command.

And if that doesn't work, software upgrades are available from several dependable sources. Not the least of which is the One we're already connected to.

I am my own programmer. I can diagnose the glitches — with others' help, if I want it. And I can install new "software" whenever I decide.

04.11

You can't be afraid of rejection.

— COMMANDER SISKO : THE HOMECOMING : Stardate Not Given

The "traveling salesman" of Terran legend is the paradigm case. The Ferengi deep space business-man (or woman) is a more contemporary example.

And the most successful ones rarely make more than one sale in ten. In other words, for every ten product presentations these entrepreneurs make, the proverbial door slams in their face nine times! That's a rejection rate of ninety percent. Or, as Sisko might have put it, a batting average of .100. How can any player cope with that?

More than not being "afraid," it's a matter of redefining the game. It means recognizing before-hand that you'll "process" ten potential customers in order to filter out the one with whom you were meant to do business. It means identifying the nine who don't need your services, so you can better serve the one who does. It means practicing on the nine, so that the tenth will truly under-stand and appreciate what you have to offer.

And what you're practicing is not your "sales presentation." What you're offering is not a mere product. What you're really "processing" is not your customers but your self.

In facing rejection, we are all like the salesman. Overcoming it is a process of affirming one's self-worth despite the outcome. Selling that to ourselves is the real success.

Rejection is a loving process for refining Who I Am. I acknowledge the Self within me that can't be rejected because The Universe already accepts it.

04.12

It is the struggle itself that is most important. It does not matter that we will never reach our ultimate goal. The effort yields its own rewards.

— DATA : THE OFFSPRING : 43657.0

Data's statement can stand quite nicely on its own, thank you. Nothing further is necessary…

Except, perhaps, for this footnote:

Religious traditions on many planets have envisioned a kind of personal salvation which claims to be a once-in-a-lifetime event. One's vow of submission to a certain deity's authority, or one's performance of a particularly heroic deed, was enough to secure the Eternal Reward.

Admittedly, there are turning points in our lives. Certain actions or realizations may stand out as life-transforming events. Religions are right to celebrate these decisive moments by giving them some kind of sacred status.

But this kind of recognition also gives the impression that the struggle is over. Or that the struggle is worthwhile only as a means toward an end. Data properly reminds us that our salvation lies in doing, not in having done.

We should be suspicious of life goals that are too close, too easily achieved. The voyage whose destination is always just beyond the horizon is the only one that can reward us eternally.

Perfection is a verb, not an adjective. I reaffirm my commitment to the never-ending voyage of self-discovery and self-improvement.

04.13

I believe someone once defined a compromise as a solution that neither side is happy with.

There are periods in every society when doctrinal purity is thought to be a great virtue. "Compromise" becomes a dirty word. Remaining true to "the party line" at all costs, whether religiously or politically, is the ideal.

It is also the cause of incessant dysfunction, if not ongoing violence – from the stalemates in our legislatures to full-scale planetary wars.

"Compromise" is the ancient art of pro-actively mapping out areas of common interest, identifying values and goals we share, and using them as steppingstones to tolerance and mutual agreement. In the process we can expect to arouse passions; we will adamantly define some things we simply can't live without, both physically and spiritually. But as sentient, empathetic creatures, we usually come to understand why some lines cannot be crossed, and others can.

And the truth is, we can still maintain our ideals; we can still go on working passionately for the things we believe in, even while acknowledging that others don't share all of our views. The "art" is to make the adjustments and sacrifices we can all "live with," in order for us to *live with one another* – in a world where we can no longer live apart. Admittedly, neither side may feel particularly thrilled at first, but history invariably demonstrates that compromise is best in the long run.

And, by the way, if you think we're talking only about societies and nations here, think again.

Learning to live with our differences is a virtue. Out of diversity I find solutions I'd never discover by myself. Give-and-take is the way I keep, not lose, my integrity.

04.14

You cannot put a price on life!

From a purely practical point of view, it's hard to disagree with Picard's statement. We know, for example, how impossible it is to predict the course of someone's life. A person born into poverty may end up giving more wealth to his community – in service if not money – than a dozen self-indulgent millionaires. Intelligence hasn't been a reliable gauge of someone's "worth" either. Nor have good looks, or racial qualities, or social standing.

Not to mention how wrong we can be in valuing our own lives. Even those of us who harbor doubts about our self-worth may go on to play decisive roles. Or at least go on to decide that our lives aren't really so bad after all.

But practical considerations are not, finally, what makes Picard's statement true. The fact is, we have no business trying to judge the worth of a person's life in the first place. The Universe has its own "reasons" for creating us all. How any individual fits into the wider Scheme of Things is not merely beyond the human capacity to know (or Vulcan, or Betazoid). It is *beyond knowing*.

What lies deep within each of us – deeper than all the external descriptions of Who We Are – is not subject to evaluation. Let's remember to treat each other that way.

I will not judge others – or myself – by any standard of "value." We exist; The Universe has given us the right to be here. That is enough.

04.15

I have considerable leeway to bargain in these circumstances: Name your terms.

— **QUARK** : THE SEARCH, PART I : 47212.4

In many ways, living is similar to running a business. And we, like Quark, are self-employed entrepreneurs, if only because our *lives* are ultimately our business. No one else is responsible. We are the managers and the custodians. We sit behind the big desk, and we mop the restroom floors. Our choices make it a success, or lead to bankruptcy.

Much depends on wise bargaining. Everything is subject to negotiation. Even goods that are "free" often require that we change our attitude in order to receive them.

Most things, however, will cost us something out-of-pocket. And surprisingly, The Universe allows us to set the terms. We can agree in advance what we're going to give up in return for what we get. Or we end up paying later.

The safest terms, as countless other entrepreneurs will testify, are based on a by-the-book, pay-in-advance contract. By investing a certain amount of time and effort, we can usually predict what our "return" will be. Progress may be slow, but it's steady. We get exactly what we earn.

But there are also times for risk, for taking advantage of opportunities even when we can't predict the outcome. And just taking those risks, for the sake of our own spiritual progress, can yield the biggest payoff of all.

Life is a bargain. The Universe has given me power to set my own terms through the "considerable leeway" (options) my life continuously offers me.

04.16

It wasn't just me. It never is.

— **CAPTAIN KIRK** : STAR TREK BEYOND : CIRCA 2263.3

The "hero" is a common figure in the lore of most sentient species, partly because our heroes' greatness often serves to make up for our own lack of it, but more importantly because they inspire us to keep trying, keep improving, to duplicate their dedication if not their achievements.

And yet, if history's genuine heroes were still around for us to ask how they achieved their greatness, few would claim all (or even most) of the credit. The majority would be humble enough to acknowledge that they'd never have succeeded without others' contributions, that contemporaries and fellow crewmembers played essential supporting roles, and that, as adages throughout the galaxy have affirmed, "We stand on the shoulders of those who precede us."

The irony here is that a statement like "It wasn't just me" can just as easily be used to spread the blame for failure as explain one's successes. So what the young Captain Kirk is saying isn't merely about sharing either the credit or the blame. It's the bold assertion that all of us must rise or fall, succeed or fail — and yes, sometimes live or die — *together*.

As adages throughout the galaxy will also affirm, striving to achieve one's goals in the company of others who are likewise striving for them is the key to success. *And* to a fulfilling life.

It isn't just me who is battling addiction, or self-doubt, or health issues, or lack of purpose. It never is. I take solace in that fact, and strength from the countless others who share the same journey.

04.17

What we don't know about death is far, far greater than what we do know.

— CAPTAIN JANEWAY : EMANATIONS : 48623.5

Religion was invented, some have said, in order to explain death. Even today, religions that claim to know what happens after death are the most popular. Books about near-death experiences are best-sellers. And holosuites that simulate scriptural visions of Paradise (or visitations with ancient gods) draw the longest lines — especially on planets where ordinary life is harsh.

The Twenty-Fourth Century offers little more "proof" of life-after-death than do the claims of earlier traditions. And as much as death is embraced by science as part of the natural order, it remains mysterious. Perhaps the most realistic approach is to simply *accept* that Mystery, without needing to know what death holds for us.

Because the more important question is, What do we know about *life?* How do we take advantage of this physical existence of ours to the fullest extent possible?

Even the scriptural accounts of an afterlife teach us less about death than what's important about life: That everything we do or think takes us to higher or lower levels of fulfillment; that connecting with The Universe's deepest resources is the way we experience heaven; and that if we follow our chosen Path with sincere effort in this life, then what we still don't know about death will hardly matter.

What I do know is this: If I take full advantage of my life, what follows will be no less fulfilling.

04.18

The honor is to serve.

— LIEUTENANT WORF : PEAK PERFORMANCE : 42923.4

The injunction to "be of service" is so prevalent throughout the spiritual archives that it ranks alongside food, clothing and security as a Primary Need.

The idea of serving others is not some burdensome call to fulfill ones "duty." It's not an obligation to repay others what you may owe them for years of childhood nurturing or a good education, or for the benefits of living in the Federation. The call to service comes as a natural, voluntary response, at the point in one's life when others' needs are suddenly understood to be as important as your own. It represents the emergence of a new self, a higher self. In spiritual language, it is "the birth of one's own divinity."

G.B. Shaw, a playwright living on 20th-century Earth, described it in these terms: "This is the true joy in life," he wrote, "the being used for a purpose recognized by yourself as a mighty one; the being thoroughly worn out before you are thrown on the scrap heap; the being a force of Nature instead of a feverish, selfish little clod of ailments and grievances complaining that the world will not devote itself to making you happy…"

Or more simply, "The honor is to serve."

I affirm and celebrate the fact that others are part of what I am. Their needs are part of my needs. My service to them is a gift to my higher and better Self.

04.19

The enemy of my enemy is my friend.

— CAPTAIN KIRK : STAR TREK / INTO DARKNESS : CIRCA 2259

The reason for quoting the young Captain here is not because of the inherent wisdom in this familiar adage, but the *lack* of it. And because of Spock's retort: "An Arabic proverb," he said, raising a critical eyebrow, "attributed to a prince who was betrayed and decapitated by his own subjects."

Spock might have added that this particular form of execution was carried into Earth's 21st Century by descendants who also betrayed their own religion, but that's beside the point. What he was saying is that genuine friendship grows out of positive goals and interests, not what we're against. True friends share a vision of the future where both deserve a place at the table, not in spite of any differences but *because* of them.

So how are we to understand Kirk's statement? Was he only joking? Or was he essentially agreeing with a more recent proverb which claims that "Desperate times call for desperate measures"?

There's no doubt Kirk understood his own desperation at the time. He knew how we often grasp for straws when confronted with life-or-death decisions, how easily we give in to solutions that may benefit us for the short term, but doom us in the long run. So, in repeating the old proverb the Captain was actually issuing a warning: We mustn't let desperate situations cloud our judgment, or force us into a proverbial Pact with the Devil simply to save our own skin.

And it's not just *our* skin, ours alone, anyway. Others are at risk, too. Others have a stake, because the battles we fight for our lives, for our very souls, are inevitably intertwined.

In the midst of those battles we discover who our real friends are.

My Inner Voyage depends on joining hands with those who share my long-term goals... goals that stand for something, not against.

04.20

This is important – you and I. Things change, but not this.

— CAPTAIN SISKO : FOR THE CAUSE : Stardate Not Given

In the midst of constant flux, we can find solace and strength in the stability of our relationships.

Not that our personal relationships don't change. We learn, we grow, we find new interests, we set out on new paths – all of which can't help but impact how we relate to one another.

But not *whether* we relate to one another.

Stable relationships aren't based on personalities, but on the person. We don't commit ourselves to the surface features someone may exhibit. (Actually, some of us *do* commit ourselves to physical beauty or wealth, or having similar likes and dislikes; but we're trying to overcome that kind of superficiality, aren't we?) It's the self behind those impermanent features we are engaged with. It's the core individual whose identity continues through all the changes, the person who remains the same in spite of all the extra pounds and wrinkles and social upheavals.

The ability to see through those "exterior things" – even past our personal disagreements – is not only the sign of a mature relationship, but a measure of our spiritual growth. To remain committed to another person is to understand something essential about our*selves*.

The opportunity to form a new relationship is a gift from The Universe. Maintaining my connection to another person affirms the higher Self within me.

04.21

Honesty is usually wise.

— DR. McCOY : FOR THE WORLD IS HOLLOW AND I HAVE TOUCHED THE SKY : 5476.3

As most of us know, "Bones" was a master at stating the obvious. And yet what seems so obvious in this statement really *isn't*.

Because McCoy wasn't merely applying his dry sense of humor to the old maxim that "honesty is the best policy." The fact is, honesty is only *usually* wise, not always. Sometimes honesty can be too strong a medicine. Most of us can absorb the full truth only in small doses. Which means we ought to think twice before dispensing it to others – especially if there's a chance we're doing so with less than the purest of intentions.

On the other hand, honesty is still the best policy overall, despite the rare exception. If we cannot rely on one another's words, lasting relationships are impossible – whether economic, political, or personal. And how true we are to our words is a primary gauge of our character, for our own reference if not for others'.

In one of Earth's oldest sacred languages, the term *dabar* could mean either "word" or "deed," as if to point out that speaking is also an action, and our acts are one way we can speak to one another. Being "honest" therefore applies as much to our behavior as our words. And striving to make one match the other is wise.

Not usually. *Always.*

I will strive for honesty in both my words and my actions, for each depends on the other.

04.22

I can't help them. I can help you.

— CADET TILLY : THE BUTCHER'S KNIFE CARES NOT FOR THE LAMB'S CRY : Stardate 1403.4

The first half of this line from Michael Burnham's over-talkative cabin-mate on the *USS Discovery* is symbolic of the feelings we all experience after hearing news reports about others facing doom or disaster. Whether we're separated from them by oceans or intergalactic space, whether their dire situation results from a natural calamity or internecine warfare, we're often too far away or too ill-equipped to come to their aid. We feel helpless.

The cadet rightly reminds us that we aren't.

Because even if *we* can't help, others can. It may not be possible for us to personally assist in rebuilding the infrastructure on a distant, hurricane-devastated island, or to house refugees from a war two continents away. But we *can* support the organizations and neighboring countries that are in a position to help. We may not be prepared to intervene in an abusive relationship or rescue someone from the clutches of a debilitating addiction or depression, but we *can* seek out intermediaries who have the familiarity and professional expertise to do so.

We are, as offspring of the same universe, responsible for one another's welfare. The fact that we often cannot help personally, is no excuse to not help at all.

My spiritual well-being depends on fostering the well-being of others. If I can't help them directly, I will find ways of helping them indirectly, through those who can.

04.23

You reveal yourself best in how you play.

— Q : HIDE AND Q : 41590.5

. . . And the person to whom we reveal ourselves best, if we're paying attention, is *us*.

For example, do we spend much of our "rec time" in escapist entertainment, or in sleep? If so, then it's possible we're running away from something in our present lives, or in our past.

Must we always seek the company of others in order to "have fun"? Then it's likely we feel incomplete or uncomfortable in our own presence.

Do we require competition in all our games, and are we upset if we don't win? Then chances are we feel insecure about who we are at some deep level, and we must continually "prove ourselves" in order to feel worthy.

These are simplistic analyses, of course. But the point is, what we do in our "time off" is a kind of self-portrait. By being more conscious of that portrait, we not only gain greater self-knowledge, we gain more self-control.

Play is a chance to experiment on ourselves without the usual pressure to perform. Through play we can test another way of being, release another side of our personalities, find strengths we never knew we had.

We set the precedent for serious self-transformation – by not being so serious about it!

Play means not having to perform my "usual" role. This week I will put aside at least one day to play, and thereby meet the more relaxed and joyous "me" within.

04.24

Concentrate on getting well... Feel the connection... Our strength is your strength... We're all one circle. No beginning, no end.

— THE COOPERATIVE : UNITY : 50622.4

First, let's acknowledge that these lines were spoken to Chakotay by ex-drones who once served in the Borg Collective. For the Commander to put his life into the hands of such a group was clearly a desperate measure. But let's also recognize that there are times in our own lives when equally desperate measures are required.

Whether we're battling a life-threatening illness, or gripped by an addiction, or grieving over a personal tragedy, we too may find that healing eludes us. Our own strength seems utterly inadequate. We lose the will to live.

An ancient spiritual tradition teaches that, when we're suffering or gravely ill, each visit from a member of our community contributes one-sixtieth to our full recovery. In other words, healing is a cooperative process. We are meant to draw strength from those around us.

And it's not simply a matter of accepting their "well-wishes." Once we begin to concentrate on recovery, we can consciously extract healing energy from them, especially when several are gathered together for our benefit.

We are not weaker for relying on one another in this way. We are stronger. And so are our relationships.

The best medicine for my healing is the help of other people. I will gladly offer my own presence as a conduit to recovery when others are suffering.

04.25

I have found myself and my place. I know who I am.

— SPOCK : THE FINAL FRONTIER : 8454.1

Here is the affirmation we all long to make someday, the "place" we all want to be in, the sense of identity that's beyond physical location, or time, or circumstance.

One ancient spiritual tradition called it *gnosis,* from the Greek word for "knowing." It means knowing not only Who We Are, but what our purpose is in the grand Scheme of Things. It means seeing ourselves not merely as others might describe us, but as The Universe envisions us.

It is a humbling, yet empowering view. Because knowing our place gives us permission to play our unique role to the fullest, while allowing others to play theirs. And like pieces in a jigsaw puzzle, our lives suddenly… *fit.*

The question is, how do we arrive at this place?

The path is different for everyone. And yet the same. It involves what another ancient tradition calls "following your bliss." The fact is, The Universe wants us to know Who We Are, and what our unique purpose is. And its surest clue is that feeling of lasting fulfillment we get only when we pursue certain kinds of activities and not others – the inner sense that *this* is The Way and not that.

Which is not to say things will be easy, or that we'll always be happy. Only that we know it's worth the effort.

I am a "work-in-progress." I may not fully realize Who I Am yet. But I'm in the process of finding out; I'm on the way to my "place." And that is enough for now.

04.26

I'll accept the judgment of history.

— CAPTAIN PICARD : THE WOUNDED : 44429.6

There comes a point in our lives when we recognize, finally, how fallible we are. We're not perfect. We can't know everything. We simply do the best we can under the circumstances… and we go on.

But what's amazing is how often "doing our best" fails miserably – or at least yields nothing tangible. At other times it's our half-hearted efforts, or even those miserable failures, that eventually bring the most positive results.

The fact is, we have no surefire way to pre-determine the long-term effects of our actions. We don't know all the variables. We can't predict with any certainty how our behavior will intertwine with the actions of others, whether the consequences will cancel each other out or develop some cumulative effect. No computer ever built can follow any single action to its ultimate "conclusion," much less chart the complex tapestry we weave together.

To accept the judgment of history is to recognize that the outcome is not in our hands. The Universe is the final arbiter of what we do. And the *best* we can do, it turns out, is less a matter of our actions than our commitment to keep "doing," to keep learning, to keep unfolding our own spiritual histories – and simply trust The Universe to take it from there.

I act, and I release the results to be whatever they will be. I accept the consequences as an ever-renewing lesson about my life.

04.27

Is truth not truth for all?

— NATIRA : FOR THE WORLD IS HOLLOW AND I HAVE TOUCHED THE SKY : 5476.4

We're good at giving lip-service to the concept of Universal Truth, or "equality under the law," or the idea that we are all essential parts of The One.

If only we could act that way.

Because when it comes to applying these lofty ideals, we start making exceptions and re-adjusting the scales. In Earth's history this was called "the double standard." The law was applied only to the masses, not to princes or politicians or the police. The right to vote was only for people who owned land, or had a certain skin color or belief system or bank account. There was one standard for ourselves, and another standard for "everyone else."

Traces of these policies exist even today, if only as the residue of our continuing struggle with an *inner* double standard: With our tendency to see faults in others that are really projections of our own faults; with our suspicion of strangers and aliens that really represents a fear of forces within ourselves we don't yet understand; with our dislike of individuals (or whole races) that results from the fact that we have not yet accepted who *we* are.

When we're courageous enough to notice this double standard in ourselves, we should consider it a call for personal growth. Take heart: It means we're ready.

I will apply the same standards to myself as I apply to others – remembering patience and forgiveness, as well as truth and justice.

04.28

Whatever you need is what I have to offer.

— NEELIX : CARETAKER : 48315.6

This is no slogan for boot-lickers, no song to subservience, no advice to submerge our own will beneath the changing tide of someone else's. Because, for one thing, it's possible to serve other people without losing self-respect, or neglecting our own needs.

More important, we must keep in mind that "need" is not the same as "want." Genuine need is not some passing fancy. It is long-term, primal, rooted in Who We Are. What others want from us is only rarely what they need. And vice versa. Discerning the difference is a skill. Applying that difference is the mark of great wisdom.

The Universe offers us whatever we need. (And sometimes even what we want!) But it also calls upon us to supply the needs of others – both out of gratitude, and to keep our own pump primed. The truth is, offering to fill another's need fulfills *our* need. And their need, on occasion, is specifically to fill ours. In fact, what others offer us – freely, willingly, seemingly out of the blue – is often The Universe pointing to a need we didn't even know we had.

To live in this interdependent circle of need and fulfillment is to experience a "community" that's both practical and spiritual. In it we discover the one need that must precede all the rest: Each other.

I enjoy supplying what others genuinely need. I affirm the giving-and-receiving that makes my life purposeful and enriching.

04.29

My mind to your mind. My thoughts to your thoughts.

— SAREK : BATTLE AT BINARY STARS : Stardate 1207.6

What has become known as the Vulcan Mind Meld was nevery meant to be an act of imposing one's will on another. Or, as was a common practice before quantum communications became the norm, "hacking" into someone's mental data banks to steal their private thoughts and memories.

"Melding," in contrast, is the cerebral equivalent of the bodily unions where the sensual and emotional needs of consenting partners are fulfilled, ideally, in tandem with one another. And in the same way one partner might leave behind traces of DNA in the other's body, mind melders would transfer elements of their own experience and personalities into the others' subconscious. Sarek described the procedure when he explained how he implanted part of this own *katra* – similar to the "soul" in Earth-based spirituality – into the mind of the young girl who would grow up to be Commander Burnham, as she lay near death after an attack by renegade Vulcans.

Some of us, too, require equally extreme measures when we've been emotionally wounded, especially in cases where our spiritual health is at stake. Whether we are witnesses to another's life-threatening wounds, or we ourselves are the ones in jeopardy, it is the duty of the spiritually aware to intervene. Sharing one's most intimate thoughts, one's own spiritual near-death experiences – so to speak – is how the healing process begins. Breaking down the emotional barriers between us, acknowledging our essential oneness, is the path to our mutual survival.

I thrive spiritually as I "meld" with others. My strength to their strength. My understanding to their understanding. My compassion to their compassion.

04.30

It's human nature to love what we don't have.

— ENGINEER LA FORGE : ELEMENTARY DEAR DATA : 42286.3

Actually it's *more* than human nature. It's a function of sentience everywhere. "Awareness" not only means being conscious of what is, but of what could be. Or what we *could have.*

There are dozens of sayings – from "The grass is always greener on the other side of the fence" to "The farther the star, the more it sparkles" – that reflect our drive to possess more. Trouble is, once we *do* possess more, we suddenly find ourselves looking for the next fence to jump, the next star to reach for. We never seem to be satisfied.

What's worse, our very success reinforces the notion that what's worth possessing are things that can be seen and touched. We become fixated on the material world.

We must learn not to take the objects of our desires so literally. The greener grass and the distant stars – or our neighbor's new shuttlecraft, or our neighbor's wife – are almost never what we really want. These are symbols, chosen by our subconscious because they are so visible, so touchable. They remind us that we aren't satisfied.

Because what we *really* want is more knowledge and understanding. What we would truly love is to keep growing, to keep pushing the boundaries of who we are.

Until what we possess, at last, is our Self.

I realize that my desire for "things" represents a deeper longing to explore and develop my personal skills and qualities. The greener grass is within me.

CORRESPONDING TO THE MONTH OF

May

05.01

To take a risk or play it safe... how precious the right to choose is. Because I've never been one to play it safe, I choose to try.

— CAPTAIN PICARD : A MATTER OF TIME : 45349.1

Living, thinking, doing – these have always been the greatest teachers. They are the seeds of our growth.

We must trust our own capacity to learn from, and be transformed by, the choices we make. The Universe does not oppose us. Nothing holds us back but our fears, our self-imposed limits, our failure to try.

Too often we dismiss our own dreams. And yet those dreams represent The Universe's invitation to spread our proverbial wings, to leave the safety of the nest, to soar higher. After all, we don't really control our dreams, do we? They rise like a wellspring from some deeper source. Ignoring them chokes off our own life-changing energy.

The Inner Voyage affirms those deeper sources, that wellspring of energy. It also trusts that when we risk the first step toward our dreams, the next step will become clear, then the next, and the next – as if a light begins to illumine the path ahead of us. If one route is blocked, another opens up. If we enter unfamiliar territory, a guide appears.

And one of the rewards is that we become guides for future voyagers. Our example, our journey, emboldens others. And that, in turn, should make us even bolder.

I am inspired by each new challenge. I will follow my dreams, not so much for where they may take me, but for what they may teach me.

05.02

But then again, all good things must come to an end!

— Q : ALL GOOD THINGS : 47988.1

If it's true, this would surely seem to be one of the most depressing statements ever.

Why must all good things end? Why can't goodness, once achieved, be kept forever? Why are the times of rest and peace so short-lived, and the struggle so unceasing? Why shouldn't we be able to enjoy the blessings we've toiled our whole lives for... indefinitely?

We're forgetting one important factor here: Our own responsibility for what happens.

Because in most cases it's not as if someone else is taking away the "good things" we've earned. It's in our natures to extract what we need from the present situation, consolidate what we've learned, enjoy our new level of achievement... and then *move on.*

Which simply means that all good things come to an end only if we want them to. And the truth is, even what's "good" has only so much to offer us before we tire of it, before we need a new challenge. We may not be consciously aware of that need. Like a child whose parents tell him it's time to leave the carnival, we may protest and sulk a bit. But we are only following an even greater good: The path to our own spiritual destiny.

The good is there to enjoy, and to encourage me to keep moving along my Spiritual Path. The end of one good thing is the beginning of another.

05.03

Brute force isn't going to do it!

— LIEUTENANT TORRES : FACES : 48784.2

The scene was not uncommon in the "movies" of the mid-Twentieth Century. An actor would be tuning in a station on an old vacuum-tube radio, adjusting its dials, unable to get it to work until — *whack!* — he'd spank it like some disobedient child. Suddenly the radio would crackle to life, the broadcast now coming in strong and clear.

A good, old-fashioned whack may be primitive and irrational; but it also strikes a familiar chord. It symbolizes our own frustrations with making things "work" — not only inanimate objects but our relationships with each other. And if patience and persuasion can't get the job done, well, there's always brute force, right?

Force, however, can never be the final answer. Even when applied to individuals (or nations) who are clearly wrong. Even when the results seem to justify its use.

Because the negative effects of coercion don't simply fade away. *And* because the crucial lessons about finding ways to live together as interdependent communities won't have been learned — not by those who were coerced, nor by those who did the coercing.

All appearances to the contrary.

And that's the real danger: That appearances will fool us into thinking the underlying problem is solved. Or that slapping the radio won't make the problem even worse.

Resorting to force is our common enemy. The battlefield is in my heart. The strategy is love.

05.04

I know you're afraid. I just want you to know that, no matter what happens, I'll be here with you.

— KES : PHAGE : 48532.4

Sometimes it's not our words people need. It's not even our assistance — whether in the form of financial help, or taking over their responsibilities if they're sick, or "fixing things" that happen to go wrong.

It's our physical presence.

How easily we forget that the quality of our lives depends less on external conditions than our internal experience. When we listen to our fellow crewmember tell us about a job-related problem, or a broken relationship, or concerns over their health, it is rare that he or she wants help in finding some concrete solution. We share our tragedies because it's our *feelings* that need "fixing."

By listening to another's woes, by acting as a sounding board, we bring healing. Simply "being there" for another can work miracles. Sharing the same physical space, without uttering so much as a single word, can express all that another person longs to know: *You are not alone.*

A beloved scripture ends with the words, "I am with you always." It's reassuring enough to remember that we remain linked to The Universe at some deeper level. But nothing speaks louder than our willingness to stand in for that Divine Presence... here, now, in the flesh.

My greatest gift to my loved ones is not in doing, but in being; not in my presents, but my presence.

05.05

Don't believe your eyes.

— CAPTAIN JANEWAY : CARETAKER : 48315.6

It's not that we should *dis*believe what we see. It's just that we shouldn't define Reality solely in accordance with what our eyes tell us.

The Changeling is perhaps the most graphic example of the fact that visual data isn't enough. Humans possess at least four additional senses because no less could insure the species' survival. Some humans – and several other species – possess still more senses, from telepathy to precognition. Different evolutionary histories have encouraged different combinations of these abilities; and each species develops its own characteristic set, usually long before consciousness has emerged.

Some scientists suggest that consciousness itself developed as just one more "sensory ability" – the ability to rise above the physical senses in order to better analyze the data they provide, and in that process to perceive one's *self*. Our "spiritual sense" is simply a natural extension of this new perception: That information about the physical world is limited and sometimes downright deceiving; that much of what's important to our survival comes from a deeper, non-material source. And if our spiritual sense is a bit under-developed at this point, perhaps we should start "believing" our ears and our eyes a little less.

I affirm that there are ways of "hearing" and "seeing" that transcend my physical senses. I will develop those abilities through regular meditation.

05.06

One of the most important things in a person's life is to feel useful.

— CAPTAIN PICARD : RELICS : 46125.3

We're not going to consider our *own* desire to feel useful here. Most of us are well aware that performing a valuable service fills an important need in us; that helping others makes *us* feel good. Today's task is to remember that *others* need to feel useful, too.

Look around. Consider the younger members in your community – brothers or sisters, school children; even the youthful "gangs" that seem to populate every planet. Know that all of these growing selves are searching for roles that affirm their worth, their value in some wider scheme. That is their birthright as sentient beings. And if we – all of us – can't offer them positive roles for acting out their self-worth, they will invent their own.

And what about those at the other end of life's spectrum? Have we found *them* roles, too? – so they might continue to express their lifetimes of learning and experience? Or is it enough to simply find them a "retirement home"?

One of our most important spiritual qualities is an ability to imagine ourselves in other people's shoes. We know what it feels like to be needed. Now imagine *others* wanting to feel the same way.

Now find a way to do something about it.

This week I will ask both a child and an elder to play a valuable role in a family or community project. I willingly accept the possibility of failure.

05.07

I have been told that patience is sometimes more effective than the sword.

— LIEUTENANT WORF : REDEMPTION, PART I : 44995.3

To act, or not to act; that is the question.

Then again, *not* taking action is also an act. Which means it's an option that should at least be considered.

Starfleet officers – even trainees – often find this option the most difficult. After all, leaders want to appear "decisive." Doing something suggests assertiveness. *Not* doing something seems weak and indecisive. Egos therefore become more important than strategy. And it's not just a matter of appearing strong to others. It's our own conceit that no conflict or issue can be solved unless *we* have a hand in it.

And yet strategy depends on precise timing, on waiting for just the right moment. To be drawn into a fight we're unprepared for, or to let someone else set the terms for an engagement, can be a crucial blunder. Not striking back – or "turning the other cheek" as one of Earth's Holy Ones once described it – can set in motion forces that are far more powerful than swords or phasers.

Sometimes these forces for reconciliation are already in motion. Things will often "take care of themselves" if only we'd let them. But first we must keep still long enough to remove our ego, to listen to the guidance of The Universe... to be patient.

I will act, not re-act. With each new day, I will practice the patience that allows The Universe to work in and through my actions.

05.08

The end cannot justify the means.

— DATA : REDEMPTION, PART II : 45020.4

Six words. Four basic components. The same ones, in the same order, are embodied in a thousand different languages. So often does it appear throughout the galactic record, in exactly this form, that it can lose its impact.

Fortunately, there are a few effective variations.

Like: Nothing good can be accomplished if the methods are evil. Or: When we set the goal, we thereby limit the options we can employ to achieve it. Or from scriptural sources: One cannot arrive in the Holy City through the Gates of Sin. Or this, from Vulcan: To separate the destination from the journey is not logical.

Or perhaps the most radical variation: The destination *is* the journey; the end, the means.

Which is simply to say that we can't arrive at our goal except by living out its effects in the present. We cannot make war to achieve peace. We can't isolate people in prisons in order to free them from their anti-social tendencies. And we certainly can't be saved by letting others make our choices for us, by letting someone else save us.

"Means" is everything. Getting there is *being* there. Working toward salvation is being saved.

Actually, the "end" could never justify the means. It's just what gets us out of our chairs.

I will set goals not so much for the conditions I hope to achieve in the future, but for the conditions they will create now, as I work to achieve them.

05.09

You have got to make use of what you have. If you need a hammer and you don't have one... use a pipe!

— **MAJOR KIRA** : RETURN TO GRACE : Stardate Not Given

Kira's advice isn't meant to remind us of our innate creativity, or to inspire us to be inventive — although that would certainly be good advice. Her words are aimed more at our need to accept who we are, and the specific weaknesses and limitations implied by that.

After all, many of us weren't born with hammers in our hands. Or silver spoons in our mouths. On the contrary, a lot more of us were born with (or we've managed to develop!) some pretty serious handicaps.

There was a time when use of the word "handicap" was frowned upon. However, the word need not be taken negatively. In certain sports, for example, a "handicap" is a disadvantage that a player willingly accepts in order to make the game more fair, to "level the playing field." A severe handicap might even be self-imposed, so that a player might push himself all the harder, and thereby improve his competitive skills more than otherwise.

Perhaps we come into this life having accepted or imposed such handicaps on ourselves — in order to push our own limits, to find and exploit personal qualities and inner resources we might not otherwise realize we had. Why not look at life that way?

The most important "hammer" is not the one in my hands, but the one within me. I accept what I do not have, so I might make better use of what I do.

05.10

What you want is irrelevant. What you have chosen is at hand.

— **SPOCK** : THE UNDISCOVERED COUNTRY : 9521.6

Our choices have a power of their own. And once set in motion, the events that flow from our choices can turn in unexpected and sometimes unfortunate directions.

We may offer the usual excuses: There were physical factors we couldn't have foreseen. Other individuals complicated things; they weren't supposed to get involved.

Sometimes nothing we do will improve or reverse a bad situation. And we end up saying things like, "If only I'd known!" or "This isn't how I planned it."

The harsh truth is, what we originally intended often turns out to be irrelevant. Sometimes *worse* than irrelevant. Because if we continue to dwell on how the situation "should've" turned out, on what we "wanted" to happen, we can lose touch with the realities we must deal with now.

We can take solace in our good intentions later. In fact, people have a surprising capacity for forgiveness if they learn what we'd *hoped* to do, despite the fact that we damaged them by what we actually *did*.

In the meantime we must take responsibility for what's "at hand," for the consequences of our previous choices. Because accepting responsibility is also a choice — one that carries its own power to harm, or to help us grow wiser.

I affirm the power I wield — for better or worse, for both myself and others — by making choices. And I will be stronger for accepting their consequences.

05.11

The answer to the puzzle is... too simple for most humans to understand. All life, all consciousness, is indissolubly bound together. Indeed it is all part of the same thing.

— LWAXANA TROI : HAVEN : 41294.5

How easily we are fooled by the apparent complexity of nature — and the seeming complexity of our own lives!

We're baffled by the hidden agendas in our relationships, appalled at how little we know of ourselves, frustrated by unforeseen events that turn our best-laid plans into smoldering ruins. So we invent the notion that life is terribly complicated, that it's a physical struggle between separate, opposing forces we'll never fully understand. And we thereby "explain" our own inability to cope.

In science, however, the best and most powerful explanation for any phenomenon is the simplest one that accounts for the most data. The idea that our physical lives spring from consciousness, and that our consciousness springs from a much deeper source that underlies all life, is just such a simple but powerful explanation.

What appears so complex are only manifestations of The One. By envisioning ourselves bound together with the same Consciousness that created the universe, we are no longer separate entities. Spiritual growth — both communal and individual — begins with this realization.

Beneath the surface, Life is One. No matter what challenges I face today, I will envision myself linked at the deepest levels to everything around me.

05.12

Our species can only survive if we have obstacles to overcome... Without them to strengthen us, we will weaken and die.

— CAPTAIN KIRK : METAMORPHOSIS : 3219.4

Most of us, frankly, don't look forward to the obstacles life keeps throwing in our path. We'd prefer things to go smoothly. We'd rather proceed in a straight line than stumble toward our goals on a zig-zag course, or find ourselves pushed backward.

The roadblocks we face, the unexpected turns, the doors that slam after seeming to open in welcome — all of these obstacles can frustrate, depress, or even anger us. It can be reassuring to remember that The Universe is still in control, still guiding us. And sometimes the roadblocks are put there specifically to force us in another direction, onto a path where things will go smoother, where the doors along the way will remain open and welcoming.

But sometimes there is no other path. Sometimes the obstacles must be dealt with directly, and either we overcome them and succeed, or we don't and we fail.

We must be content at such times to realize that these too are meant for a purpose. Even our failure to overcome them can teach and strengthen us. Pushing against a mountain is doomed only if we think we're actually going to move it. If we do it simply to keep in shape, we succeed!

The obstacles in my life are meant not so much for me to move, but to move me to become a stronger person. They are opportunities to grow spiritually.

05.13

Our only influence is by example.

— CAPTAIN PICARD : HALF A LIFE : 44805.3

It's fortunate so many of us put less of a premium on what other people say, than on what they do.

Because "practicing what we preach" holds us all to a higher standard. And because the best measure of what we believe can be found in our behavior. If we give lip-service to certain principles, but we don't follow them in practice, is anyone really fooled for long?

History and personal experience demonstrate that lasting "control" over others cannot be achieved through force, or by threats of hellfire, or even through the Rule of Law. All we can do – all we *must* do – is simply live our lives as we would want others to live theirs; to act as if our Articles of Faith can only be formulated in actions; to *embody* the truth, not merely embrace it.

There is tremendous power in teaching others by embodying one's principles. Witness the fact that the Most Revered Ones throughout the galaxy have rarely been warriors or politicians. Neither are they unapproachable sky gods who rule over us from a distance, as if direct contact with us would somehow contaminate them. Rather they were individuals who modeled a lifestyle, who earned our respect precisely because they lived among us. And what *they* could do, so can we.

I will let my whole life stand for what I believe, trusting that others will see, and perhaps follow, the light which The Universe embodies in me.

05.14

The ability to recognize danger... to fight it or run away from it... that's what fear gives us. But when fear holds you hostage, how do you let it go?

— CAPTAIN JANEWAY : THE THAW : Stardate Not Given

The last part of the Captain's statement hides a clue. Because if we *can* "let it go," fear can't hold us hostage in the first place. At least, not without our permission.

Which means *we* are ultimately in control, not our fears. The ability to overcome them is already in our possession.

Imagination is part of it. Picturing ourselves doing the very things we fear can be a powerful tool for developing confidence and courage. From speaking in front of large groups to climbing great heights; from high-pressure job situations to red-alert battle conditions – whatever your fear may be, guiding yourself through a mental simulation sets the psychological precedent for overcoming it.

And it's not necessary to totally eliminate our feelings of fear, either. The key is simply to *not let them stop you.*

The other part, of course, is testing yourself in real life. What's important here is not expecting immediate success, but rewarding yourself for even the smallest move in the right direction. Simulate, test, reward… simulate, test, reward.

Only we can hold ourselves hostage. The fact that we so often do just means we still have something important to learn.

My fears hold me back until I have learned the lessons they are designed to teach me. I will meditate, learn, thank my fears and then release them.

05.15

Do you know what helps me when I'm freaked out? Talking.

— CADET TILLY : LETHE : Stardate 1412.3

Here, the *USS Discovery*'s loquacious Cadet employs a distinctively mid-20th Century term to describe a condition that's all-but-inevitable whenever we're under great stress, when life seems to be coming at us from all sides and we're not sure what to do.

Getting "freaked out" may be a more contemporary way to put it, but the way Tilly *deals* with it is hardly new. In fact, the method is as old as speech itself. And even if we can be certain our subconscious mind is working diligently on a solution to whatever challenges we're facing — and it *is* — our conscious mind isn't always kept in the loop. Talking can make a crucial difference.

For one thing, the unbridled energy that boils up when we're severely stressed or nervous is harnessed and put to positive use. More importantly, the neural pathways used in speech are directly connected to our subconscious. So by talking, our problem-solving efforts are given an open channel into our conscious mind. That's why we refer to this process as "talking it out." By using another person as a sounding-board, we can progressively bring *out* what was hidden and realize something previously unknown. Sometimes in the sudden flash we call a "revelation."

Not that what's "revealed" is automatically the answer to our problem. Sometimes talking makes us aware of our *un*healthy thoughts and unrealistic solutions. But openly exposing them to ourselves is a good start. Getting help can't begin until we realize we need it.

Expressing my innermost thoughts is part of my healing process. I will find others with whom I can talk things out, and who can talk things out with me.

05.16

We will do what we have always done... We will find hope in the impossible.

— SPOCK : STAR TREK BEYOND : CIRCA 2263.3

Some things can't be done because that's just the way things are. We can't jump off tall buildings in our birthday suits and fall skyward. We can't dance in the vacuum of space clad only in leotards.

But some things are "impossible" only because we *think* they are, or because so many people have already tried and failed, and some of those same people have rationalized their failures by claiming that whatever they tried to do just can't be done, and that's that.

Fortunately there are a few of us who regard "the impossible" as a challenge to *try*, as inspiration to become the first to succeed. Spock's "hope" represents a kind of faith that all things are possible — or at least worth attempting — if we refuse to back down whenever challenged, if we are willing to test a new approach and keep at it, if we have the *chuzpah* to disregard the "conventional wisdom," the prejudices, the nay-sayers and excuse makers... if we would only listen to the voices cheering for us, even while others may be jeering.

And if the only one cheering for us is, well... *us*, that's a start. Because if you cheer for yourself long enough and loud enough, somebody else is bound to join the chorus. Not the least of whom is The Universe.

What's "impossible" is often more of a mindset than a reality. I will look at the obstacles in my life as a reason for hope, and motivation to try.

05.17

When a man is convinced he's going to die tomorrow, he'll probably find a way to make it happen.

— GUINAN : THE BEST OF BOTH WORLDS, PART II : 44001.4

The self-fulfilling prophecy is one of the most insidious – and at the same time most miraculous – facets of the human mind. "As a man thinketh," the Terran proverb goes, "so he *is.*"

The fact is, human beings view reality through a variety of filters based only in part on direct experience. Perhaps more important is what we've been told as children. Because, just as we learn our primary language before we're even aware of it, we also absorb our basic world-view: Whether it's out to destroy us or save us; whether other life forms are competing with us for slices of a finite "pie" or sharing the infinite resources of an infinite universe.

Fortunately, ever since the link between matter and consciousness was proven experimentally, we've known that we can change our "filters" – and therefore reality itself – by changing the way we think. If it's true that a deep-seated belief in our imminent demise makes us succumb more easily when our life is threatened, the opposite is equally true.

More than most of us realize, our lives are truly in our own hands.

I accept full responsibility for what happens to me... both now and in the past. I will change my circumstances by first changing the way I think.

05.18

Once you detach yourselves from your emotional responses you come closer to controlling them. Eventually they will be eliminated altogether.

— LIEUTENANT TUVOK : INNOCENCE : Stardate Not Given

First of all, Tuvok is not talking about eliminating emotions. He's talking about eliminating emotional *responses* – those knee-jerk, psycho-physiological reactions that can cloud our judgment and interfere with performance.

The distinction is critical. Because even Vulcans recognize that emotions serve a purpose in most other humanoid species. Emotions draw our attention to events and situations that have potential importance for us. They help us mobilize our physical energies so we can effectively deal with those events and situations. But they are singularly ineffective by themselves. We must also bring our mental and spiritual resources into the response process.

Unfortunately, we can't do so unless we see our Self as separate from our emotions, as a "higher" Being merely using the language of emotion. This is the "detachment" Vulcans (as well as Earth's Buddhists and Hindus) refer to.

In time, like training wheels on a child's bicycle, our emotional reactions cease to be necessary. We know what's important without having to *feel* it. Our bodies respond without our emotions having to slap us awake. And we can save our emotions for better things.

I am not my emotions. I will seek to understand the messages they are sending me, and then I will release them.

05.19

...In the end all that matters is how we feel and what we do about it. Because either way we're the ones that have to live with the consequences.

— LIEUTENANT DAX : REJOINED : 49195.5

As one of Earth's old "television" shows put it, *This is Your Life.* And, we might add, yours *alone.*

Because no one else can feel your feelings (though a Betazoid can empathically reproduce them). No one else can see through your eyes, (though a Vulcan mind-meld can replay mental "snapshots"). Nor can anyone else think with your mind (even if it's true that we're all linked through some greater Consciousness).

So when Dax insists that the only thing that matters is how we feel, and what we do, she's not suggesting we totally disregard others. She's simply reminding us that no one is as directly affected by our own decisions and actions as *we* are. We cannot be faulted for looking to our own welfare first, to our own needs, our own growth.

This isn't as selfish as it sounds. Because by acknowledging "consequences," Dax also reminds us that consideration of others is an essential part of our decision-making process. Not only are others affected by what we do, their response to our actions affects us in return. And may continue to affect us throughout our lives.

I am responsible for my life. I consider my own feelings first, but the extent to which others impact those feelings is a sign of my spiritual growth.

05.20

May fortune favor the foolish.

— ADMIRAL KIRK : THE VOYAGE HOME : 8390

It's always humbling, if not infuriating: What we think ought to happen often turns out to be completely wrong. Our most carefully-conceived plans, our most logically-constructed schemes, end up in the porcelain dumpster.

And then some fool comes along with nothing more than a hunch – or worse, a *vision* – and everything magically falls into place for him.

Throughout galactic history, the most revered prophets and visionaries were originally re-garded as "fools." Maybe because others couldn't see the possibilities, or only the negative ones. Maybe because the majority were operating strictly on what was "rational" or "practical"; on what could be deduced from "the facts."

But facts represent only a narrow band on the spectrum of reality. "Foolish" is a term people use to describe whatever lies outside their own perceptual spectrum. It's also a label for imposing that narrow vision on others.

Not that others' myopia should restrict *us*. We must learn to trust our own insight, our own intuition. Which doesn't mean acting on every idea that pops into our heads. It simply implies a willingness to take seriously what might at first seem foolish. And, along with our prophets, to be willing to "act like fools" for what we believe in.

I will act on the vision The Universe instills in me, considering others but not substituting their vision for mine. And I will accept the consequences.

05.21

There's an old horse-trader's adage about putting too much weight on a young back. ...Don't want it to break under pressure.

— CAPTAIN PICARD : PEN PALS : 42695.3

There are scores of similar sayings throughout the Quadrant. While horses figure in only a few, all make an analogy between the loads borne by a primitive culture's beasts-of-burden and the "weight" we ourselves carry through life.

And the analogy is simply this: Just as a young animal must become accustomed to lighter loads before taking on heavier ones, we too need to "build up" to more demanding responsibilities and concerns. Especially spiritual ones. The reason should be as obvious as learning the alphabet before reading The Classics. The corollaries are less obvious.

The first corollary is that we shouldn't judge others by the spiritual progress *we* may have made. Regrettably, many of us treat other people who are just becoming aware of their spiritual responsibilities as if they should know better whenever they make a mistake. We hold them to standards of discipline and ethical behavior we ourselves have only recently taken on. As one of the ancient Holy Ones advised, we must "...forgive them, for they know not what they do."

Secondly, we too still have "young backs" in many ways. So we shouldn't put too much pressure on our*selves* either.

The Inner Voyage isn't easy. Let's take it one step at a time.

I must develop basic spiritual skills before mastering the more advanced ones. The "weight" given me by The Universe does not exceed what I can carry.

05.22

You must have faith that the Universe will unfold as it should.

— SPOCK : THE UNDISCOVERED COUNTRY : 9521.6

Just as some variation on The Golden Rule is found all across the known universe, so too is this sentiment.

The Universe is lawful. Though we may not always know why a specific event happens as it does, we can rest assured that present circumstances are the inevitable, lawful result of prior events. Even wormholes and "future causation" are part of this matrix.

Sentient life is no less lawful. Our consciousness, our "inner lives," are also embraced by causation. This isn't some straightjacket we wear; it is the very foundation of our transformation.

Because if we're not happy with our present circumstances, there are specific steps we can take to change them, however painful or difficult they might be. Our realization of this fact should empower us.

It is also empowering simply to recognize within all these laws the existencee of a deeper, unseen Reality which underlies the universe. And since every event is an expression of that Reality, there are no accidents. Spiritual Paths acknowledge this as "grace," or "the Divine Plan." Events conspire toward Life, toward growth, toward wholeness.

And as it is with the universe, so it is with you.

I will live as if everything that happens is purposeful. My life and my growth are as natural and necessary to The Universe as they are to me.

05.23

May the great bird of the galaxy bless your planet.

— LIEUTENANT SULU : THE MAN TRAP : 1531.1

There's been lots of speculation through the years about what Sulu meant by his reference to the "great bird of the galaxy." Was he referring, indirectly, to the Enterprise and the positive legacy it left behind on its pioneering flights of exploration? Or maybe to some other starship?

Was he drawing on religious symbolism, where the bird represents Spirit — or, in some traditions, God? Or was the "great bird" of Sulu's blessing, as some historians theorize, a legendary figure from the past, perhaps even a specific visionary from Earth's pre-Federation era?

Whatever the case, the bird is a meaningful symbol for the inner workings that bless us with spiritual growth. In many cultures, birds represent nurturing and guidance. We can imagine ourselves hatched into a cozy "nest" with others like us, force-fed while we grow in self-confidence and strength — and sometimes "taken under wing" when the world outside seems too frightening.

But at some point it becomes necessary to leave the nest and spread our own wings. In some cases we are literally pushed out — and it ends up being for our own good, because only then do we find out what we were destined for: To fly, to soar… even as the great bird does.

I am grateful for the nurturing of The Universe. As I learn each new lesson, I understand I will be sent out to test my spiritual wings. But only when It knows I'm ready.

05.24

Never stop seeking what seems unobtainable.

— THE WRAITH : ROGUE PLANET : CIRCA ECE2153

Ever since the entities collectively called the *Pah-wraith* became the sworn enemies of all those with corporeal form, it shouldn't surprise us to find one of them cynically offering advice that amounts to beating one's head against the wall. After all, working toward goals that can never be achieved not only wastes precious resources, it is ultimately demoralizing.

For someone learning a new skill, especially, it is essential to set short-term, *attainable* goals. It's called "taking baby steps." Teachers start with easier problems requiring little time to solve, slowly build their students' confidence and competence, then assign progressively harder, longer-term tasks as they demonstrate repeated success.

But at some point the truly wise teacher will assign a problem that is unattainable, no matter how hard and how long her students work at it. Why? Because the wisest students, the ones who end up excelling at their professions, are those who have not only learned about succeeding, but about defeat. They find out how to deal with frustration, how to spend weeks or months at a task only to fail, then pick up the pieces and go on. So in the process of failing they often discover resources they'd never have found otherwise: Like inner strength and patience, new friendships and supporters, and perhaps a deeper relationship with The Universe.

And sometimes — often enough to make all those failures worthwhile — they also discover that the goals they once thought were unobtainable… the lost causes, the fools' errands, the impossible dreams… really *aren't*.

Sometimes it is the attempt itself, and the things I learn through my efforts, that make a goal worth pursuing — whether or not I ever achieve it.

05.25

Therapists are always the worst patients. Except for doctors, of course.

— DR. CRUSHER : THE LOSS : 44356.9

This isn't just about therapists. Or doctors. It's a meditation for people who think they know so much about the process of healing – or about relationships, or religion, or gourmet cooking – that they find it almost impossible to admit that they might ever need anybody else's help.

In short, it's a meditation for, and about, *us.*

Because all of us have some kind of "specialty." We've all become experts about some facet of life, either by studying it, or living through it, or because it's our job. And all that expertise gives us the sense that no one else could possibly know the subject like we know it.

Which may very well be true. But it's also true that we can never know everything. And we can almost always benefit from the fresh insight that only someone else can provide – someone not as emotionally involved, not as committed to the way things are "supposed to be done."

Some of our greatest scientific advances have come not from senior professors at The Academy, but from their newly-recruited research assistants. That doesn't mean the elders are no longer needed. It simply means that our own hard-won knowledge, combined with another's insight, may yield the answer neither of us could find alone.

I am only one of many people on this Voyage. My own knowledge is essential, but not always sufficient. I am grateful for the help of others.

05.26

War is never imperative.

— DR. McCOY : THE BALANCE OF TERROR : 1709.1

Though McCoy was referring to the clash between nations, war is ultimately a product of our *inner* conflict. If we would only practice peace in our personal lives, war not only wouldn't be "imperative," it would be inconceivable.

Unfortunately, there are enough people who *don't* practice peace to ruin things for everyone else. And even if we've learned not to respond to these aggressive types out of anger or revenge, shouldn't we at least give them a taste of their own medicine? In fact, don't we have a responsibility to forcefully "teach them a lesson"?

No… because overcoming force with greater force only teaches an aggressor that he wasn't powerful enough. Meeting angry words with *more* angry words only justifies feelings of animosity. The cycle inevitably escalates.

We can break that cycle only by doing the one thing the aggressor doesn't expect – because it's the last thing *he* would do in the same situation: Reach out in love.

One of Earth's Sacred Ones advised us to "turn the other cheek" after being assaulted. Which doesn't mean simply allowing oneself to be whipped into submission. It means standing your ground, staring into the soul of the other person, believing so strongly in the divinity of "the other" that the aggressor can't help but see it himself. *That's* the way to teach him a lesson.

I stand for peace in all I do. I believe in the goodness hidden in others, and I believe in my own.

05.27

You should know the dangers of opening old wounds.

— ADMIRAL KIRK : THE WRATH OF KHAN : 8130.3

There are reasons why we sometimes don't heal our wounds, why we bury our painful experiences under a false pretense of "It's okay" or "It didn't really bother me" or "I just don't have time to deal with this right now." There are also reasons for suppressing the memory of pain altogether, as if we weren't wounded to begin with, as if the events that hurt us never really happened.

And the usual reason is: We weren't ready to learn from them at the time.

There is nothing shameful or demeaning about this. The adult who was abused as a six-year-old child couldn't have learned anything at that tender age, wasn't spiritually equipped to transform his or her pain into something more productive. At age twenty perhaps. Or maybe thirty.

The point is, sooner or later our old wounds must be reopened so that genuine healing can take place. And even when we finally think we're ready, it's still dangerous work.

Because we must be prepared to feel the pain again. We must seek to understand ourselves and the others involved, both as the people we were and the people we are. And we must forgive.

Most of all we must be committed to assuming full responsibility for our feelings and our actions, to stop affixing blame and start taking control.

Know the dangers. But seize the opportunity.

I am not the person I was. I have grown. I am ready to heal my wounds and grow even more.

05.28

If there is a Cosmic Plan, are we not part of it? Our presence at this place, at this moment... could be a part of that fate.

— COUNSELOR TROI : PEN PALS : 42695.3

Even though we're all busy working on our own personal plans and goals, we must never lose sight of the wider Plan of which we're part. Because as we grow more spiritually aware, it's only natural to begin receiving occasional "casting calls" from The Universe – offers for us to play some important role in a larger cosmic drama.

At such times other people's needs, or even some life-transforming event, must take precedence over what we happen to be doing at the moment. It may be frustrating and sometimes painful to put aside our own "work." We may be so wrapped up in our own lives, or so convinced we're already doing something important, that we'll even pretend not to hear this call. But our response is crucial.

For one thing, if we expect to receive assistance from the Spiritual Network, if we believe that people often come out of the blue to help us just when we need it – and they often *do* – we too must be willing to perform the same service for others.

But there's also this: The Cosmic Plan does not call on us arbitrarily. More often than not, what we assume is only a side trip on our Voyage turns out to be exactly where we needed to go, and teach us exactly what we needed to learn, at exactly the right time.

I am part of the Cosmic Plan. I am grateful for all the help The Universe gives me on my spiritual path, and I gladly offer assistance to others when called.

05.29

Logic is the beginning of wisdom, not the end.

— SPOCK : THE UNDISCOVERED COUNTRY : 9522

…And knowing the *limits* of logic is the next step.

Clearly, there are places where even the most skilled application of logic cannot penetrate. One such place is referred to by romantics as "the human heart."

One needn't be romantic to recognize that our minds are more than "intellect." Even Vulcan culture acknowledges that the biological system which supports all our rational firepower has its own needs, its own "language." And if certain Vulcan rituals seem to be among the most *il*logical in the galaxy, it is because those rituals speak to an entirely different component of the Vulcan mind.

In fact, for most sentient beings the concept of "mind" includes affective components. Emotional "well-being," for example. Or a sense of meaning and purposefulness. A connectedness of one's self to others and to something that transcends space and time. In a word, wholeness.

To recognize these components is only logical. But logic alone can't satisfy them. "Wisdom" is the art of dealing with the whole person, the whole community, the whole universe… as if every part plays an essential role.

Because they do.

I will honor those dimensions in others, and in my self, which lie beyond the limited horizon of logic. I celebrate my whole self.

05.30

We all create God in our own image.

— COMMANDER DECKER : STAR TREK/TMP : 7412.6

The story's the same on every planet that is home to sentient life. Insofar as a Supreme Being is envisioned at all, that Being is initially seen in the "likeness" of the life forms who envision it.

Naturally, this god "evolves" as their understanding evolves. To begin with, it is simply bigger or more powerful than they are. It will have arms, legs, ears and eyes, even though these appendages and organs are not necessary to the god's actions or awareness. It will also have emotions – which usually means the god tends to be jealous and vengeful as well as compassionate and forgiving.

Just like it did in the course of human history, the Being eventually becomes more than a mere extension of what we are, and represents the very best we can be. This is often symbolized in miraculous events wherein the Supreme Lord enters the planet's history to save its inhabitants from their baser qualities.

But as progressive as this new "image" is, it still largely depends on the scope of our imagination. That's why idols and images ultimately cannot save us. Instead, we must open ourselves to the Source that can draw out the potential we never realized we had – the capabilities that elude us precisely because we can't yet conceive of them.

Though, fortunately, we can *connect* with them.

I submit to the Mystery that is Ultimate Reality. Even as I envision the best I can be, I do not limit my spiritual growth only to what I can imagine now.

05.31

There's no relative direction in the vastness of space... It's easier than you think to get lost.

— COMMODORE PARIS : STAR TREK BEYOND : STARDATE 2263.2

As many of us look at it, the notion of "finding our way" presumes that we already know the direction we should be going. After all, only then can we correct our course if necessary, or confirm that we're on the right heading to begin with.

But what if, in the face of all the options out there, with the mind-boggling array of pre-defined paths to chose from, or the vast, unexplored reaches of space to tempt our curiosity, we just can't decide how to proceed? Worse, what if there *is* no direction, no obvious up or down, no left or right by which to orient ourselves – or, as Yorktown's Commodore warns, we're already in danger of being "lost"?

Let's remember that being on the right course isn't about pointing ourselves at some location in space. Having "direction" isn't about heading toward a specific destination. It's about listening for the guidance that comes from within, about connecting with the inner resources Earth's eastern religions describe as "following your bliss" and western traditions refer to as that "still, small voice." It's about a Way of Being, a spiritual grounding that keeps us mindful of our place regardless of the "relativity" and vastness that surrounds us.

In the end, it's not about *where* we are, but *who*.

I am never truly "lost." I am on my Path as long as I am determined to keep moving, keep growing.

06

06.01

The needs of the many outweigh the needs of the few.

— SPOCK : STAR TREK / INTO DARKNESS : CIRCA 2259

What The Universe continually affirms is that every one of us is bound together in an interdependent Web of Life. No single individual is so isolated that his existence doesn't matter, or that his actions affect no one else.

Yet every higher life form enters the material world with the same Prime Directive: Survival of self. In its biological infancy, each individual is preoccupied with its own needs, usually to the exclusion of others.

Personal growth, however, begins with the realization that others *can't* be excluded. Making others part of Who You Are becomes increasingly essential. Throughout the galaxy, wherever The Inner Voyage (or some other "spiritual path") is practiced, its success depends on a radical redefinition of "self." Slowly, by stages, we incorporate others: Family, friends, mates, community, all life forms, the universe. The boundaries separating us gradually disappear until others' joys and sorrows become *our* joys and sorrows... their needs, our needs. And vice versa.

Ironically, those who lose their narrower self – even to the point of sacrificing one's life, as Spock would do decades later with the very same words on his lips – insure a legacy that makes the ancient promise of immortality seem egocentric by comparison.

Today I will practice inter-dependence by putting the needs of others first. I will make at least one new friend, or re-connect with a friend I've neglected.

06.02

You are not alone. Do you understand? We are in this together now!

— CAPTAIN PICARD : LOUD AS A WHISPER : 42477.2

What is the most significant moment in your personal history? In human history? In the history of the galaxy...?

Best answer: It's the point at which we finally realize that our lives, our destinies, cannot be separated from one another. It's the revelation that, from princes to paupers, from Klingons to Cardassians, we are all in this struggle together.

One of Earth's pre-modern cultures had a very specific word for this life-long struggle: *Jihad.* Often mistakenly interpreted as an armed conflict against one's political or religious enemies, the "greater" meaning of the word referred to the struggle *within oneself* – the effort to redeem one's own soul from inner turmoil... from greed and anger, from sloth and selfishness.

Even in the case of armed conflict, the real enemy is never the other individual or group. It is our own primitive tendency to divide ourselves, to build walls rather than bridges. It is the worldview in which we see one another as material rather than spiritual beings, as competitors wrangling over a finite slice of the pie instead of fellow workers in a universe of unlimited possibilities.

The fact is, we need each other. And those who come to this realization share the responsibility for setting an example others will be inspired to follow. Do *you* understand?

I understand that the real struggle is within us, not with each other. I will look there for the things I must change – and there for the strength to change them.

06.03

Don't be afraid of your darker side. Have fun with it.

— COUNSELOR TROI : FRAME OF MIND : 46778.1

"Darker" is one way to describe it. But the darkness has less to do with a certain "side" of us than how little we understand it. And what we don't understand, we fear.

When we act in ways we can't explain, or when our emotions surprise us, chances are we're operating under the influence of this "darker side." Our surprise – or, in some cases, our embarrassment – should be seen as a cry for help, a call to get back in touch with that deeper, more "primitive" region which comes to us courtesy of the Animal Kingdom. And to deal with needs and feelings we've probably repressed for the better part of our lives.

Not that we're being asked to suddenly vent all those repressed feelings on the world. What our darker side requires of us is simply to acknowledge and respect its existence, in the same way an adult admits to the inner legacy of the child he/she once was.

In fact, just as the adult can have fun by recapturing the spirit of that child – the anticipation of each new day, the endless game-playing and exploring, the sense of wonder – we can also have fun with our "primitive" side.

When was the last time you climbed a tree barefoot, or danced around a campfire? Or spent an entire day eating, sleeping or snuggling with someone you love?

I will set aside time to honor the physical needs and emotions that are an essential part of who I am.

06.04

Why does everyone say "Relax" when they're about to do something terrible?

— ENSIGN KIM : NON SEQUITUR : 49011

Perhaps the most cynical answer to Kim's question is, "To tempt us to lower our shields just before they fire the photon torpedoes."

But the truth is, people more often tell us to relax when they're about to do something on our behalf – something they sincerely believe is for our own good. Perhaps they think they know better. Or they suspect we're about to make a mistake, and since they're more experienced in certain matters we should stop worrying and let them handle it.

What's so "terrible" is not so much the possibility that things may turn out badly. It's the fact that we'd rather do it ourselves. We *need* to do it ourselves.

Our jobs may not give us a choice. But when it comes to our own personal lives, we mustn't allow others to act for us. Even if they know better. Even if we'd prefer to relax while someone else does the difficult work.

Not only must we insist on our right to "learn by doing," we must remember that others have the same right. Not only must we be allowed to take the risks and make the mistakes that lead to our own personal growth, we must guard ourselves against doing the things for others that might prevent *their* growth.

I no longer depend on others to do for me what I should do for myself. I can offer advice to others, but what they end up doing is up to them – and The Universe.

06.05

Notice your mind working... how it plans for the future, visits the past. Notice those thoughts and set them aside. Turn your attention to the white light that is your breath.

— LIEUTENANT TUVOK : BASICS, PART I : Stardate Not Given

Our minds are wondrously precise, potentially flawless instruments. Below the surface of our awareness, the mind works constantly — managing our bodily functions, tracking events in the world around us, analyzing past actions and consequences in order to plan our future.

Trouble is, we can interfere with the flow of that process by trying to do consciously what is best left to our *sub*conscious. Knowing when that's happening is tricky, of course. But if we experience feelings of unfocused fear, or can't seem to concentrate – or perhaps we're uncharacteristically "grumpy" – it's more than likely that our conscious mind is pushing itself into areas where it doesn't belong.

Tuvok's instructions summarize a meditative exercise (known as *v'passana* on Earth) which is designed to free our subconscious from such interference. The first step is to simply "notice" that our mind is doing its job already, to accept that, and then calmly direct our attention elsewhere.

Focusing on our breathing is a galaxy-wide technique for concentrating so strongly on one activity that distractions, even consciousness, temporarily fade away. That's when we do some of our best work!

I breathe in calm, I exhale tension. I breathe in clarity, I release confusion. I am refreshed!

06.06

Over the years I've learned that sometimes you just have to punch your way through.

— CAPTAIN JANEWAY : PARALLAX : 48439.7

The word "punch" may derive from a pugilistic sport once popular on Earth, and still practiced on several other pre-technological planets. As the Captain uses it, however, punch is neither violent nor even physical. It's something we *have,* not something we do.

"Punch" is a state of mind. It's the recognition that barriers exist only if we allow them to stop us; that meeting resistance is a sign that we're making progress; that opposition means we're on the verge of a breakthrough. And when we finally *do* break through, it's not so much because we've beaten the opposition as outlasted it.

The most important characteristic of punch is not power. It's persistence. Overcoming our addictions or grief or personal flaws rarely happens in a single swing. It's a struggle over time – a fight in which we renew our determination each time we're knocked down, celebrate every moment we manage to stay on our feet, and continuously affirm the meaning it gives our lives.

"Punching our way through" is less about right hooks than the right attitude; less about hammering our opponents than forging our own character. And sometimes the sweetest victory is simply making it to the final bell.

Today I will not back away from the fight. I will stay in the ring, go the distance. I will feel my strength and my joy increase as I finish each daily round.

06.07

An answer? I don't even know the question!

— CAPTAIN KIRK : STAR TREK/TMP : 7412.6

It's a common problem. Our search for knowledge is rarely thwarted because we can't find answers. More often it's because we haven't asked the right questions.

How we ask is critical. Sometimes, for example, our questions make assumptions that immediately point us in the wrong direction. Like the question, "Which religion is true?" We assume that a religion describes an objective reality, and, like some scientific equation, if it's not accurate it must be "untrue." But the truth is, religious traditions are more or less subjective means for linking us with realities and resources that are beyond these finite packages we call "words." And what successfully links one individual to those resources may not work for another. Asking if it's "true" misses the point.

Other questions contain similar misleading assumptions. "Which planetary race is superior?" "How can I achieve happiness?" "What's the best way to earn love?"

The way we formulate our questions restricts the answers we can generate, or even whether an answer exists at all. Too often we limit the possible responses only to what we expect, or what "fits" with previous knowledge.

Instead we must learn to ask in ways which free The Truth to reveal itself. We must risk being surprised, challenged, even offended. That is the price of growth.

The Universe is ready to answer fully only if I will open myself fully. If I seek, truly, I will find, truly.

06.08

If you could experience the Link, you'd know why nothing else matters.

— CONSTABLE ODO : BEHIND THE LINES : 51149.5

We're going to regard what Odo says here less as a positive recommendation than a cautionary statement. Because any activity that becomes so consuming that "nothing else matters" can be downright dangerous.

True, we need some method for looking at our lives from a wider perspective. Whether we're connecting with our "Higher Source" or simply reviewing our long-term goals, we often come to the realization that much of what we do is trivial, or wasteful, or even self-defeating. But we can also trivialize our whole life if this "wider perspective" ends up making our daily activities seem pointless.

The purpose of going on what some have called "The Hero's Journey" was never to enter some higher dimension and stay there. It was to discover the Truths we could access only in that realm, then bring them back to *this* life. Likewise, in one of Earth's oldest traditions, the highest achievement is not just to reach Nirvana, but to return to human existence and help others find *their* way.

Genuine encounters with divinity are marked not by a desire to leave this world. They're marked by a greater respect for it, and by a deeper commitment to living in the present as completely, joyfully and gratefully as we can.

I experience the Link by feeling the presence of resources and loving relationships all around me, above me and within me, each day of this life.

06.09

Perhaps you would be happier... in another job...?

— DATA : UNIFICATION, PART II : 45245.8

Data's question, though made in jest, is a serious one – serious enough to ask ourselves on a regular basis: Is our work making us happy? Is it personally fulfilling... or simply a task we must engage in to "earn a living"?

One of Earth's ancient languages preserves the notion that our careers are meant to be an expression of Who We Are on the deepest levels. Ideally our work should be our vocation – literally our "calling" – from the Latin word *vocare,* meaning "voice."

The Universe, if we listen, is calling us to do something: To prepare for a life's mission; to perform a special task as only we can. No employer, no corporation – not even The Federation – can call us to this job. The most they can do is provide an avenue for it. And if that avenue doesn't exist, then we must create it for ourselves.

Fortunately, if The Universe needs a job done, it will also supply the energy and the means to do it. Which is why we must concentrate first on what *kind* of work might make us happy, on what "mission" would best express the unique capabilities within us. Once we begin to follow that path – a spiritual path, really – The Universe assigns us more than a "living." It gives us our life.

My work is what I do... what I do... what I do. I will strive continually to make my job part of my life's work, and my life's work my job.

06.10

When one has a difficult job to do, personal reasons can be quite an incentive.

— GUL DUKAT : INDISCRETION : Stardate Not Given

There are many things we must do in life, even if we don't feel particularly inspired to do them. Our jobs, for example, or our responsibilities to family. Or perhaps a project we volunteered for out of some perceived "duty."

Some of those tasks are difficult and ongoing. Others would be quick and easy once started; yet even these we often put off because we "can't work up the energy."

We could quit, of course. We could decide not to finish the task, to *un*-volunteer our services. But that course is usually more damaging – to our own integrity and self-respect if not to our relationships. So we must somehow find the inspiration, despite the challenges. We must invent our own "personal reasons."

And fortunately we *can.* Because in every task there is something to be gained, something meant specifically for our benefit, something that fuels our spiritual growth.

We have only to identify the potential lessons. Or we can add our own "selfish" goals, to use the upcoming job as an excuse to learn new skills, expand our knowledge.

Or we can simply reaffirm that The Universe is still guiding us. And our inspiration comes from trying to find out where.

It is natural to feel burdened by the difficulties that lie ahead. But I feel even more uplifted knowing how much wiser and more experienced I'll be afterward.

06.11

I can only speculate about my programmer's motives.

— THE DOCTOR : THE CLOUD : 48546.2

Fact: We, individually or collectively, did not create the universe. Neither did we create our own existence, or the rules by which we and the universe operate. We can only discover and apply those rules — and then only by going boldly out, as voyagers, on Life's Grand Adventure.

The Reality that "programmed" these rules into the very nature of things transcends our finite lives not merely by some theoretical order of magnitude. It is not simply wiser or more powerful — or any other superlative description we might think of. It is utterly beyond our comprehension precisely because we cannot "think" in the terms that apply to it.

The most we can do is to make analogies and inferences. Or, like the holographic doctor, to "speculate."

Not that we should. One of Earth's pre-Stardate cultures (compared by some to early Klingon) considered such speculation as *dhanna* — idle conjecture that can't be proven, and more often ends up creating division among the people.

Better to accept that there are some things we will never know, to cultivate an appreciation of The Mystery... and then to simply get on with our lives.

I will spend my time on those things I can affect or learn from, and not pretend to know what is beyond my capacity to know.

06.12

Stop being so rational. Try using your imagination once in a while.

— ENGINEER LA FORGE : THE NEXT PHASE : 45892.4

There's a subtle difference here. If someone "stops being rational," that's not the same as "being *irrational*."

Irrationality is the condition of seeming to use reason and logic, but making deductions that are unsupported or downright mistaken. Like the paranoid schizophrenic who argues that we are all Romulan secret agents: He purports to use logic, yet refuses to acknowledge the unfounded assumptions his argument is based on. That's irrational.

Geordi isn't asking anyone to defy the rules of logic or refuse to consider possible mistakes in their thinking. He is simply reminding us that there are ways of "knowing" which don't involve evidence and deductions and linear thought. Our imagination is one such way.

The visions that flow from our subconscious are not merely fantasies we create. They can display vital information about us and our world in non-verbal form. Often that information contains answers we've been seeking through rational methods, but haven't had enough data to "compute." Or maybe we have all the data we need without knowing it consciously. And maybe we've been blocking it because it leads to a conclusion we're uncomfortable with.

Our imagination can break through these conscious barriers... if only we would stop *thinking* now and then!

My imagination is one more resource for accessing the truth. I will use it to complement my rationality.

06.13

In spite of human evolution, there are still some traits that are endemic to gender.

— COUNSELOR TROI : THE ICARUS FACTOR : 42686.4

In several ancient Terran and Klingon texts, we find prayers to various dieties which read something like, "Lord, thank you for not making me a woman."

No doubt there was a time when these prayers were taken literally. After all, being a male in some societies was a distinct advantage. As traditions evolved, however, such prayers became less and less statements of male "superiority" than affirmations of one's sexual identity, male *or* female. The woman devotee could just as fervently pray, "Lord, thank you for not making me a man."

Within this affirmation is the realization that each of us could have been born as the opposite sex. Our gender in this life may not be an accident, but neither is it essential to our deeper, spiritual being. We wear our sex as clothing.

Still, it's clothing for life. Our outer wear makes us different from half the population. And those differences, as the Counselor says, are "endemic." They're given. We can't ignore them.

What we *can* do is realize that they serve a purpose. Not only in terms of our species' survival, but in providing lessons we couldn't have learned otherwise. And one of those lessons is about learning to wear your clothing with pride.

My sexual identity is a gift from The Universe. I will find the joys, and celebrate the unique lessons, available to me only through this gender.

06.14

Never hide who you are. That's the only way relationships work.

— SCIENCE OFFICER STAMETS : MAGIC TO MAKE THE SANEST MAN GO MAD: Stardate 2136.8

It's the oldest crime in the book — the Book of Relationships, that is… pretending to be someone you're not in order to convince another person to form a friendship they might otherwise reject.

And it's not just private individuals who conceal who they are for fear of revealing some personality defect or past wrongdoing. It's the public official who trumpets his supposed care for the middle class while working to benefit the rich or those who got him elected. It's the corporation that flaunts its philanthrophy when all it really cares about is its profit margin and stockholders. It's the nation that seeks a "mutually beneficial" alliance only to cement its own power.

In the short run this may be a savvy strategy. Because most of us would like to believe the best about others. Or maybe we're just plain gullible, swayed by appearances rather than substance.

In the long run, however, the truth will come out. Our moral malfeasance and personal shortcomings are exposed despite our pretenses. The self-serving motives of politicians, companies and nations can't be hidden forever. And the real crime ends up being less about our individual faults or corporate agendas than the fact that we orchestrated a cover-up. We painted ourselves as magnanimous when we were mere money-grubbers. We deceived our partners. And ourselves.

Being open and transparent is the best policy not just because it's the "only way relationships work," but because it's the only way to gain our greatest power… over Who We Are.

I will reveal my true self to others not only to forge bonds with those able to see me for what I can be, but to see myself more clearly through their eyes.

06.15

It can be a challenge to feel grounded when even gravity is artificial.

— CAPTAIN KIRK : STAR TREK BEYOND : 2263.2

The complaint is so common that it's become a refrain in the litany of our lives: Nothing seems real or "natural" anymore. We live in a world spun from technology and holographic reproductions. We consume food reconstituted from bio-engineered ingredients, wear clothing composed of synthetic materials. The earth benfeath our feet has been replaced by asphalt and concrete, or the wire mesh flooring of starships in which gravity is supplied not by mass but by artificially generated force fields.

The very idea that we should "feel grounded" acknowledges a primal need to be connected to something solid and enduring, something we can count on despite the artificiality and constant changes which otherwise dominate our lives. And when we *don't* have this natural stability, we must create it.

Rituals can fill this need. By carving out a sacred space in our daily lives… a corner of our cabin, perhaps, with photos of loved ones or cherished mementos that connect us with our own past… an easy chair where we can rest and read words of inspiration, or a floor mat on which to meditate at the end of the day. Simply by doing one thing intentionally and regularly that feeds our souls, that connects our finite selves to The Infinite, we can find the ground that supports and restores us, no matter how hectic our lives, regardless of how artificial.

I will strive to carve out regular opportunities to reconnect with what is real, what is enduring, to what abides despite constant change.

06.16

We shield it with ritual and customs shrouded with antiquity.
It brings a madness which rips away our veneer of civilization…
the time of mating.

— SPOCK : AMOK TIME : 3372.7

The saying repeated on Earth is more to the point: "Love makes us do stupid things." And compared to our usual preference for suppressing emotion, to remain rational and logical and "civilized," love *is* a kind of madness.

But it is also entirely natural. The instinct that drives us to form loving relationships and physical unions has played an essential role in our species. It deserves to be celebrated in ritual and custom, and enjoyed in our personal lives.

Not that our particular brand of the Vulcan *Pon farr* gives us permission to let our instincts run rampant. We are still fully responsible for our actions, whether they are products of our reason or the effects of our glands.

On the other hand, by acknowledging this "madness" we can be prepared for it. Better yet, we can transform it. Because the rush we feel at the sight of physical beauty is really an avenue for connecting with all people, and all creation. The passion that rises within us comes from the same pool of energy we can use to fuel our daily work, to inspire our spiritual growth, to feel the Life this Universe has granted us… to feel how truly precious it is.

The "madness" of love is The Universe's open invitation to renew my connection to all people and all Life. I accept.

06.17

Without cooperation we will get nowhere.

— CAPTAIN PICARD : THE CHASE : 46731.5

Even if we *could* handle the entire assignment on our own, we shouldn't. Even if no one else could match our ability, perform the task as efficiently, or finish it as quickly — we should never insist on doing any job by ourselves when we could include others.

Because community is our ultimate destiny. We cannot claim to be responsible for "only our own souls." Our lives are too intertwined with, and dependent upon, others. Even the rare individual who no longer requires spiritual guidance must still seek out other people on which to demonstrate his or her spiritual skills. Personal transformation doesn't happen in a vacuum.

But neither does it require diluting our individuality in a communal melting pot. Cooperation isn't about suppressing the strong, personal qualities we've developed to this point. It means using them to their fullest.

Sharing one's skills and unique perspectives in community is actually the fullest expression of our individuality. As Picard might explain it, "where" is a location that can be defined only in relationship to others. "Nowhere" is the place we end up when we think we can go it alone.

In the sacred language of ancient Bajor, the translation of the word closest in meaning to "hell" is *no place.*

My personal skills become most valuable when I use them cooperatively. My individuality is refined and redeemed through my relationships with others.

06.18

I fell in love with you without knowing how lonely it would be to live without you!

— NEELIX : JETREL : 48832.1

Much as we try, we can never make "deals" with our affections. We can't calculate our love, divide it up, send some of it here, some there, or withhold it until certain conditions are met.

We can't, that is, without doing serious damage.

Our emotions have a definite logic of their own. Not that they're always "right" or appropriate. Not that we shouldn't control how we express them. It's just that we can't determine beforehand exactly how we're going to feel about something or someone. Or how strongly.

We hear people say, "I refuse to get involved with anyone because I might get hurt." Or "I'll care for somebody only if I get something out of it." Or "If you won't love me, I won't love you." This kind of emotional deal-making doesn't lead to control; it leads to denial. Our emotional responses and affections don't stop; we only end up suppressing them. And eventually losing touch with our*selves.*

That's serious damage.

Admittedly, affections are risky. We can be hurt by love. We can give more than we "get" — assuming we're keeping score. But that's the cost. And holding back our love costs far more.

Genuine love flows through me, not from me. My joy is not in keeping it, but keeping it flowing... unconditionally.

06.19

The important thing is to cherish whatever time we have together, whether it's a day or a decade.

— KES : JETREL : 48832.1

Often we can change things. Often we can't. And all-too-often we spend so much time brooding over what we wish we could change that we fail to enjoy what *is.*

This tendency to let our "real lives" slip through our fingers while we brood (or fantasize) is especially evident in our relationships. Either we have such high expectations for our friends or mates that we fail to appreciate who they are, or else we never find any friends or mates to begin with. Or maybe we're lucky enough to have plenty of friends, but we spend so much time wishing we had more time with them that we can't enjoy the time we *do* have together!

It's good to "want more," to have high expectations, as a first step toward a new, more enriching reality. But those expectations must not blind us to the riches we already have. Because we gain far more by learning to cherish what is, than by constantly striving after what's new.

Better yet, we also develop a skill that pays off in every other area of our lives. To "cherish" something is to experience it fully, to extract all the goodness and joy available to us right now if only we would open ourselves to it. And once we do, days and decades lose their importance, because living in the present is as good as it gets.

I will learn to cherish my days rather than count them, to enjoy what I have before asking for more.

06.20

I'm still recovering from all those desserts I had last night!

— COUNSELOR TROI : LIAISONS : Stardate Not Given

Whatever the currency, we pay dearly for our addictions. It's a weakness common to most sentient species. And the possibilities cover the spectrum: From drugs to sex, from gambling binges to shopping binges, from over-indulging in desserts to over-indulging our careers.

Chances are we'll hear warning bells before others begin to notice. Whether it's a psychological signal like guilt, or a physical one like pain, we can thank our own subconscious for trying to get a message through to us.

The worst thing we can do is ignore that message. Dismissing our inner warnings can induce a self-inflicted schizophrenia which makes it even harder to regain control of our lives.

The next worst thing we can do is "rationalize" our addictions. Enlisting logic to support our unhealthy habits is like rewriting the Constitution to empower a dictator.

The best thing to do, it turns out, is to openly admit when we've lost control over some aspect of our lives. It is also the hardest part.

The consolation is, we're in good company. Because virtually everyone has suffered from an addiction at one time or another. And those who choose the road to recovery often come to know themselves – and therefore The Universe – better than most people ever will.

If I lose control I can regain it – with the help of others, and with the awesome strength within me.

06.21

Don't think about it. Just do it.

— COMMANDER SISKO : EXPLORERS : Stardate Not Given

Do we think about walking, moving… breathing?

We *can* think about these things, of course. But unless we're just starting to learn (or re-learn) these functions, we've probably mastered them well enough to release conscious control. In other words, we just *do* them. And we thereby free our conscious mind for other things.

This process of "mental releasing" isn't meant only for motor control functions. It applies to *life* control functions, too. For example, we don't need to exert conscious control in order for the universe to continue delivering its blessings to us. We should be grateful, certainly, for the material and spiritual riches we enjoy. But concentrating on *receiving* those riches, as if we need to remind The Universe to do its job, is more likely to short-circuit the process than insure speedy delivery.

Similar to our own physical bodies, the Body of Life has many natural processes we can "release" once we acknowledge that they are flowing, or that they simply exist. Like the process of personal growth. Or the process of receiving just what we need, right when we need it. Or being exactly where we should be at exactly this moment, on our own one-of-a-kind spiritual journey.

Some things we do by just letting them be done.

The Universe is taking care of me right now. I am walking The Spiritual Path without having to think about each step. I am doing it. It is being done.

06.22

You can't make someone love you.

— COMMANDER RIKER : TRUE Q : 46192.3

Oh, but how we try! Flowers, lavish gifts, dinners — we offer these baubles as if they are personal qualities someone can fall in love with! Yet, ironically, the things we do to "win" a potential lover are often the very things we will no longer do once the victory is achieved. The flowers and gifts are merely "start-up costs" for the relationship, rarely indicative of the lifestyle we intend to live afterwards. Are people really fooled?

Constantly. But not for long. Because drawing attention to ourselves in this way is really pointing at someone we're not. And the people who are likely to be attracted by this sham are the people who, in the long run, we wouldn't want as friends or lovers anyway.

All we can ever offer anyone else — the only thing that's genuine, that's representative of the relationship someone can expect from us — is ourselves, is Who We Are. Or perhaps Who We're Trying to Become, assuming we *are* trying.

The bottom line is simply this: Be real. Be yourself. Be patient. Do what's in your heart… but only if it's you and not merely the means to an end. The person — soul mate, lover, friend — meant to find you, *will.*

Or maybe they have already.

I attract those relationships that represent my own current development. If I present the real "me" to the world, I will attract others who are also genuine.

06.23

***We think of ourselves as the most powerful beings in the universe.
It's unsettling to discover that we're wrong.***

— CAPTAIN KIRK : ERRAND OF MERCY : 3198.4

Now and then we get into the groove. We're on a roll. We feel like nothing can stop us, nothing can
go wrong.

Maybe it's because, for once, we're doing all the right things. We're meditating regularly; our
attitude is optimistic and confident; we interact with people on a positive, respectful, supportive
basis, and they respond in kind. And then we hit the proverbial Brick Wall.

Because it's the last thing we were expecting, we fall apart. Having forgotten what adversity was
like, we lose our resiliance. And not only are we unable bounce back, we end up falling lower than
ever before.

Call it a Spiritual Reality Check. Occasionally we need an unsettling, or even humbling, experience to keep us grounded. For humans, in fact, it's the essence of our identity: Human, humble,
humus ... of the earth. That's what the word means.

Keeping ourselves in proper perspective – filled with divinity, yet subject to the vagaries of
material existence – is actually a source of strength. So, too, is being openly and joyfully appreciative
for what we have, what we are.

Including the fact that we are *not* the most powerful beings in the universe.

***Omnipotence would quickly grow boring. I am grateful for challenges, and the
resources to face them.***

06.24

I am proud of what I am. I believe in what I do.

— ENSIGN CHEKOV : THE WAY TO EDEN : 5832.3

This time we'll start with our daily affirmation, by repeating Chekov's words just as he spoke them.
Go ahead: Say them to yourself. Out loud. And *loud*.

Now once more... and *mean* it this time!

Unfortunately, some of us can't seem to "mean" it, no matter how loud we shout. After all, what
if we *aren't* particularly proud of what we are? What if our lives are full of activities we *don't* believe
in – at least not passionately? Most of us are still searching; we're far from perfect; we're still on that
long, laborious journey to becoming the person we'd like to be. Surely we're not being asked to lie
to ourselves, to pretend to be something we're not.

Actually, there's no need to pretend. To realize you're on that journey of "becoming" is a proud
tradition in itself. To recognize that you're imperfect, that you're still searching, is to believe in the
Self within you which *is* perfect, the Self which is the culmination of your search.

Besides, we aren't being asked to be proud of the outward roles we may play in this life –
whether teacher or Starfleet crewman or migrant spacedock worker. Our deepest pride comes from
what we already are, what each of us will always be: A child of The Universe. To repeat Chekov's
words is to be transformed by that.

So once again, say it. Out loud. Loud. And *mean* it.

I am proud of what I am. I believe in what I do.

06.25

Peace in your hearts. Fortune in your steps.

— COMMANDER CHAKOTAY : INNOCENCE : Stardate Not Given

As we grow spiritually, the practice of well-wishing becomes almost second nature. And it's not simply a matter of respecting the laws of karma.

It's true that wishing good fortune on others brings more positive effects into one's own life, just as hoping others will meet disaster creates negative karma for oneself. But that's not *why* we wish others well.

After all, when we pray that others might be blessed with life's riches, it's not like we're giving away the store; and it's not our store to begin with. Wishing someone happiness and peace isn't offering them anything they don't already deserve as children of The Universe.

What it *does* do, however, is draw us into closer alignment with The Universe. Its plan for healing and salvation now becomes *our* plan. Its mechanism for enlisting consciousness in the ongoing task of creation becomes *our* mechanism.

If we are sincere – if we can wish peace and good fortune even upon our "enemies" – the Universe will trust us with the power to make those wishes come true. Our very thoughts begin to transform the world.

By then, they will have already transformed us.

Today I will verbalize to others the blessings that I know The Universe holds in store for us all. I will be patient as my well-wishing slowly takes effect.

06.26

The Prime Directive has many different functions, not the least of which is to protect us.

— CAPTAIN PICARD : PEN PALS : 42695.3

We often regard the policy of non-interference as a measure to protect other planetary cultures from us. After all, throughout history, the policies of colonial powers were frequently responsible for the destruction of their supposedly "less-advanced" neighbors. By not allowing those societies to undergo their own natural evolutions, their imposed development was artificial and temporary at best. Not to mention that unimagined treasures and traditions were sometimes lost forever.

But *we* have much to lose, too, by forcing ourselves on other planetary cultures. Jumping into a situation without knowing the full story can be dangerous. It can entangle us in ways we can't foresee. Besides which we often react emotionally rather than objectively in such encounters; and by the time we understand all the facts, the damage is done.

Each of us would do well to learn the personal application of The Prime Directive, too: Not to react emotionally, based on superficial evidence, to conditions and events in other people's lives. Not to assume that we are more "advanced" than somebody else, and therefore we must know the answers to their problems. And, most of all, not to interfere with the natural course of growth and change.

Unless we're absolutely certain their asking us for help is *part* of that course.

Not only are other people's lives sacred, where they are in their lives is sacred. As part of the universal community, I will lend help. But only if I'm asked.

06.27

I am not concerned with pleasure. I am a warrior!

— LIEUTENANT WORF : JUSTICE : 41255.6

In a sense we are all warriors. We strive to defend what's right and true. We struggle for peace and wholeness, both in our communities and in our selves. And we must work daily toward these goals with a sense of discipline and duty — as if achieving them matters more than the personal inconvenience and sacrifices they inevitably require.

Not that we can't enjoy things along the way. Not that achieving these goals shouldn't be pleasurable. In fact, what most of us learn is that Right and Truth and Wholeness yield the greatest pleasures, the highest bliss, the deepest fulfillment. It's just that aiming specifically for the pleasure at the end of our struggle, instead of concentrating on the struggle itself, is the surest way to miss it.

Many ancient spiritual practices made a similar mistake. Spiritual novices were often told that our final goal was "getting to heaven." But the real goal should have been — and still is — doing the things that, if done mindfully and wholeheartedly, will result in what is meant by "heaven." In other words, heaven isn't the goal, but the by-product of having achieved our goals.

And therein lies a world of difference.

Today I will focus on being the best person I can be, not because of the pleasure I expect to gain, but because that's the goal I set for myself.

06.28

We come in peace. That's why we're here.

— COMMANDER BURNHAM: THE VULCAN HELLO: Stardate 1207.3

The irony with this statement is that it was understood by most Klingons of that era as a threat. Members of that Empire saw peace as a fatal condition in which there were no longer any opportunities to prove oneself, no further quests or character-building battles. No *honor.*

And the Klingons had a perfect right to see it that way, insofar as they interpreted "peace" as the kind of quiet serenity that might describe a graveyard.

From the Starfleet perspective, however, to "come in peace" means to seek a relationship with another person, community or culture, confidently expecting to discover shared values and interests that might lead to joint commercial ventures and other projects of mutual benefit. The challenge, of course, is to introduce oneself in such a way that the other party understands that the hoped-for relationship will not be one-sided, meant to exploit or even subjugate them — and, in consideration of the Klingons' native belligerence, that an alliance isn't being sought out of fear, or from a position of weakness. Hence the preemptive display of overwhelming force that came to be known as the "Vulcan Hello."

In Earth's Hebrew and Islamic traditions, the words *shalom* and *salaam*, often translated as "peace," are closer in meaning to the concept of "wholeness." It's the condition where everything works together for the greater good, even when there is occasional dissention or dysfunction.

And sometimes, *because* there is.

I will strive for wholeness in every new relationship, seeking to understand others' differences as new perspectives and talents that may complement my own.

06.29

Parted from me and never parted. Never and always touching and touched.

— SPOCK : AMOK TIME : 3372.7

Relationships are a mystical thing. Admittedly, there is a physical dimension: A being together, a "touching" and being "touched" – if only in the sense that we respond physically to one another's presence. Our brain waves literally change; our senses reset themselves at measurably higher levels of sensitivity.

But there is a spiritual dimension, too. And it's not just that the mere thought of another person can generate these same physical responses. Or that, when we're separated from a loved one, we can find emotional comfort in our memories of them. Special relationships go deeper than thoughts and memories. They open up avenues of communication and connection between what The Ancients called our "souls."

In truth, our souls are already connected. A caring, committed relationship simply lowers the veil that gives us the illusion of being "separate." We become increasingly aware of an identity which transcends our bodies – even our location in time – so that, despite our parting, we are never parted. We are always "touching."

Relationships are therefore opportunities to explore our own spiritual roots… in others… in The Universe. And the ultimate discovery is Love.

I open myself to the mystery – and the treasures – which lie hidden in my relationships to others.

06.30

The needs of the one outweighed the needs of the many.

— ADMIRAL KIRK : THE SEARCH FOR SPOCK : 8310.3

Spock wasn't wrong when he willingly traded his own needs (i.e. his *life*) for "the needs of the many." Far from it. As Spock would later say, his sacrifice was the most logical thing he ever did, the high point of his Starfleet career.

And yet, Kirk reminds us, there are times when saving a single life can justify putting many others at risk. Not because that one life is so much more valuable than anyone else's. Rather, it's because the attempt to save that one life affirms what is most valuable about *all* of our lives.

Our own identities grow not by feeding our individual egos, not by becoming increasingly concerned with ourselves and our private, selfish needs. Our personal growth, paradoxically, depends on exactly the opposite – on becoming increasingly *un*selfish, on seeing others' needs as inseparable from our own.

The now-legendary Search for Spock was therefore more than a rescue attempt focusing on one individual. It was a symbolic act, a galaxy-wide demonstration that caring for one another is what gives our lives meaning.

As another legend summarized it, "All for one, and one for all." That is the solution. And both halves are equally essential.

There are no impenetrable boundaries between myself and others. Their needs affect mine, and mine theirs. We thrive in community, or not at all.

07

07.01

It only knows that it needs. But like so many of us, it does not know what.

— SPOCK : STAR TREK/TMP : 7412.6

Like most animal species, we are designed for action. Despite our capacity for thought, our nerves, bones and muscles are meant to move, to run, lift, climb… *do*.

Most of the time, however, we "do" without ever knowing why. Sensing an inner call to be "about something," we give ourselves over to jobs and activities that soon absorb all our waking hours. But all this busy-ness is like a drug. It numbs our sneaking suspicion that we *don't* really know what we're about, that our deepest needs are still going unmet.

More often than not this addiction will eventually worsen to the point that it draws attention to the very message it tries to suppress. And instead of beating ourselves up for having the addiction, we should be resolving the question we've ignored for so long: What do we really *need?*

A five-thousand-year-old tradition on Earth charts our spiritual evolution through four stages of "need": From fulfillment of bodily pleasures to personal success; from a life of service to eventual liberation from every need. If we stop long enough to acknowledge that we still have unmet needs, we can feel ourselves being prodded to continue along this evolutionary journey. And if we honestly define those needs, we can take the next step: We can start "doing"… and know why.

Today I will make a list of my life's deepest needs. Each month I will review my list to see if those needs have changed, and to chart my progress.

07.02

Change is at the heart of what you are. But change into what – that is the question.

— Q : HIDE AND Q : 41590.5

In the face of constant change, it's reassuring to know that some people can always be counted on; that no matter what happens they will remain just as they are.

And yet, ironically, if someone is too predictable, too "stable," chances are they've stopped taking the risks necessary to grow and further improve themselves. We must encourage others to surprise us on occasion, to *not* adhere to our own selfish insistence on stability.

What we should seek for others, as we seek it for ourselves, is not some steady state, but steady progress. Which means having a goal for our lives – even if it, too, will evolve. If we keep our focus on that goal, what seems like a constant state of turmoil becomes a series of stages in our development. Our identities no longer coalesce around specific, unchanging characteristics, but around movement toward our life's purpose.

Pre-modern cultures on dozens of planets institutionalized this "movement toward" by giving people new names at successive stages in their spiritual evolution. The same practice today would probably wreak havoc on Starfleet records. But we *could* reward each other with new "nicknames" that reflect our continuing progress. And that better reflect the reality of who where we are now.

The "who" in Who I Am may change. "I" am the constant, as is my commitment to spiritual progress.

07.03

You know as well as I do that fear exists for only one purpose... to be conquered.

— CAPTAIN JANEWAY : THE THAW : Stardate Not Given

In its own twisted way, it's downright miraculous: Our fear can become so palpable, so intense, that it seems like a separate "personality" we carry around inside us. We can hear its nagging voice as clearly as a scolding parent, feel its icy breath on our necks, its grip like a straightjacket.

These imagined sensations are actually a sign of inner strength. For what they tell us is that we can bring a kind of "reality" to something that exists only in our minds, in order to better deal with it. The personality we've invented to embody our fear is proof that we can also create a figure to represent our courage – in fact to represent all the higher qualities waiting to be born in us.

One of the most important of these qualities is self-confidence. Ironically, without our fears to actively stand in the way – like a real-life adversary – we could never achieve genuine confidence. We would therefore be less likely to take the risks necessary to learn and grow, and to overcome the other weaknesses that prevent us from claiming our full heritage as children of The Universe.

Conquering our fear, then, is the first step. By imagining a courageous warrior within us – already imbued with the power and confidence we seek – our fear-gripped personality will slip quietly... finally... into oblivion.

I will acknowledge and name my fears. I bless them for challenging me to grow. And again I release them.

07.04

Freedom is not a gift. You have to earn it, or you don't get it.

— CAPTAIN KIRK : THE RETURN OF THE ARCHONS : 3156.2

In one sense, freedom *is* a gift. The universe bestows sentient beings with an incredible range of choices and actions – any of which can beneficial... or harmful.

Of course, the universe also "knows" which is which. And it tends to reward those choices and actions that balance individual fulfillment with communal wholeness. Conversely, it tends to punish those individuals who buy personal gain at the expense of others. Like a healthy biological system, the universe roots out selfishness and greed by making their consequences increasingly intolerable. If an individual continues to disregard others, his range of choices becomes narrowed, his actions more and more restricted until there are no alternatives available. Freedom – even though once given – can be taken away.

But the flip side is that, if one's freedom is exercised wisely, the universe responds by expanding the possibilities, *and* the rewards. Like the steward who carefully invests his master's money rather than spending it foolishly – or worse, burying it in the ground to keep it "safe" – we earn the right to exercise still more of it.

Better yet, we earn the right to become stewards of The Universe, and of the vast potential that lies within us.

I will honor my freedom by using it wisely: Acting with respect for the universe, consideration toward others, and confidence in my own unique gifts.

07.05

The first speech censored, the first thought forbidden, the first freedom denied – chains us all irrevocably.

— CAPTAIN PICARD : THE DRUMHEAD : 44769.2

No human being, according to one of Earth's beloved poets, "is an island." Which is simply to say that we can't help being affected by one another's joys and sorrows, gains or losses. Neither can the political suppression or enslavement of one people be ignored by the rest.

The Universe commands us to protect each other's freedoms if we wish to maintain our own. Another writer experienced this maxim personally during a dark period in Earth's history known as The Holocaust. "First they came for the Jews," the man wrote, referring to the Nazis, "and I did not speak out because I was not a Jew. Then they came for the socialists, and I did not speak out because I was not a socialist. Next they came for the trade unionists, and I did not speak out because I was not a trade unionist. Finally they came for me," he lamented, "and there was no one left to speak out on my behalf."

We ignore abuses of universal law at our own peril, because karma extends equally to what we *don't* do as to what we do. And if we sit idly by as others are put in chains, we will surely wear the same constricting shackles in due course.

Fortunately, the flip side is also true.

I earn my own freedom by cherishing the freedom of others. I free myself as I help to release others from their bondage – both physical and spiritual.

07.06

Amazing to think that, while we fight our war, a place of peace not only survives, it thrives!

— FIRST OFFICER SARU: SI VIS PACEM, PARA BELLUM : Circa 1306.7

On virtually every planet where intelligent life has been found, wide swaths of strife and open warfare are present even as sanctuaries of peace and cooperation exist right alongside. The fact that those who practice peace appear to tolerate members of their species living amidst terror and combat is troubling. But the real crime is that the war-mongers refuse to study their neighbors in order to learn the secrets of their success, and then wage peace with the same dedication as war.

Eons of experience have proven that more advanced societies rarely help by taking sides in others' armed conflicts, especially by intervening militarily. That's why the Prime Directive was mandated. Far better to simply shine one's light in the darkness, to influence others "by example," as Picard put it; to show the warring parties that harmony is preferable by demonstrating it in their own affairs. And then, only when asked, to instruct their belicose brothers in the ways of peace.

The same thing applies on a more intimate level, too. When our personal lives are beset by conflict, our awareness that there are others who remain serene in the face of hostility should assure us that we too can achieve serenity and self-control, if only we would learn how.

That peace exists *any*where should inspire us to pursue it *every*where. First in our own lives. Then in our communities. Then in our world.

Let my amazement that peace survives some*where *inspire me to make sure that it survives in my own life, and thrives as I teach it to others through my example.

07.07

Regulations aside, this action is morally wrong.

— SPOCK : STAR TREK / INTO DARKNESS : CIRCA 2259

We can all be considered "explorers" to the extent that we sometimes find ourselves in morally ambiguous situations we've never faced before, in which social conventions or "regulations" don't seem to apply. These are the proverbial "grey areas," the moral questions that yield conflicting answers, where the "accepted" norms just don't "feel right." Or where some Higher Law seems to override what mere mortals have decreed, and we have no earthly clue what to do now.

Before we take action, our first responsibility is to insure we're not flaunting regulations for our own selfish gain. But we must also recognize that there are some situations that require us to react in new ways, conditions in which The Universe itself may be calling on us to pioneer a new "exception to the rule," to contradict "the way it's always been done" despite threats of punishment.

"Into Darkness" isn't about aligning oneself with the Dark Side (as one tradition describes it). Nor is it about using the tactics of evil to defeat evil (which virtually all spiritual traditions condemn). It's about our willingness to go where no one has gone before if that's where our conscience leads us, to venture into the undiscovered country where the terrain is treacherous and doubt holds sway.

In the end, it's about our determination to stumble and fumble and feel our way through these moral ambiguities no matter what; and, if and when our actions are vindicated, to know that we've not only learned something essential to our own lives, we've illumined the Way for others.

It is my duty to know the regulations. But it is also my duty to question them when conscience calls. That's how regulations are constantly refined; that's how morality becomes progressively more aligned with Higher Law.

07.08

No power in the universe can hope to stop the force of evolution.

— COMMANDER RIKER : ANGEL ONE : 41636.9

Historians can point to a phase on almost every planet when the concept of evolution was vilified, or even outlawed. Some cultures still regard it as incompatible with the existence of a higher, purposeful Power.

Which only goes to show how easily we can trap ourselves in the finite boxes we build around The Infinite. Because, rightly understood, evolution is one of the primary manifestations of that higher Power. To use the language of many sacred traditions, evolution is "redemption" acting visibly in nature, and through time. It is what "grace" looks like in purely physical terms.

But it also has a spiritual, "invisible" aspect, too. Because it's an activity that goes on inside us, quietly, inconspicuously, as we learn and grow. It is the inner impulse that transforms us from the raw material of self-centered need into the refined souls whose greatest joy is to give.

To assert that nothing can stop this force is to say, first of all, that we will all be "redeemed." Spiritual transformation is our destiny, both as individuals and as communities.

Secondly, it says that The Universe is in that ultimate Captain's Chair. The voyage may be no less bumpy, but being part of the crew makes it one fabulous ride.

Whether I accept my destiny or fight it will not alter the outcome. But it will affect my happiness and satisfaction in this life. The choice is mine.

07.09

There is no correct resolution. It's a test of character.

— ADMIRAL KIRK : THE WRATH OF KHAN : 8130.3

The most common view on Earth – or at least the western view – used to be that life's major lessons were all about learning to do "the right thing," or giving "the right answer." Getting it right became an obsession, as if "it" were something outside of ourselves, an object we're supposed to chisel away at like some marble statue until it finally duplicates someone else's preconceived ideal.

Actually we *are* sculptors of a sort. But the statue we're working on at the moment is only an excuse to continue sculpting our*selves,* to refine our techniques or try new ones; to shape the person we wish to become.

The statues we produce – our achievements – are less important than what we learn in the process. In fact, if we try to carry those statues/achievements around with us as we go through life, we end up being weighed down by them, perhaps even stuck in our tracks. Or in the past.

We need to jettison the idea that "right" is something external. Right is not a resolution in the sense of an outcome or an end-product. It's our resolution, our resolve, to develop our character. It's where "correct" is not what we try to be, but something we *do*… to ourselves.

I resolve to bring my character more and more into alignment with the will of The Universe. I look forward to the tests that help me track my progress.

07.10

You know… if an Earth girl says, "It's me, not you," it's definitely you.

— DR. McCOY : STAR TREK BEYOND : STARDATE 2263.2

Intimate relationships can be fragile things. As well as mysterious and baffling. Or at least ambiguous. And while some couplings might be characterized by the statement, "Like two peas in a pod," others clearly fall under the banner of "Opposites attract."

No two relationships are exactly alike. All are ongoing experiments in finding common ground and getting along despite inevitable differences. Even relationships that seem to "click" from the first meeting can fall apart as two individuals grow and individual circumstances change. And since our social graces call for us to soften the blow of a looming separation to the extent we can, we often fabricate little white lies to explain it.

"It's me, not you" was Lt. Uhura's effort to soften the impact on an inexperienced, socially-challenged Spock. "It's definitely *you*" was McCoy's not-so-subtle effort to affix blame… on *him.*

But the reason for most break-ups is rarely the fault of one party. In fact, it's not so much anyone's "fault" as a natural, inherent potential that comes with every relationship. It goes with the territory. It's part of what makes relationships so exciting. Because it's our job to remain vigilant, to never cease the work of relationship-building and maintenance. And when one *does* fall apart, it becomes our job to humbly ask ourselves why, to learn from experience, to enter into our next intimate relationship a little better prepared, and all the more grateful for the blessings they bring.

Relationships are laboratories for personal growth. I will put in the same effort I would when learning any new skill, and grade myself accordingly.

07.11

If you do not learn from your mistakes, you will be doomed to repeat them.

— LIEUTENANT TUVOK : LEARNING CURVE : 48846.5

As it is with so many of these Starfleet sayings, the identical theme appears in a thousand forms throughout the galaxy, and dozens on any single planet.

For example: "History repeats itself for those who fail to learn its lessons." Or: "Even the victor must fight again if he learns not the cause of the war." Or, on a more mundane level: "Unless the divorce leads to self-knowledge, the suitor will marry the same spouse again."

Earth is only one of many planets on which entire religions have grown up around the idea that life's purpose is about learning from our mistakes – and that we *will* learn, even if it takes a thousand lifetimes to do it!

On the other hand, being "doomed" to repeat our mistakes is perhaps too harsh a sentence. We could just as easily look at the adage in a hopeful light: That the Universe is giving us another chance to learn a life-changing lesson, and we wouldn't want to "graduate" until we *did* learn it.

What's even more hopeful is that The Universe provides fresh opportunities for learning our lessons with every new day. All we must do is seize one, to "experiment" with another approach this time, and to never give up until we discover what works.

In fact, it's the learning of this experimental attitude that is one of life's most important lessons!

Mistakes represent failed experiments. I will take advantage of any new opportunities The Universe gives me to try again, and finally learn its lessons.

07.12

Lies must be challenged.

— CAPTAIN PICARD : REDEMPTION, PART I : 44995.3

We're not talking about what our ancestors called "white lies," those (mostly) harmless distortions of truth designed to preserve social harmony and good will by sacrificing a little honesty. Like: "Oh, Uncle Quark, I was *hoping* you'd get me another bolo tie for my birthday!"

It's the distortions of truth that support prejudice and injustice that can't be tolerated. Or the kind of misinformation that justifies one group's abuse of another: The lies about racial or genetic inferiority; the claims of moral pre-eminence, or divine mandates, or "galactic destiny."

Because the damage is not limited only to the victims of injustice. The people who know the real truth yet allow the lies to stand are damaged as well.

For one thing, their silence makes them partly responsible for the injustices that are supported by the lies. Worse, ignoring lies perpetrated by others makes us increasingly immune to the falsehoods in our *own* lives. Like the notion that we can continue to indulge in our same bad habits without any further harm. Or that our spiritual welfare (or lack of it) doesn't really affect anybody else. Or that we can put off those self-improvements we'd like to make (but haven't yet) because, well, there's still plenty of time left to repent.

If those lies go unchallenged, it is *we* who suffer.

I will challenge falsehood wherever I encounter it, both for the sake of those who may be hurt, and to preserve my own integrity.

07.13

I'm an illogical woman who's beginning to feel too much a part of that communications console.

— LIEUTENANT UHURA : MAN TRAP : 1531.1

It's a logical necessity to admit that, sometimes, we are not logical.

We are emotional beings, with emotional needs that run deeper than the roles we play and the jobs we have. We need to laugh, to cry; to feel sympathy and joy and meaning. We need to love, to *be* loved.

But there are times when we become so wrapped up in our jobs that we forget those needs. We focus so much on the practical functions we perform as members of a crew or community that we lose touch with our own individuality.

Uhura's words remind us that we must never lose sight of our physical selves – and physical *needs* – that support all our various roles and functions. Because even as we link with others, even as we redefine and expand our concept of self, even as we identify more and more with the transcendent Oneness beyond all finite selves – we are still linked to a specific person, born into a specific form, living at a specific time in galactic history.

That person will not be ignored for long, since it alone can act as our "center." It is the strong thread that binds together our experiences, our learning, our lessons.

It is the Voyager that will one day carry us home.

I celebrate the unique personhood of "me." I will not ignore the physical, emotional needs that support my ongoing spiritual journeys.

07.14

I'm just trying to keep to the essentials.

— CONSTABLE ODO : CROSSFIRE : Stardate Not Given

Let's take a few moments to consider what occupies our time and energy. If we're honest, most of us will admit that we spend the majority of our time on activities that have little to do with our life's goals, or with our efforts toward personal and spiritual transformation.

True, we have a right to occasional "diversions." Play is as important as work. But the best kind of "play" is more than a diversion. Whether we're conscious of it or not, our periods of relaxation and "fun" are really designed to give us a better perspective on what we're doing with the *rest* of our lives. Their function is to remind us what's important, what the essentials are.

And yet, with travel brochures in hand and itineraries full of "things to do," that function is defeated. How many of us return from vacation with a new sense of *vocation*?

Instead we must consciously set aside time for the task of simplifying, of reflecting on what truly matters. A weekly "Sabbath" is useful for this. Regular meditation can help enormously. We must learn to re-focus.

And the point is not to logically prioritize our activities, not to make lists, not to "decide." What's essential in our life becomes clear as we quiet ourselves, as we listen to our inner longings. As we let the Spirit guide us.

Today I will search my heart for what matters. I will concentrate on those things so that everything I do contributes in some way to their fulfillment.

07.15

The need to resort to violence and force has long since passed.

— CAPTAIN KIRK : LET THAT BE YOUR LAST BATTLEFIELD : 5730.2

Sometimes our words are more an expression of hope than fact. And the fact that Federation Starships are still outfitted with shields, phasers and photon torpedoes is a pretty good sign that the need for force *hasn't* passed.

What the Captain is really saying is that people can get along if they make the effort. There are alternatives to force, even when those involved seem utterly irreconcilable.

The process to peaceful solutions has been worked out through trial and error on dozens of planets. That process is known and tested. It works. Two or more "sides" who agree to abide by this process will invariably come to an accommodation, and often form an alliance that benefits them in ways they could never have dreamed.

But the cost is nothing less than a change in identity. We can no longer think of ourselves as members of one isolated community, one race, one planetary society. We must learn to identify more fully with our spiritual selves, *and* with that Universal Self to whom we are already connected, with whom we are already in communication – in whom an alliance has already been inked.

It's not a matter of compromising with our enemies. It's a matter of making peace with who we already are.

My deeper self is connected to everything, even to those with whom I seem to be in conflict. I will surrender to that Self, and experience genuine peace.

07.16

Some women can't resist the bad boys.

— ENSIGN SATO : THE COUNCIL : CIRCA ECE2154

Okay, let's admit right from the start that Sato's comment recalls a stereotype that 21st-Century pundits labeled as "sexist," or at least "politically incorrect." But let's also admit that the theme was hardly uncommon. Maybe because it symbolized something deeper, that transcended gender.

The fact is, *all* of us, male or female, consciously or not, are attracted to "the rebel." We admire, even if secretly, the person who "marches to a different drummer," who has the self-confidence to break a few rules now and then, to boldly go, to follow his or her own path.

And yet, to be honest, the admirers are more often women than men. It's the female of the species, after all, who has more often been subjugated, who has been kept "in her place" throughout much of history by social convention and religious restriction.

Ironically, the "bad boy" is one of the few role models women have that symbolizes a kind of freedom from those choking customs and conventions. And it's not that women (or men) want to adopt the bad boy's lifestyle. The vast majority of us reject the instability and irresponsibility which often characterizes it. What attracts us is the notion that all of us have a right to define who we are. It's the rebel's courage we admire, his willingness to persevere despite disapproval, to flaunt conventions in order to pioneer new ones.

And that's not bad, boy. That's good.

I will honor the paths of others whose "rebelliousness" opens up new horizons for the rest of us. And I will become a rebel myself if I believe what I'm doing is right.

07.17

Vulcans are revered for their accomplishments, not for the way they look.

— SUBCOMMANDER T'POL : ROGUE PLANET : CIRCA ECE2153

"Looks": Pre-Starfleet slang for one's "personal appearance"... i.e., the way we dress and arrange our hair (or shave it off); how we adorn ourselves with jewelry or tattoos (or don't); and, of course, whether we keep ourselves trim and taut and attractive, as if to prove we're not growing older.

All of these shallow projections of Who We Are are holdovers from our evolutionary origins, when signs of physical fitness and youthfulness demonstrated an ability to produce, nurture and otherwise provide for one's offspring. At some point, however, this superficial focus gave way to other symbols of personal and communal "fitness." Like educational degrees and professional honors, civic awards and career achievements. Such symbols could not be diminished by age. In fact, it's the process of aging that allows the *time* for one's achievements.

But "achievements" are actually symbols for something even deeper, something more crucial to our evolution. It's the message that what we *do* is what matters most. Action trumps appearance. Who We Are is built not on what others see with their eyes but what we accomplish with our lives.

And even that message isn't the point. It's the development of the discipline and dedication that lead to our accomplishments in the first place. It's the slow, steady accumulation of skills and insight and wisdom that we can pass on to the next generation. It's the creation of *character*.

Not only for Vulcans, but for humans.

How I "look" is a function of what I see within myself – not only what I am now, but what I can become.

07.18

May the Prophets walk with us.

— MAJOR KIRA : FASCINATION : Stardate Not Given

One needn't be "religious" to profit from the Prophets.

Stories about scriptural heroes and ancestors who claimed to speak for various divinities can be instructive for us all. Studies of sacred histories throughout the galaxy reveal themes and truths shared by virtually every tradition. Within these common elements is a larger, more universal story about the emergence of life, the advent of consciousness and the responsibilities that come with it.

Viewed from this wider perspective, the words of every tradition's Prophets begin to transcend the boundaries of time and place. If we look past the specifics, we find a rich repository of information about what makes us all tick – whether Bajoran or Klingon, Human or Ferengi. We find examples of what causes our problems, what leads to solutions, how to respond in a variety of situations, and how *not* to. In short, we learn more about ourselves — at our worst, and our best.

To listen to the words of these Prophets, to reflect on their meaning — whether or not we fully agree — is to converse with them, like we might during a long walk. After we go our separate ways, we can recall that conversation. And as often as it helps illumine our path, they "walk with us."

We couldn't ask for better company.

The story The Universe tells is written in every culture and age. I can find and affirm the eternal Truths by searching the words of all the Prophets.

07.19

I've been close to death... You don't think about who's failed you. You think about who you love, what you wish you'd done different.

— LT. ASH TYLER : LETHE : Stardate 1412.3

It's not only Starfleet voyagers who live in a world where death is a daily possibility. Back on Earth, life isn't fully guaranteed either. The machines and modes of transportation we use often put our lives at risk. Natural disasters and deadly illnesses can take us by surprise. So can thugs or terrorists or madmen who can buy a gun as easily as a gallon of milk.

We may strengthen our preventative measures. Or finally enact legislation that puts public good over corporate greed. These may give us enough peace of mind to keep death at a distance.

But listening to stories about others' encounters with death — or coming face-to-face with our own demise — may lead us to our only sure "preventative" — a change in perspective, in our values; a recognition of what truly matters; a realization that our limited lifespan makes our time that much more precious, and our family and friends that much more deserving of it.

If Hell exists, it can't be any worse than our anguish over all the opportunities we've missed to lend a hand or forgive someone's perceived failings. Or to trade an hour spent alone with our "personal devices" for one more hour with a parent or co-worker who was taken unexpectedly.

To gain that priceless perspective amounts to a spiritual breakthrough, and, no matter how many years we've already lived, the basis for a brand new life.

Today I will spend time thinking about all the significant people in my life, and choose the methods and moments when I will demonstrate my affection for them.

07.20

You could learn something from Mr. Spock, and stop thinking with your glands.

— CAPTAIN KIRK : MAN TRAP : 1513.1

The idea is not to turn a deaf ear to the call of the wild, to stop enjoying the way our passions can sometimes transport us to a simpler place where life was *felt,* not analyzed. Having "glands" — sexual or otherwise — is a gift. The point is to not let them rule our lives.

In a broader sense, the point is to not let our *bodies* rule our lives. We are sentient beings, "knowing" beings. And by knowing what purpose our glands and our bodies serve, we can give them their due without losing the self-control that makes us *us.*

One of the most ancient disciplines for giving our bodies "their due" is called yoga. From a Sanskrit word meaning "union," yoga is the practice of unifying our minds and bodies/glands into a single entity where every individual component works in harmony with the others. Practiced under a variety of other names across the galaxy, the discipline relies heavily on physical movement and balance, while paying close attention to one's "inner senses."

Ironically, we must become more conscious of our bodies and glands before we can stop "thinking" with them. We must also forgive ourselves for the times we allowed them to dictate our responses — and we ended up paying for it. Now, at least, we know better.

I will learn a discipline that helps me to unify body, mind and spirit — and I will practice it regularly.

07.21

I've never let my past lives interfere with my job.

— LT. COMMANDER DAX : REJOINED : 49195.5

As a member of the Trill species, Dax might be regarded as a living, breathing example of the ancient concept of reincarnation. In Dax's case, as with reincarnation, there is a more fundamental Self which resides in the body, yet transcends it. The real Dax isn't the beautiful humanoid we see, but the deeper entity that also "incarnates" in many other successive lives – sometimes as a female, sometimes as a male.

But unlike those of us who must be content merely to believe (or not believe) in reincarnation, Trills have first-hand experience. Dax can recall her previous lifetimes in great detail – a fact that can sometimes create serious problems.

Ironically, *non*-Trills face some of the very same problems. Because even if we don't accept the idea that we've lived before, we still, in a sense, have "past lives" to deal with. The people we are now are not the people we were ten years ago. Or even five. We've learned much since then; we've cast off bad habits and limiting beliefs (or we're trying to). And the change in us often feels like a whole new life.

As we continue to grow, the challenge is to remember the difficult lessons of our past lives, while not allowing the person we were to interfere with the better person we've become. Or distract us from creating an even better person – and life – in the future.

My previous life is a priceless repository of first-hand experience. I draw insight and perspective from that life even as I grow well beyond it.

07.22

Sometimes... you just have to bow to the absurd.

— CAPTAIN PICARD : UP THE LONG LADDER : 42823.2

Absurdity, like beauty, is in the eye of the beholder. What seems patently absurd to one person may seem perfectly logical to another. Or at least not that illogical.

Often it takes someone else's explanation or viewpoint to help us make sense of what happens in our lives. That's why our network, our community, is so important. Alone, we may not have the knowledge or experience to integrate new information. Educators have long recognized that optimal learning proceeds in a series of steps that build upon one another. Out of sequence, events and new experiences can seem haphazard, random... absurd.

Unless someone fills in the missing steps for us.

But sometimes even that isn't enough. Either no one can make us understand – that is, we just don't "get it"; or no one else understands to begin with. Which is another way of saying that there are limits to what we know. Or *can* know.

To "bow to the absurd" is not merely to acknowledge those limits, but to respect them. Because what we don't know can hurt us. "Absurd" is therefore not a label for writing something off, but for reminding ourselves to proceed with caution, to find out more if we can, and to learn to live with our own ignorance in the meantime.

Things often don't make sense. But help is always available, both from others and from my Inner Source – if only to support me while I seek answers.

Scientific progress has led many people to stray.

— PRI'NAM D'JAMAT : HATCHERY : CIRCA ECE2153

The same claim has been repeated by various "authorities" on every planet where science and technology have emerged. It summarizes the inevitable conflict between those who seek to control others by enforcing The Truth through revealed tradition, and those who endeavor to discover what's true for themselves through a direct encounter with the natural world.

The Earth's so-called Dark Ages are a case in point, where a religious Inquisition competed with a growing Enlightenment. Lesser competitions and conflicts followed for centuries, including one final outbreak of fanaticism that sought to impose a brutal form of pre-scientific tribalism while, ironically, using modern weaponry and technology to do the job.

Freedom-loving nations were right to combine their resources and fight this testament to human depravity, this destroyer of personhood and the spark of divinity within us all. And that's exactly the point: Science, far from leading people "astray," actually frees them to pursue spiritual truths. It opens us up to the deeper dimensions where nature nurtures the soul, where awe and appreciation for the physical world inspire creative expression and technological innovation.

There is no inherent conflict between science and religion, only between those who follow the truth wherever it leads and those who use science (or religion) to dominate others and remake them into clones of themselves.

Science and religion are tools that can inspire me to create both the reason and the rituals for my Inner Voyage.

07.24

If you lie all the time, no one is going to believe you... even when you're telling the truth.

— DR. BASHIR : IMPROBABLE CAUSE : Stardate Not Given

The Terran fable of the shepherd who cried "Wolf!" is retold in dozens of similar folktales across the galaxy. Like the story of the Klingon sentry who raises so many false alarms that his fellow warriors no longer respond when the real attack comes. Or the account of the Ferengi businessman who forgets to tell just enough of the truth to fool off-worlders into believing his sales pitch.

The fact is, we base our acceptance of what's true on the reliability of the source. We tend to trust our own perceptions first — what we can "see with our own eyes." We rely on other people's testimony only insofar as we respect their track record or proven "authority."

But the real crisis is not about believing what other people say. It's whether we can believe in who we ourselves are. And too often it's our own lies that end up shattering our belief: Our inability to admit when we're wrong; our substitution of a private fantasy world for "real life"; our unwillingness to take an unflinching, objective look at our own flaws and commit ourselves to the hard work of personal growth.

Before we can believe anything, we must reject our own lies. To know the truth, we must first be able to trust what we tell ourselves.

The real challenge is to be true to myself. I will be honest in evaluating my own thoughts and actions.

07.25

I have noted that the healthy release of emotion is frequently very unhealthy for those closest to you.

— SPOCK : PLATO'S STEPCHILDREN : 5784.2

Just as an infant's cries will grow louder until his caregiver responds to his needs, our own emotions often grow "louder" until we pay them the attention they deserve.

Ignoring those messages will result in either of two outcomes: Our emotions finally explode and disrupt our lives so much that we must deal with them. Or, like the infant who finally gives up and learns not to cry – _ever_ – our emotions are driven deep inside us where their energy gets twisted into negative thoughts and physical ailments.

Our health, then, depends on keeping our emotional energy where we can "see" it, where we can interpret and respond to the messages it is sending us. We do this by accepting it and releasing it, thereby letting it speak to us.

But not where others might misunderstand it.

An emotional outburst can mean something entirely different to someone else. Those closest to us, especially, can react to our displays of anger and sorrow and self-reproach as if _they_ must somehow be responsible. What's healthy for us ends up hurting them, and our relationships.

We must consider the message our emotions convey to others as carefully as the message they hold for us.

I respect my own emotions. And I will respect others by releasing my full emotions only in private, or in the company of those who won't misinterpret them.

07.26

The best defense is a strong offense. And I intend to start offending right now!

— CAPTAIN KIRK : THE EMPATH : 5121.5

The Captain isn't implying that we should stop being polite or respectful. Nor is he suggesting we demonstrate how strong we are by going out and picking fights with everyone.

He's talking about our attitude toward life. He's pointing out that many of us have an unfortunate tendency to build protective walls around what we've managed to gain – materially and spiritually; that we often become more concerned about keeping what we have than risking it on new gains; that our lives thereby become more like a defensive position than an expeditionary force.

The problem is, we can never live victoriously while in this "protective" mode. Nor can we rise to our potential if we simply react to whatever life sends our way. Instead, we must go out looking for experience, boldly exploring new territory, taking the risks required for growth.

We must also be willing to raise a few eyebrows in pursuit of our dreams and our life's mission. Perhaps other people will be offended after all. But not because we've run roughshod over them. It's because our courageous attitude forces them to wonder what they're missing.

By living fully, we can show them. Right now.

It's okay for me to be forthright in the pursuit of my spiritual goals. As I live exuberantly, even "offensively," I give others permission to do the same.

07.27

Humor… I love it!

— DATA : GENERATIONS : 48632.4

Most attempts to define humor eventually come down to this: Either you get it… or you don't.

Not everyone is blessed with a sense of humor. Some species, Vulcans included, claim to be utterly unaffected. Which is simply to say that emotions are as essential to humor as intelligence is. And while even Vulcans can "appreciate" irony and satire, most of us also have a visceral response when we "get it." The usual result is that convulsive expulsion of breath known as "laughter."

For emotional beings, how *much* we laugh is a remarkably accurate indicator of our current mental and emotional health. Because the circuits that process our perceptions of reality, that transmit the data required for thought and action, are the same circuits that allow us to feel humor. And if we rarely laugh – or we laugh at everything – chances are there's trouble in the system.

Fortunately, the same method used to diagnose our "system" can also be used to treat it. Laughing has a certifiable cleansing affect, literally relaxing muscle tension, releasing repressed energy, restoring hormonal balance.

So find something to laugh at. Daily. Make it a practice. When you find yourself not only laughing regularly, but at yourself, too, the system is probably working just fine.

I will make my daily dose of humor as important as meditating. I will create opportunities to laugh, even artificial ones, until my joy flows naturally.

07.28

There is something to be learned when you're not in control of every situation.

— COUNSELOR TROI : THE LOSS : 44356.9

Faith is as much about actions as attitude. But attitude is crucial; and one of the most crucial attitudes is trust.

We can think of "trust" as the assurance we feel that someone or something will perform as expected. Trust means "allowing" another person (or object) to carry out his/her (or its) function without our having to be involved. Trust is about letting go, about not being in control.

In a sense, we're not in control whenever we board a shuttlecraft or step into the transporter bay. Our lives are literally at risk, but we've learned to trust the pilot and the technology to take us where we want to go. Giving up control is the price we pay. It's a trade-off, a choice we make.

Unfortunately we can't always choose. Sometimes control is taken away from us, or maybe we never had it in the first place. And our lives may be no less at risk.

We can look at these situations as opportunities for learning: That we (and the world) will still survive, for example. Or that "following" has its own rewards, as does leading. Or that other people have wonderful talents if only we'll step back and give them a chance to prove it.

We may even learn that there is another Pilot in whom we can trust, and a Technology that will take us where we want to go. Giving up control is a small price to pay.

I am in the care of a higher power. I will release my need to control, and trust in The Universe.

07.29

***(The) Federation has taught you that conflict should not exist.
But without struggle, you will never know what you truly are.***

— KRALL : STAR TREK BEYOND : CIRCA 2263.3

As our most beloved stories and sacred texts have always taught us, life's greatest challenges and most frightening adversaries often turn out to be our greatest teachers. The original concept of "Satan" wasn't about devils or demons; the name/title literally meant "Adversary." It referred to the person — or the event — that put one's beliefs and commitments to the test, that forced you to take a stand.

It's no accident that the strongest among us are those who've faced the strongest adversaries. Examples include not only the battle-tested warrior, but ordinary people faced with addictions to drugs or dysfunctional relationships, temptations to do the wrong thing when nobody would ever find out, or to do the *right* thing when it might require great sacrifice.

Later in life, Captain Kirk would talk about this kind of "struggle" as the very purpose of life: To be confronted with one's worst fears; to face one's foes at the risk of death; to have one's skills tested in a setting where the results might change everything… and through that "conflict" find out who one is.

And if the results turn out to be disastrous or disappointing, to remember that no defeat is ever final.

Struggle and conflict are among the best ways to discover Who I Am, and how much more I need to learn on my spiritual journey. I embrace opportunities to test myself.

07.30

Maybe necessity really is the mother of invention. You never look for something until you need it.

— ENGINEER LA FORGE : THE MASTERPIECE SOCIETY : 45470.1

Nowhere is this more true than in spiritual matters. Many of us never go looking for a religious community or spiritual discipline because we prefer to think of ourselves as totally independent, fully self-reliant. Some will hang on to this belief in the face of all evidence to the contrary.

For others, the truth finally breaks through in the form of hard, scientific data about the "soft" boundaries that only seem to separate us — or in the realization that our solitary, one-point-in-space/time perspective on life is so incredibly limiting.

Some form of this realization, whether conscious or subconscious, is said to be why religion was invented. Ironically, because it was "invented" is precisely why many reject it.

But an invention — any invention — works insofar as it takes advantage of laws and realities that are *not* someone's invention. Spiritual disciplines, and the traditions which uphold them, can work for us to the extent that they understand these pre-existing laws and realities correctly, and they provide a mechanism whereby we can use them to live fuller, more satisfying lives.

How many other inventions do that?

More than the right job or mate or possessions, I need the right perspective. Today I will look for new resources to help me reaffirm and re-invent my life.

07.31

The trial never ends.

— **Q** : ALL GOOD THINGS : 47988.1

In some cultures, this is the very definition of "hell": To always be on trial; to continually be in the position of having to prove oneself. Or *im*prove oneself.

Can't we ever take a break from the struggle? Can't we just *be* once in a while, without any expectations?

Yes. And as a matter of fact, *that's part of the trial!*

Because knowing when to stop is just as important as knowing when to keep going. Taking breaks to "process" our learning, to reward ourselves for our efforts, to simply relax, is as crucial as our day-to-day struggles.

Actually, as we go deeper into our Inner Voyage, the greatest temptation is to *not* take these necessary breaks. Ancient religions, which were often closer to the natural cycles of struggle and rest, instituted frequent feasts and celebrations for exactly that reason. One of Betazed's early spiritual disciplines, going well beyond Earth's "sabbath day," insisted its members take four days of rest for every five days of work or study. (Or face four days of confinement!)

The point is, what we are on trial for is our current level of spiritual development. That trial is as continuous and automatic as breathing. But without time to consolidate, to simply enjoy who we are now, we can easily be found guilty of losing what we thought we'd gained.

I will remember to sentence myself to rest and re-creation. My own testimony will help me judge when it's time to continue my spiritual work.

08

August

08.01

I don't pretend to tell you how to find happiness and love when every day is just a struggle to survive. But I do insist that you do survive.

— EDITH KEELER : THE CITY ON THE EDGE OF FOREVER : 3134.0

This is bliss: To understand that human life is a series of starts and stops, gains and losses, painful struggle and sweet grace; and to pronounce all of it "good." *All* of it.

But sometimes in the depths of struggle and loss we can lose our perspective. We forget The Big Picture. We are no longer able to envision the smooth sailing beyond the storm-tossed seas of the present. Life seems hopeless.

Our Inner Voyage is of little value if it cannot help us overcome these inevitable periods of hopelessness. And the Voyage teaches us that, at such times, forgetting The Big Picture is actually the beginning of recovery. Because we are forced to remember that we must still live day by day. To get "from here to there" requires living fully in the present moment, concentrating on the details, taking one step at a time. And rediscovering that the source of genuine fulfillment is not some outward goal but within ourselves.

Inner bliss will come. Whatever our problems, "This too shall pass." What lies beyond is worth living for. Even if, in the meantime, the best we can do is survive.

This is my pledge: I will survive, and I will thrive. The days ahead will make all my struggles worthwhile. I hope, therefore I am.

08.02

If the universe is truly endless, then are we not striving for something forever out of reach?

— CAPTAIN KIRK : STAR TREK BEYOND : CIRCA 2263.3

If every answer only leads to more questions, why ask? If every destination we reach only opens up new and more distant territory that must be explored – usually at great risk or cost – why begin the journey in the first place?

When we compare infinite time and space with our own limited lifespans and capabilities, it's tempting to react by withdrawing into well-defined boundaries, by saying "enough!" We thereby declare that our present body of knowledge is all we really need to know, that one holy book contains all the Truth that matters, and *this* way of life is the only path to happiness or fulfillment or salvation.

But again, life is about the journey, not the destination. If stability is admittedly a primary human need, so is The Quest. We are spiritually deprived when we suspend our searches, stifle our natural curiosity, stop seeking new horizons and new knowledge.

And the fact is, *we can have both*. We can find stability by grounding ourselves in the Reality behind the appearances, even while continuing the endless explorations that may sometimes seem to contradict that Reality, but eventually end up deepening our understanding of it.

I affirm that my pursuit of what may seem forever beyond my reach is exactly what keeps me moving, keeps me alive!

08.03

I've learned that our work, in the end, means very little. Our real legacy is the children.

— DEGRA : STRATAGEM : ECE12.12.2153

Who knows? Maybe each of us will continue to live on in some spiritual afterlife when this physical one is over. Or maybe not. Maybe we'll exit our bodies at the end of our alloted years, then be re-born for yet another lifespan, and the process will go on for untold generations to come. Or not.

What we *do* know is that our actions in this current life can make a lasting difference, perhaps for generations, maybe until "the end of time." And the best place to start, the clearest way to see the difference we can make, is in the lives of our children.

Even if those children don't share our specific DNA, even if they're not biologically "ours," investing in the present generation can pay big dividends for the one that follows… and for the next, and the next, *ad infinitum.* We do this not by giving them work-free lives filled with comfort. We do it by providing them with a good education, by motivating them to begin their own searches for meaning and mission, by demonstrating that our voyages into our selves can make our communal journeys richer and more harmonious; and by striving to become the best we can be, that they may be inspired to become the best *they* can be.

And in the process, hopefully, we inspire them to do the same for *their* children. Whether or not they share DNA. Whether on this Earth, or on worlds yet to come. *Ad infinitum.*

I am living my life not only for myself, but for those who follow. What I endeavor to leave them are not accomplishments, but an example.

08.04

Whatever my personal feelings, I simply cannot interfere.

— CAPTAIN PICARD : HALF A LIFE : 44805.3

We are all connected at the deepest levels, consciously and subconsciously; that much is now certain. So it's no wonder we find it difficult not to become involved in other people's lives. We are *already* involved. But it's especially tempting to intervene when our experience allows us to see an approaching danger others don't see coming. How can we just stand by and watch?

The Prime Directive – this mandate of non-interference – is nothing if not gut-wrenching. It is often far more painful to allow another person to suffer than to undergo the suffering ourselves. But the fact is, there are well-defined stages of growth in the evolution of sentient life. Some of these stages are chaotic, painful and risky. These are potential "breakthrough stages" when a whole people stand at the threshold of self-discovery and redemption.

There is no substitute for living through such experiences, even if painful. Outside interference can set a species back generations. Individuals can lose years of growth.

And sometimes the individual is *us.* We can ask for help, yes. We can expect guidance. But if we are to have our own breakthroughs, we must earn them. We must *learn* them. And we must give others the same chance.

I will gladly help when asked. But I must not do for others what they must do for themselves. And I pray for the wisdom to know the difference.

08.05

Look at us! We're each fighting with ourselves!

— LIEUTENANT TORRES : FACES : 48784.2

Most of us never get the chance to witness, much less experience, what B'Elanna Torres learned when her core personality was ripped into its two competing components. In her case, the two halves were Klingon and Human. But they could just as easily have been male and female, or animal self and spiritual self. The lessons are the same.

And the key words are, "Look at us!"

Because when our primary personality components fall out of harmony with one another, when they *dis*-integrate, they are not so much attempting to destroy each other as trying desperately to call attention to themselves.

The first thing we must do, therefore, is stand back and look. Not join the conflict, but seek perspective. The mode of communication may be primitive, yes; but what is all that fighting trying to tell us? What primal needs are going unmet in our "Klingon side"? In our human half?

The fact is, conflicts within us are appeals to remember and honor the positive qualities that each of our personality components brings to the larger unity of our Self. They are calls to restore balance, not to "take sides."

And as it is with us personally, so it is with our communities. So it is with our world.

My conflicts – external and internal – are signs that I need to work on myself. I accept the challenge.

08.06

I don't believe in no-win scenarios.

— ENSIGN KIRK : STAR TREK / PREQUEL : CIRCA 2258

One of life's saving graces is that we sometimes learn more from our failures and defeats than our successes and victories. Pain and loss are simply the price we all pay for some of life's most important lessons.

What hurts even more than losing – because there seems to be no lesson to draw from it – is the situation in which *no*body wins. And it's amazing how often things turn out this way! Unresolved. Unfinished. Check, but no checkmate.

But maybe there's a lesson even in these frequent "stalemates." Maybe some struggles aren't about winning, but *enduring* – despite no permanent victory. After all, we can't give in to selfishness and greed just because the temptations never stop coming.

Or perhaps the lesson is that our idea of struggle is mistaken to begin with. Perhaps what we see as "conflict" is really no conflict at all. Because more often than not, the people we think we're competing against are those with whom we most need to join forces in a common quest.

No-win situations call us to transcend the apparent conflict to the point where we redefine what we're really fighting against, where "winning" is no longer the goal. And that's the point, paradoxically, where everyone wins.

The stalemates in my life tell me that I have not yet learned something vital to my growth. I will open myself to the messages they contain.

08.07

Take good care. But more importantly, take good care of those in your care.

— CAPTAIN GEORGIOU : THE BUTCHER'S KNIFE CARES NOT FOR THE LAMB'S CRY : Stardate 1403.4

With these concluding, pre-recorded, post-mortem words to Michael Burnham, Captain Georgiou is reminding each of us to keep our priorities straight.

We all have an inherent right to take care of ourselves, to ensure our own material and spiritual well-being, to pursue our own creative dreams and professional goals. But in doing so, we must never lose sight of *why*. Because, in the end, we are individuals *in community*. Our greatest psychic rewards, our most enduring achievements, come from service to others.

And not just because others may rely on us. True, some of us have children who can't yet provide for themselves, or elderly or disabled dependents who require our assistance. We may be business leaders or crew chiefs without whom our organizations could not function.

But even children and other assorted subordinates (i.e. most of us!) can be said to have people "in their care," often including those who exercise authority over them. The care we take in our jobs, however lowly, can make a crucial difference in our company's bottom line. How we care for those with whom we come in contact, from family and friends to total strangers, contributes to our society's overall health. In fact, the number of those in our care is limited only by the responsibility we accept for improving others' lives… in our neighborhoods, in our universe.

I take good care of myself, so that I am better equipped to care for others.

08.08

There comes a time in every man's life when he must stop thinking and start doing.

— CAPTAIN SISKO : PARADISE LOST : Stardate Not Given

Elsewhere in the record, Sisko points out the benefits of having a plan, a "blueprint," for our activities. Whether for a single project or our whole trek through life, a plan provides inspiration and guidance. It helps bring us back to our original vision whenever we get off track.

But some of us *over*-plan things. We try to anticipate everything. We leave no room for mid-course corrections, or for taking advantage of unexpected opportunities. Worse, some of us have a tendency to keep planning as a way to put off doing. Which is not unlike the student who continues his "higher education" year after year in order to avoid actually getting a job.

And yet, once the basics are learned, getting a job is the best form of higher education. Likewise, once our plans are roughly outlined, actually carrying them out is the best way to refine and perfect them.

In reality, "doing" is simply an extension of "thinking." Planning is the intellectual part. Applying that plan adds the physical dimension. Both have their own inherent logic. Each is incomplete without the other.

As the saying goes, we change our lives by changing our thinking. But only when thought becomes deed.

My plans are imperfect. My information is incomplete. But I have faith that The Universe will guide me and supply what I lack – if I start now.

08.09

If an event were important enough to be recovered, why would it be forgotten?

— DATA : VIOLATIONS : 45429.3

Like many quirks of being human – or at least being sentient – our tendency to forget events in the past (before we recover/remember them) is difficult to understand. Why do we forget things that may be critical to our mental health or personal growth? Why must we forget at all?

Actually, unless there are organic factors like brain damage, memories of past events are never forgotten completely. Our minds simply place certain memories beyond the reach of our consciousness. Recovery is temporarily "disabled."

Not that those memories don't continue to affect us. Our subconscious often draws on suppressed memories to make its decisions – or give us hunches. Our attitudes toward other people and toward the world may be influenced by such memories as well. Often profoundly.

Whatever the case, we can trust that something purposeful is going on. Some memories, for example, may elude us until we're better equipped to deal with them emotionally. Or until we have more information, or more experience, or more patience. Sometimes not remembering is meant to trigger the very question Data asks.

And in searching for the answer, we may learn something about ourselves we would never have known otherwise.

My forgetting is as purposeful as my remembering. If a memory is blocked, I will ask "why," and open myself to what The Universe wants to teach me.

08.10

We can use all the friends we can get.

— CAPTAIN JANEWAY : STATE OF FLUX : 48658.2

The fact that Captain Janeway was only repeating an old cliché makes the message no less true.

But what *does* diminish the message is the selfish twist we sometimes give it, as if the only thing friends are good for is our "using" them – usually to help us get out of the sticky situations we've gotten ourselves into.

Friends are good for that, too, no doubt. But friendship is a two-way street. It's as important for us to help our friends get out of *their* sticky situations as it is for them to help us. That's because our wholeness and happiness depend as much on serving others as being served.

More important, as we grow spiritually, we recognize the need to expand our horizons, to transcend our self-centered interpretation of events, to see our own lives in relationship to the larger Web of Life. Friends – fellow voyagers – provide that wider perspective. They enlarge our experience as we help enlarge theirs. They affirm our inherent wisdom, as we do theirs. They provide encouragement, show us alternatives we might otherwise miss, and sometimes give us holy hell when we need it.

The wider our network of friends, the more "useful" we become to The Universe for carrying out its goals. And therein lies the ultimate Friendship.

Today I will seek not so much to "get" a new friend as to be one. I will help others along their journeys, and perhaps they will accompany me in mine.

08.11

I sometimes ask those kind of questions… Who am I? What am I doing here? What's my purpose in life? …Doesn't everybody?

— KES : PROJECTIONS : 48892.1

The surprising answer for many of us is, well… *No.*

Either the thought simply hasn't crossed our minds to question the meaning of life – which, admittedly, is rare. Or we've asked those deeper questions, found them too unsettling (or flatly unanswerable); and we've made the conscious decision not to ask them anymore. End of story.

There's something to be said for the latter view. Why bother delving into such questions if no final answer is forthcoming? Or if it only makes us more cranky and confused? Or worse, what if we end up deciding that life is meaningless after all? Better to take things as they come, embracing both the joys and sorrows, living fully in the moment.

In fact, even for those who find a reflective approach more fulfilling, *not* asking the deeper questions can be a good thing. Because we find our answers to Who We Are only by actively *being* Who We Are. We decide what we're doing here by first doing *some*thing. We discover our purpose by feeling that something we've done has meaning.

In other words, if we would spend our time being, doing and feeling instead of asking, the answers would take care of themselves soon enough.

It is good to ask, but better to be. Before I can reflect on my life, I must give myself experiences to reflect on. Today I will stop talking and start doing.

08.12

What you were, and what you are to become, will always be with you.

— Q : ALL GOOD THINGS : 47988

It's easy enough to accept that *what we were* remains a part of us, if only in our memories. What's harder to swallow is that *what we are to become* is also within us.

Try looking at it this way: Beyond the present, in the "no time" of eternity, our core identities (sometimes called "souls") are already everything they were capable of becoming. Like an old-fashioned laserdisc that contains an entire audio/visual story etched into its surface – or in this case an infinite number of possible stories – our souls are inscribed with all the life journeys we will ever take.

Back in the "now," the laserlight of time is pinpointing only a specific instant in the course of one of those journeys. If we could somehow get outside of time, however, we could see the culmination of all our journeys, as well as the evolved Self we will have become by then.

As it turns out, we *can* get outside of time – in our daily meditations. This is where we meet our Higher Self, the self who has already made the journey, who already knows what we were, are, and will be.

By drawing on that future perspective, we can help ourselves in the present. Doing this is not cheating. It's a matter of choosing one of the better stories on our laserdisc.

"My highest potential is already present within me." As I concentrate on this thought, affirm it and release it, I turn potentiality into reality.

08.13

You might as well sit back and enjoy the ride.

— CAPTAIN KIRK : METAMORPHOSIS : 3219.4

We are strengthened by struggle. We grow through facing life's challenges, hooking up with new resources, and working to change our conditions for the better.

But some conditions *can't* be changed. Some things that happen simply can't be controlled. The only thing we can change in these cases is our attitude about them. The only thing we can control is how we react.

An Arabian parable is told about a farmer who can't seem to rid his garden of weeds. Finally he travels to the Caliph's palace – several days away by camel – to seek the learned advice of the royal gardener. The wizened old man listens, then offers several suggestions. The farmer thanks him, goes home and tries each suggestion… without success. He thereupon travels back to the palace to complain that he has tried everything, and still he has weeds.

The royal gardener scowls, thinks for some minutes more. "There is one last thing you can try on your weeds," he says at last. "You can learn to love them."

When we can't rid our gardens of the weeds, when the voyage is underway and there's no stopping now, we can still make a choice. We can decide to accept the circumstances or the experience, and then extract whatever goodness and growth The Universe has prepared for us.

I will seek to change what I am able, find goodness in the rest, and trust The Universe to care for me no matter how bumpy the ride.

08.14

There are times when men of good conscience cannot blindly follow orders.

— CAPTAIN PICARD : THE OFFSPRING : 43657.0

We can read Picard's words as a statement with mainly political or military significance – the kind of guiding Principle that might have come out of Earth's well-known Nuremburg War Trials, perhaps, or Bajor's Lasting Peace Convention. But even for politicians and soldiers, what it comes down to is the primacy of following one's own sense of Right.

Because the bottom line is, we never lose responsibility for our actions. Being under orders, or "under the influence" – or under some other kind of compulsion – does not free us from the fact that we still have a choice. This is not merely some judicial edict so that people can be held "legally accountable." It's a spiritual necessity. Deciding the kinds of actions we will and will *not* perform is precisely how we create Who We Are.

Which doesn't mean we should never follow orders. We have jobs. We make commitments to perform certain functions in return for certain benefits. We may not enjoy everything we're asked to do. But enjoyment isn't the criterion. Measuring our orders against a Higher Order *is*.

If we find ourselves questioning every order given to us, we probably can't see that Order clearly. If we find ourselves questioning *nothing,* chances are we're blind.

The "orders" I am given are valuable opportunities to analyze and fine-tune what I believe in. I will trust my own sense of right to guide my response.

   BOLDLY GOING ON YOUR INNER VOYAGE

08.15

There's nothing wrong with a healthy fantasy life. As long as you don't let it take over.

— COUNSELOR TROI : HOLLOW PURSUITS : 43807.4

Soon after its entry into the Third Millennium, Earth suffered through what later became known as The Lost Decades of Virtual Reality. Following dozens of advanced civilizations before them, humans became technologically adept at simulating real-life experiences.

People could "travel" to exotic places without leaving home. They could refine their mental skills and physical abilities against computer-programmed competitors. They could also experience endless pleasure with sexual playmates whose only purpose was their satisfaction. Or they could feel the darker thrills of slicing imaginary enemies in half – or even killing "virtual copies" of real people.

The social effects of this technology took little time to surface. The problem wasn't just that virtual reality could never quite capture the realities of genuine social interaction. (If it even tried.) It was that virtual reality became a very efficient training ground for anti-social behavior.

The lure of our fantasy lives has always been strong. Which is a good thing, since fantasy is one of the most powerful mental tools for redesigning our own futures. We just need to remember that, with every fantasy we indulge in, *that's* what we're doing.

I will use my fantasy life to lay the groundwork for the future I intend to create.

08.16

We can hardly hate what we once were.

— COMMANDER RIKER : THE LAST OUTPOST : 41386.4

We do not overcome our problems by hating them. We can't forgive ourselves and move on to the next phase of our lives if we continue to despise the person we were – even if we recognize the evil and the outright lies in our past.

For one thing, we have a right to despise the behavior, but never the person. For another, the basis for forgiving and forgetting is love, not hate. To love the person we once were, in spite of the weaknesses and "sins" attached to that person, is the most powerful prerequisite for loving ourselves now. Our current state, after all, may seem as imperfect and corrupt to the person we will become, as our past state of corruption appears to the person we are at present.

Besides which, that "past self" was our bridge – our only bridge – to the wiser, stronger, more experienced person we've become. If anything, we should be grateful, not hateful. If that person didn't have the roots of goodness in him back then, beneath all those flaws and imperfections, we couldn't have come as far as we have.

To love ourselves – past, present, and future – is to realize and accept what The Universe is doing to us.

To love others, is to *mirror* what The Universe is doing to us.

I celebrate the divine re-creation of my Self. I lovingly embrace the person who brought me to this point, and turn to meet the person I will become.

08.17

I'm a doctor, not a decorator!

— THE DOCTOR : PHAGE : 48532.4

The Voyager's dour-faced doctor must've had a dozen cranky rejoinders similar to this one. Elsewhere in the record we hear him insisting that he's "not a doorstop," nor "a counter-insurgent," nor "a sex surrogate."

And we can sympathize with his obvious impatience as he fires off these retorts. Because, like The Doctor, we too have been asked to do things we consider "beneath us." We too have been treated by someone as if we were cheap labor for any service they might suddenly require.

No wonder we take offense. After all, we know what we're good at — and what we're *not* good at. It's only natural to get a little annoyed when we are assigned to projects that don't make the best use of our time and talent.

In response we might consider setting our fellow crewmembers straight. Maybe they just don't know what our true talents are. Or perhaps they're misusing their authority over us.

But we should also consider the possibility that these people are guiding us toward new and useful experiences that will increase our versatility. And our self-confidence.

It's often no mere "coincidence" that a certain job will be assigned to us that seems utterly unrelated to our personal or spiritual growth. And only later do we realize it was precisely what we needed, at just the right time.

I am a novice, not an expert! – at least in most subjects. I know The Universe is providing valuable lessons for me, even if I can't yet see the connection.

08.18

There will be time to grieve. This is not that time.

— CAPTAIN LORCA : SI VIS PACEM, PARA BELLUM : Circa 1306.7

The events in our lives often seem to assault us at warp speed, from multiple sides, and with hardly a moment's respite. No wonder our thoughts can "get jumbled," as Engineer Stamets described it.

All the more so when we witness bad things happening to good people... or sometimes to *us*. And even though we'd like to stop and rage about how unfair life can be, to grieve for our losses, ongoing events often leave no time for expressing our feelings. During such sustained assaults, we have little choice but to focus on our assigned duties, to remember that others are depending on us to respond to what's happening in the moment with all the experience and skill we can muster.

It is enough to know that we *will* have the opportunity to process our suppressed feelings at some point in the future. In fact, that process has already begun on a subconscious level, even while the crisis continues. The Universe has not left us without resources for surviving these challenges, sometimes rewarding us with new insights and strengths we might never learn otherwise.

Grieving is one of the ways we begin to recover and integrate those lessons and insights from our deeper levels. The process may be noisy at first, exploding with all the fury and emotion that are natural to our bodies' healthy functioning. But "getting it out" only peels off the top layer. Below that lies not only our consolation, but our Higher Self and the clues to our moving forward.

I have faith that, on the far side of every crisis, my spiritual wounds will be healed, through sharing my feelings with others, and by opening myself to a caring Universe.

08.19

Running may help for a little while, but sooner or later the pain catches up with you. And the only way to get rid of it is to stand your ground and face it.

— CAPTAIN SISKO : THE WAY OF THE WARRIOR, PART II : 49011.4

The wisdom of Sisko's statement seems compelling enough. More so because he himself *lived* it.

And perhaps now is the time to point out that all the sayings and comments which inspire these reflections have the ring of truth for the same reason. They aren't merely theories, or some office-bound counselor's idea of how things ought to be. Nor are they "revelations" from some ancient text. They are the fruits of experience. They have been lived.

Which is how Benjamin Sisko learned this lesson. He discovered first-hand that we can no more run away from the events that hurt us than a criminal can "run from the scene of the crime." Because the scene that matters most is the one within us. Everything we do is recorded in our minds and in our hearts. Everything in our past remains present – as emotions and attitudes… as Who We Are.

Fortunately, when we *stop* running, that too is recorded. Taking a stand, facing the pain, finally dealing with the negativity in our lives also becomes Who We Are.

And we are stronger for it. Not in theory. Not because that's how it ought to be. But because we lived it.

No matter how painful the events in my life, I can live through them. The person I will become once I've faced my past is worth my present struggle.

08.20

Worlds may change, galaxies disintegrate; but a woman always remains a woman.

— CAPTAIN KIRK : THE CONSCIENCE OF THE KING : 2817.6

It's reassuring to know that some things don't change. The speed of light in a vacuum. Acceleration of mass due to gravity. The Trans-Warp Constant.

And our own personal constants. Like the soothing effect of a mountain stream. Or the simple delight in the laughter of children at play. Or the fascination of soft backlight on a woman's hair.

Whether these are scientific "laws" or genetically-programmed response mechanisms isn't what matters. Like Captain Kirk's unflagging appreciation for the opposite sex, they are simply the things we can count on no matter what else might change.

We need a core of such "constants" to keep us grounded. Part of the strategy for transforming our lives, in fact, is to claim the territory we've come to know – what works for us, what doesn't; what generates certain feelings, and what doesn't – and then to venture out from these "strongholds," adding *new* constants, continually claiming new and higher ground, defining the things we can count on no matter what.

And if the galaxies around us start to disintegrate, we can always find refuge there. At least until the dust settles and we boldly go out again.

Over the next week, I will make a list of all the things I know well enough to call my "constants." Each month I will review my list, and add to it.

08.21

It will be my job to anticipate your needs before you know you have them.

— NEELIX : CARETAKER : 48315.6

In cultures across the Quadrant, a statement similar to this one is spoken — and understood — not in any literal sense, but merely as a way of emphasizing one's commitment to "be of service." Most of us, after all, sincerely want to help others. But we need to go beyond words.

Try this exercise on a friend or loved one, or even a fellow crewmember: Spend a day — the *full* day — making that person the focus of your attention. Wait on them. Spoil them. Put yourself in their place and imagine what they might want you to do — not what *you'd* like to do, but what they would like if only they weren't afraid to ask. And then do it. Expect nothing in return. At the end of the day tell them you'd gladly do it all over again.

The point is, we need to *practice* serving others. In our spiritual transitions from ego-centered selfishness to a broader, "inter-connected self," the hard work of service can sometimes feel un-natural and even unfulfilling. The ego will whisper "Hey, why knock yourself out?" and "They don't really appreciate it anyway." And the clincher: "What about your *own* needs? Don't you deserve a little attention, too?"

You do. And it will come eventually, inevitably. That's how the universe works. The fact that you'll no longer require it by then is, as Neelix might've put it, "frosting on the cake."

I will do something wonderful for someone today — joyfully, without being asked, without expectations.

08.22

The true test of a warrior is not without. It is within.

— LIEUTENANT WORF : HEART OF GLORY : 41503.7

A "fighter" is an individual who fights battles. A "warrior" is one who knows that battles are merely tactical encounters in a much wider conflict.

The warrior also knows that the real conflict isn't over possessions or planetary dominance. It's the struggle to overcome one's inner demons. It's about discovering that the physical conditions of one's life — what's "without" — are only mirrors to show us what's "within."

There are several important corollaries, the first of which concerns commitment. Because we must commit ourselves to the long-term. The struggle goes on for a lifetime.

That's why, secondly, we must be willing to lose a battle now and then if it preserves us to fight a more important battle later. Or if the real lesson is about losing. Or letting someone else win if it serves a higher purpose.

Tactical choices like these shape the people we become. They teach us the value of sacrificing short-term gain for higher goals. They are tests of our discipline, our connection to others, our connection to the deeper reservoirs of grace, of genuine peace.

That is why we go to "war" in the first place. And why the supreme victory is over our own minds and hearts.

I am committed to the life-long effort to become my Self. My greatest ally is The Universe.

08.23

Live now! Make now the most precious time!

— CAPTAIN PICARD (as "Kamin") : THE INNER LIGHT : 45944.1

One way to determine if our lives are in proper balance is to look at the emotional weight we give to the past, present, and future.

We often hear about those who "live in the past." We know how seductive it is to reflect on years gone by as if they were some kind of Golden Age. To be fair, "selective memory" can be a way to acknowledge all the good we've gained from past experience. But it can also be a sign that we've become less optimistic about our future.

On the other hand, being *too* future-oriented is just as unhealthy. In always looking toward the horizon, we can easily miss the present passing beneath our feet. And the irony is, in planning for this glorious future of ours, we'll imagine ourselves living in that "present" to the fullest; but by the time we get there we won't know how. Because we won't have had any practice doing it!

If only as "practice," then, we need to concentrate on the "now." We need to look beneath our feet *now*, consider how blessed we are *now*, feel the warmth of the relationships and the love that surrounds us… *now*.

The past no doubt had its golden moments. The future may be even more glorious. But the present is the only time we'll ever really have.

Today – all day – I will be present to the present.

08.24

The problem is not in the stars, but in ourselves.

— GARAK : THE DIE IS CAST : Stardate Not Given

Earth's most famous playwright, Shakespeare, was among the first to put it in the poetic terms Garak quotes here. And it's true: When things go wrong, when we're not happy with our lives, we tend to look outside of ourselves for someone – or some*thing* – to blame. Other people are usually at the top of the list. But once we realize that others are really no more in control than we are, most of us end up shaking our proverbial fists at The Universe. Or at least at "the stars."

It's understandable why we do. The stars are a potent symbol for "the way the universe operates." After all, powerful forces are obviously at work, distant forces that were here long before we dropped in, and they seem to shine on our lives in ways we may never fully comprehend. The best we can do is try to "align" ourselves with them, to figure out their signs and cycles and conjunctions. But the bottom line is, *they're* in charge, not us.

Which – again, symbolically – is true. It's also why the primitive craft of astrology still has its fascinations. But even astrology places final responsibility for our lives on us. Because it's still *our* job to learn the rules. And we can act in harmony with those rules, to find the hidden opportunities in them. Or we can pretend they don't exist.

In which case we have no one to blame but ourselves.

"The stars" represent What Is. My "problem" is to accept What Is, and organize my life accordingly.

08.25

I have no idea what I'm supposed to do! I only know what I can do!

— CAPTAIN KIRK : STAR TREK / INTO DARKNESS : CIRCA 2259

Sometimes what's right – what we're "supposed to do" in keeping with custom or convention or sacred tradition – simply isn't clear. All we see ahead are the available options, the things we *can* do. Some might turn out well, many are destined to fail, and we have no idea which is which.

Kirk's frustration at having to make a decision in this sorry situation tells us two things. For one, considering what you *can* do is usually a good place to start. After all, it makes little sense to dwell on what can't be done. Once you've determined a course of action is impossible, there's no use wasting precious time wishing things were otherwise, or fantasizing about what can never happen.

Secondly, Kirk's statement is testimony that we need to spend more time learning what our traditions have taught us, why custom and convention call us to act in certain ways under certain conditions – *before* those conditions arise. Not because these traditions are always "right," but because they've been right more often than not over decades and centuries of practice. They're a useful fall-back position, especially when there's no time to weigh options.

But know this: Our actions not only reflect tradition, they continually *refine* our traditions and customs. What we do will either prove the rule, or carve out a new exception, a "subset" of the rule.

We mustn't be afraid of going against what we're "supposed to do" if we've had time to consider other options, if we believe another course is better. And if we're willing to accept the consequences.

My spiritual mission is not simply to follow the time-honored trail, but to risk blazing new ones... not only for my sake, but for others'.

08.26

Bickering is pointless.

— SPOCK : MIRI : 2713.5

Fault-finding, negative criticism, verbal sparring – all these forms of petty argument get us nowhere. Worse, they prevent us from getting *some*where: From moving beyond our frustration with the problem to the search for an acceptable solution; from getting past our state of conflict to the process of reaching compromise.

As long as we let bickering hold us back in this way, it *is* pointless. But our irrational arguing also has a positive aspect – one that Vulcan logic can all-too-easily miss: Our bickering keeps us talking to one another. Because what's even worse than bickering is to stop talking for good. We can never end our conflict and find a solution unless we remain in communication.

And the fascinating thing is, people who are bickering with each other usually understand this, even if subconsciously. We know it's in our best interest to avoid breaking off relations and thereby give our darker sides an excuse to demonize the other person. Illogical as it may seem, bickering can keep us in contact until we finally realize what we *should* be talking about: How to begin working together on the problems facing us.

Bickering is a kind of raw energy – pointless energy. That is, until we seize the opportunity to transform it.

The moment I catch myself bickering with someone, I will remember the message my subconscious is sending me: We need each other to find a solution.

08.27

The lasting peace begins here.

— GUL MACET : THE WOUNDED : 44429.6

Centuries ago, there was a ballad with the refrain, "Let there be peace on Earth, and let it begin with me." Bajor's last Cardassian governor echoes this sentiment, not in the sense of expressing hope for one particular planet, but in the simple recognition that, for peace to be achieved anywhere, it must start *some*where.

And there is no better place to start than in our own hearts and minds. Right here. Right *now*.

There are risks, of course. To lay down all our weapons – whether physical, verbal or emotional – leaves us vulnerable and defenseless. On the other hand, peace will never come unless someone breaks into the cycle of violence and counter-violence. Often, the riskier that break, or the more unexpected and shocking and even "unwise" it may seem, the better the chances that peace will catch on.

Unfortunately, peace will never fully "catch on" until a transformation occurs that makes violence and vengeance unthinkable to begin with. And "here" – in our hearts and minds – is where that transformation must take root. Because no matter what shape our world is in, despite the groups and governments and galaxies still waging war, we can at least achieve *inner* peace.

And then the world – inevitably – will follow.

I refuse to let the world's strife derail my efforts to change myself. I will seek peace in my own life and relationships, and let my example inspire others.

08.28

How do we know about any of us?

— DR. McCOY : STAR TREK/TMP : 7412.6

The short answer to the good doctor's question is: We *don't*. If only because we rarely allow it.

We routinely keep secrets from one another, perhaps hoping to use what we know for our own private gain. We hide behind our own personal cloaking devices, thinking that if others saw us as we really are, they could never love us. Deception is the name of the game.

We even manage to deceive our*selves*: Pretending we're in control when we're not; learning to suppress our emotions until we no longer recognize them; assuming we've conquered certain passions or overcome temptation when we simply haven't been tested yet. It's no wonder our own behavior sometimes comes as a shock. We hardly know who *we* are, much less others.

Not that we *can't* know. Ideally, in an atmosphere of openness and acceptance, we could all present an accurate self-portrait of ourselves to the world – both our flaws and our strengths – knowing that no one is perfect. Just because most people won't do that is no excuse for *us* not to. In fact, our own fearless self-revelation can be a catalyst for communal change, the example that gives others permission to be themselves, too.

Try setting the trend. And let go of the results.

I must know myself before I can begin to know others. I will openly display who I am, thereby encouraging others to do the same.

08.29

It is often helpful to find elements of commonality.

— DATA : LIAISONS : Stardate Not Given

Socialization is only part of it. We are programmed by eons of evolution to notice differences. That's how we instantly recognize people, how we identify objects, how we separate what's important to our survival from what's not.

But this handy survival skill can also raise barriers. Because when it comes to people, differences often take on special meaning. Skin color, facial features, distinctive clothing or customs — all these warn us that we're in unfamiliar territory. We don't know what to expect. Yellow alert; be ready to raise shields!

What we're encountering here isn't our prejudice but our ignorance. Biology has hard-wired us to feel a "discomfort" in such situations that's meant not to drive us apart but to make us want to learn more about each other.

Master of protocol that he is, Data points to the proper procedure. The most productive relationships begin by naming the things we share. What common interests and goals might outweigh our differences? How can we see ourselves as fellow voyagers, not as competitors?

Biology never has the final word. Our intelligence is designed to complement and refine what our bodies tell us. In the end, that's what makes the real "difference."

Each time I meet someone new today, I will search for – and name – three things we have in common. I will relate to him or her on that basis.

08.30

If we're going to be damned, let's be damned for what we really are.

— CAPTAIN PICARD : ENCOUNTER AT FARPOINT, PART I : 41153.7

Let's get one thing straight: The Universe does not damn us. The Universe does not seek to condemn us or destroy us, or threaten us with eternal punishment.

It may negatively reinforce certain actions, yes. But karma is designed to refine and improve us, not punish. Karma is a manifestation of Grace.

Damnation, on the other hand, is a concept invented by people. It reflects an inability – or refusal – to recognize the divinity within others because of certain "unacceptable" actions or beliefs. Or because of some superficial reading of who they are.

It's almost certain that we will be "damned" by someone at some time. After all, we can't do what we need to do and end up pleasing everyone. Nor should we try. To continually compromise our beliefs and behavior in an effort to make ourselves more "acceptable" to others is not only an act of self-repudiation, it is not possible to begin with.

Picard offers a better approach. Since someone is going to damn us no matter what we do, why not earn that damnation in the course of doing what we think is right? At least we'll maintain our own self-respect.

And if we listen carefully, all that "damning" starts to sound more and more like… applause.

I can't please everyone, but I can please myself. If I am doing what I believe in, the condemnation of others cannot touch me.

08.31

The real world doesn't always adhere to logic. Sometimes down is up. Sometimes up is down. Sometimes when you're lost, you're found.

When Burnham spoke these lines (as a convicted mutineer), what she no doubt meant was that the laws of an infinite cosmos don't always conform to what we finite beings consider "logical" or "expected." Members of some spiritual traditions might've made the same point by citing a cherished passage from one of their sacred texts: "The Lord works in mysterious ways."

And it's true. How The Universe performs what we often call "miracles" – turning defeat into victory, for example, or healing our spiritual wounds, or saving our sorry souls – sometimes surpasses all human understanding. That's because we can't imagine how fiercely a seemingly impersonal universe endeavors to insure our continuing growth, how much it "hates waste," as Captain Lorca put it; how it will take whatever little good it can find in us and use that as a foundation for turning our lives around.

When circumstances seem most chaotic, when our world has been flipped on its head, when our previous experience tells us all is lost… sometimes that's the very turning point The Universe has been preparing for us all along. It's the spiritual breakthrough all the seemingly random events in our lives have been leading up to without our realizing it, the transformative moment we finally discover our true purpose, our life's mission, our *selves*.

And by admitting that possibility up front, by keeping that expectant faith, we help make it so.

I admit that my view is limited. But I have faith that The Universe can make me whole… even if I don't know how, even if I'm not sure when.

09

September

09.01

In this galaxy alone there's a mathematical probability of three million Earth-type planets. And in all the universe three million million galaxies like this one. And in all that... only one of each of us.

— DR. McCOY : BALANCE OF TERROR : 1709.1

We are defined not by our specific location in space and time, not merely by the fact that our consciousness is localized here and not somewhere else. We are defined by what we've learned, by what talents we have, by the opportunities only our lives can provide.

Even the rare "duplicate selves" some voyagers have encountered elsewhere in the universe are not really duplicates. Rather, they are chances to further define our true selves, to discover the unique, core identity which makes us *us* – despite all outward appearances.

It is as if The Universe is calling each of us to reaffirm our own uniqueness, to identify and reclaim Who We Are… and then to be that person no one else can be.

A story told by one of Earth's "Pious Ones" recalls a teacher named Zusya. His students asked him why he couldn't be more like their role model and prophet, Moses. "When I arrive at heaven's gates," Zusya replied, "the Holy One will not ask me why I was not more like Moses. He will ask, Why was I not more like *Zusya?*"

I will treasure the lessons uniquely given for me to learn. I affirm and celebrate the person whom The Universe is calling me – and me alone – to become.

09.02

There's no harm in keeping both eyes open.

— DR. BASHIR : DISTANT VOICES : Stardate Not Given

As DS9's doctor suggests here, sometimes our own anatomy provides the most valuable clues about Life.

And not just Human or Vulcan or Klingon anatomy. All across the universe, from simple organisms to complex, species with only a single eye are virtually non-existent. The vast majority have exactly two eyes. Why is this?

In a few cases, it's because two eyes provide two entirely different points of view. Some creatures can see not only what's ahead, but what's behind; not only what's on this side, but that. In most species, however, each eye has roughly the same field of vision, but the "offset" between them is just enough to provide a sense of perspective, to recreate in our minds the dimensionality that exists in the world.

Caught on yet? The lesson is that a single "viewpoint" isn't enough. Looking at things from at least two perspectives increases our ability to survive, if not thrive. It's not just that we see more of the world around us. The world becomes a qualitatively different place. We don't just see "things," we experience the space *between* things. We experience relationships, visualize new possibilities.

Bashir was understating the case. Keeping both eyes open is not merely harmless. Without that kind of vision, one of Earth's holy books warns, "the people perish."

I see only as I open my eyes to different perspectives. I know only as I test my ideas against others. I grow only as I seek options, and make choices.

No choice. You say that frequently. Does that... comfort you?

— SEVEN OF NINE : EQUINOX, PART II : Stardate Not Given

Such an easy excuse: "But I had no choice!"

Yet almost without exception, whenever we make this claim, what we're really saying is that we preferred another alternative. Or that others in our position would've done the same thing. Or that our decision was dictated by habit or culture, or "nature." It was... *automatic.*

The Inner Voyage, however, is designed to make us conscious of what was once "automatic." After all, we can't take control of what we do thoughtlessly, without even being aware of the process. First comes awareness, then control.

Not that we always *should* take control. If we had to think about taking every breath, if we had to consciously tell our hearts to beat, most of us would be fertilizer by now. Some things are better done *for* us than *by* us.

But making the choices that affect our lives, that help define the kind of people we are, are not among those things. In fact the really tough choices – the ones we too often hand over to someone else – are the very opportunities The Universe gives us to take responsibility, to transform Who We Are. The moments we think we have no choice are exactly the moments when our power to choose can blossom.

Find a time and space to be still. Be open to The Infinite. You may lose count of the options!

As I connect with my Source, I open myself to new alternatives, new choices, and a new, truer Self.

When has justice ever been as simple as a rule book?

— COMMANDER RIKER : JUSTICE : 41255.6

An ancient holy book put it this way: "Justice, *justice,* shall you pursue." Not "happiness," as a more recent political document would suggest, but justice.

In other words, do what's right, do what's best for all concerned, and happiness will naturally follow. Put happiness first and justice will occur only by accident. If at all.

Of course, *how* to pursue justice is no simple matter, even if there are rule books (and holy books) that presume to tell us. For one thing, our self-interest frequently clouds our perception of what's "best" – especially when others may be impacted. But the larger problem is, how can we be absolutely certain what impact our actions will have on others? Not to mention on ourselves. Starfleet records – like each of our personal histories – are full of good intentions that ended up having precisely the opposite effect.

Which is precisely why the pursuit of justice is a spiritual pursuit. Because it encourages us to transcend our narrow, purely physical view of things; to realize there is a wider perspective that "sees" what's best for all; and to strive, somehow, to gain access to that perspective.

Or rather, to let that perspective gain access to *us.*

Pursuing justice means affirming that I am part of a larger Web of Life. I open myself to the rule book which is that Web. I will endeavor to act as its agent.

09.05

Well, no offense, Ma'am. But where's the fun in that?

— CAPTAIN KIRK : STAR TREK BEYOND : CIRCA 2263.3

Early in his career as Captain of a Federation Starship, Kirk is put on the spot when Yorktown's Commodore offers him a promotion to the Admiralty in recognition of his outstanding leadership abilities, not to mention the recent acts of bravery that literally saved Yorktown. The young captain wonders aloud whether the duties of the new position would prevent him from further explorations of the galaxy in the company of his crew. When the Commodore explains that he'll essentially be helping to pilot the entire Federation rather than a single starship, Kirk declines her offer with characteristic humor.

And not only does the Commodore completely understand Kirk's reluctance, so should we. Because what's most important about our jobs — about our own vocation, our *calling* — is the passion we bring to it, along with the passion it continues to generate within our souls. More than prestige and pay raises, if "advancement" in our career comes at the cost of giving up the very things that attracted us to a job in the first place, it is our spiritual duty to reject it.

Sometimes our biggest promotion comes precisely when we realize where we "fit"; that what we're doing *now* is our real mission in life… at least until it stops being "fun." And the greatest honor a superior officer can bestow is simply to allow us to *keep* doing it.

Others may have a vested interest in what I do with my life. But in the end, it is my decision alone, and my passion that will help me decide.

09.06

Thinking about what you can't control only wastes energy and creates its own enemy.

— LIEUTENANT WORF : COMING OF AGE : 41416.2

There's a prayer that appears in the sacred writings of nearly every planetary race, the essence of which is this: "Holy One, let me try to change what *can* be changed. Prevent me from trying to change what cannot be changed. And give me the wisdom to know the difference."

It's easy to see why such a prayer is almost universal. None of us wants to waste our time and energy on projects that are destined to fail. We'd rather invest ourselves and our efforts where they'll have a reasonable chance at paying off. If nothing else, it's simply a case of managing our resources, of being practical.

But there are also spiritual implications. If we try to move a mountain that can't be moved, (but we *think* we should be able to move it), we begin to see that mountain as "the enemy." Its refusal to move must be deliberate.

Or worse: Maybe it's not just the mountain. Maybe the whole *world* is against us. Or maybe we're not "worthy." Maybe there's something wrong with us.

Persistence is good. Our willingness to take on ever greater challenges strengthens us. But knowing when to quit, or when to not even try, can be just as important.

Sometimes we need The Universe to help us decide.

I accept the fact that I can't change or control everything. I will seek guidance to know what those things are, and what I can do instead.

09.07

I have to hope that whatever happens here can serve as a bridge between our civilizations.

— CAPTAIN GEORGIOU: THE VULCAN HELLO: Stardate 1207.3

Sometimes our first encounters with another person – or culture, or religion – do not go very well. Accustomed to our own ways of doing things, to our own familiar circle of friends, we may be shocked by newcomers' attitudes or behavior, if not merely by their "looks."

Our feelings of dismay and discomfort aren't meant to send us fleeing for the nearest exit. They're designed to jolt us out of our comfort zones, to infuse us with the energy to confront our assumptions and knee-jerk reactions to The Other, to fuel a search for better understanding.

Although we are accountable for our actions *as individuals,* it's wise to remember that, in our initial encounters with others, we are often perceived as "representatives" of whatever sub-group we may belong to… our social standing or "class," for instance, or our gender, political affiliation or spiritual tradition. Whether being judged in this way is "fair" is beside the point. It happens.

And the fact that it *does* happen is no reason to avoid these encounters. Think of each one as another opportunity to reflect on the best and highest aspirations of your particular sub-group, to be guided and emboldened by those ideals even if you don't always reflect them; to feel your friends' and compatriots' "presence" surrounding and strengthening you as you enter uncharted space. To feel that what you're doing in the present can be a bridge to a brighter future for us all.

I will remember that I am not only an individual, but a representative of my wider community, and an incarnation of the sacred spirit that seeks unity, not division.

09.08

You never know what conditions you might encounter. You must be prepared for anything.

— LIEUTENANT TUVOK : LEARNING CURVE : 48846.5

In one sense, we can't be "prepared for anything." At least not with pre-rehearsed counter-measures and programmed responses. The amount of information we'd need to know is simply too great. Besides, it's impossible to prepare for what we can't even imagine, right?

Tuvok admits as much when he warns us not to make assumptions about future "conditions." Yet he still advises us to "be prepared." Isn't this, well… *illogical?*

Not if we remember that proper preparation also includes what Picard called "readiness." And that's a matter of attitude. It's the mental framework that expects the unexpected, that's willing to accept new challenges as the cost of learning. It's the faith that we will survive, and that if the conditions are too much for us to cope with individually, then there are other resources we can turn to.

And there *are* such resources. Other people, for instance. Not to mention the resource within us: The One whereby we are already linked with others; the One that already "knows" the conditions we'll encounter even before we encounter them. And the One through which we are, even now, empowered to cope with anything.

I prepare myself for the unexpected as I link with other people, and as I connect with that Source of wisdom and power that lies within.

09.09

He will triumph who knows when to fight, and when not to fight.

— COMMANDER RIKER : THE LAST OUTPOST : 41386.4

Triumph, fighting, *not* fighting… all of this sounds so belligerent, so militaristic, hardly in keeping with another Starfleet sentiment about war never being "imperative."

But even as we find peaceful ways to deal with conflict, war and warriors still symbolize something crucial about our existence: Our need to struggle against those forces that prevent us from achieving our highest potential.

In the midst of that ongoing struggle, we must take regular breaks (i.e. retreats, sabbaths) to rest, to gather our own forces, to plan new strategies. Of course, the success of any strategy ultimately depends on an honest, steely-eyed evaluation of our strengths and weaknesses.

Because there are times when picking a fight can only harm us. Like when we carelessly assume we've beaten an addiction, or overcome some other wasteful habit; and we stroll into enemy territory only to discover how easily our untested defenses can be stripped away.

There are also times when we've renewed our strength, disciplined our troops; and now the only way to assert control of our lives is to go back and confront the enemy. Our eventual triumph isn't so much "won" as reaffirmed. Because the real victory has been achieved already – within us.

My spiritual growth emerges from struggle. I will carefully choose opportunities in which I can test, refine and confirm the personal qualities I seek.

09.10

There's only one first time for everything, isn't there? And only one last time, too.

— JAKE SISKO : THE VISITOR : Stardate Not Given

"Firsts" are more significant than many of us realize. Not only consciously, but *sub*consciously, they become signal beacons on our Inner Voyage. They are the turning points, the personal breakthroughs, the spiritual "revelations." They symbolize the thresholds of transformation beyond which our lives can never be the same again.

Because our subconscious naturally elevates these events, we should strive to make them positive experiences. Or at least be aware of them when they happen.

We can also be aware of "last" times, too – as in the last time we smoked, or the last time we did something dishonest, or yielded to some other temptation.

In fact, by consciously labeling some event as "the last time," we can increase the likelihood that it will remain so. Unlike "firsts," however, last times are easily reversed. We can always repeat actions we thought we'd stopped, and the change we hoped for is effectively cancelled.

A better approach would be to make every hoped-for change into a "first." The last time we lit up a cigarette becomes the first time we took control of our habit. And if we yield to temptation again, at least we see ourselves moving in the right direction. Instead of endings, we concentrate on beginnings. Life is about doing, not undoing.

Every day offers opportunities to do something for the first time. I will use this day to change my life.

09.11

You're good at building things. I'm good at blowing them up.

— LIEUTENANT REED : UNITED : CIRCA ECE2154

This off-hand comment may have been intended as a joke when Malcomb said it. But a related observation by Spock, centuries later, proved how deadly serious the message is. "As a matter of cosmic history," Spock mused, "it has always been easier to destroy than create."

What both statements represent is the dialectic between creation and destruction. It also calls to mind the sad, simple fact that evil can undo so much good so easily. After all, technological progress and affluence are achieved only at great cost to a society; and yet a small band of terrorists can bring down in mere minutes a skyscraper that took years to build, along with thousands of people inside. A single saboteur can blow up a bus, or a starship. The kind of "nuclear exchange" once feared on Earth can decimate entire planets, bringing unique cultures and whole civilizations to an end.

The same sad imbalance holds on the personal level as well. Our own hard-earned property and possessions can be lost in a single "act of nature" or one random act of violence. And if that's the case, how can life ever be fair? Or, put another way, What is The Universe trying to tell us?

The answer that's so easy – yet so hard to accept – is that the material world is not what's most important. That's the by-product, the "reality" whose existence depends on a still deeper reality. We cannot protect our "things" with other *things*. We must undergird our monuments and our technology with a spiritual foundation. That's what we must "build." And only that will protect us.

Material things are secondary. My true foundation lies within. I will help others find theirs, too, so we may go on building... together.

09.12

You get to live your life the way you deserve to... not at war, but at peace.

— SCIENCE SPECIALIST BURNHAM : INTO THE FOREST I GO : Stardate Circa 1523.5

The significance of this line lies partly in the statement itself, partly in the response it drew from Ash Tyler. "I found peace," the Lieutenant replied, taking Burnham's hands in his, "right here."

The peace to which both were referring isn't really about the end of a war, or the absence of conflict. True peace can exist even in the midst of war, despite ongoing conflict. Because it does not flow from temporary, external conditions. It comes from within. It's the inner sense we get when we realize we're on the right path, that even if we stumble now and then we're still making progress; and that there is another person, or perhaps many others, on the same path, whose presence on that journey acts as the firm footing, the stabilizing force in our lives, if only for a time, if only to embody what the universe provides already, without our even asking.

It's true that intimate relationships can and do offer a kind of "grounding" for inner peace. But other people can falter and lose their balance, too, sometimes taking us down with them. Which is why our most important foundation must be our relationship with the Ground of All Being, with the unchanging laws and the Ultimate Reality our external conditions are based upon.

Let us focus on that relationship first, allow that greater Consciousness to permeate ours, and welcome the quiet assurance it brings.

I am increasingly at peace as I align myself with The Universe. I deserve it!

09.13

Even logic must give way to physics.

— SPOCK : THE UNDISCOVERED COUNTRY : 9521.6

No matter how many intellectual trophies we accumulate, The Universe always finds some way to bring us back down to earth.

And that's a good thing. Because we can become so smug, so puffed up by our own mental prowess, that we begin to think our intellect is what saves us. Feelings are irrelevant. Relationships are beside the point. Solutions to life's problems are simply a matter of collecting data and putting it under the microscope of Pure Logic.

At least this approach uses logic purposefully. Too often our mental calisthenics become an end in themselves. We enjoy playing mind games, solving all kinds of problems "in theory" while ignoring the fact that the ultimate test is whether our solutions work in the real world. Our ancestors called this "living in an ivory tower."

Spock's reference to "physics" is a call to come down from our ivory towers. Our mental and spiritual studies, after all, become useful only as we can apply them in our everyday lives. That's the reference point for all our learning, all our growth – individually and collectively.

Whenever our knowledge collides with physics, The Universe is simply telling us to try something else until we get it right. Otherwise all our knowledge amounts to, all we *are*, is just "theory."

Learning becomes genuine knowledge as I test it in my life, refine it, and grow more confident in it. In the process I feel The Universe testing and refining me.

09.14

Part of being human is learning how to risk new experiences… even when they don't fit into your preconceptions.

— ENGINEER LA FORGE : INHERITANCE : 47410.2

Think of "being human" as shorthand for "fulfilling your highest potential." Human, Klingon, or otherwise.

This potential is a quality all sentient beings share, a treasure bestowed on each of us by The Universe. Unfortunately, it also lies buried beneath the complex programming our species has evolved for its biological survival. As amazing as that program is, it can take us only so far. In fact, if we assume that our highest potential is defined strictly in terms of biology, the program will effectively block any further growth. We become like stunted caterpillars, content to crawl when we could be soaring like butterflies… unwilling to emerge from our cozy cocoons when divine transformation is our destiny.

Unlike the caterpillar, our transformation requires our assent. And the best way to give that assent is to break free of our preconceptions: To imagine that we can soar even if we've spent most of our lives crawling; to allow a new concept of our world and ourselves to emerge, even if our present concepts are comfortable, familiar, safe.

The caterpillar can't imagine being a butterfly, yet becomes one. How much higher might we soar if we *can* imagine it!

I grow not by staying comfortable, but by leaving my cocoon. I earn my spiritual wings not by flying close to the ground, but risking the heights.

09.15

Stop trying to kill each other, then ***worry about being friendly.***

So often we get things backwards. We speak before thinking, act before considering the consequences. Or we *don't* act, missing an opportunity we should've taken.

Of course there are also times when we must speak or act — or not — without having time to properly analyze the situation. We may have little more than intuition to guide us. (Not "impulse." *Intuition.*) We accept the fact that mistakes are fairly common in these cases; and most people will forgive us if they think our original intentions were good.

What's *not* easy to forgive is when someone premeditates an action they know is wrong, trusting that they'll be forgiven later. It's shocking how many people routinely do this. It's even more shocking to catch our*selves* doing it.

That's because we corrupt our sensibilities if we cynically use divine grace in this way. To hurt others, intending to make up afterwards, is to "play act" at forgiveness. It leads to the pretense of regret, not heartfelt sorrow. It stifles the sincere desire for change that produces genuine transformation. The people we end up hurting most is *us.*

On the other hand, if we premeditate reconciliation and friendship with other people, we also become reconciled with our own feelings. And with the divine nature within us.

If I pre-plan my actions at all, it will be to do only those things for which I will not require forgiveness.

09.16

You are going to have to make some hard choices about your future. And you can't make them if you're going to ignore the truth.

Spock and Tuvok would readily agree. Because making choices involves logic. Unfortunately, if the data we use is faulty — if we haven't input "the truth" — the most flawless logic will still yield an incorrect conclusion.

Even the most advanced Ship's Computer ultimately depends on the quality of the information fed into it. Perhaps the early computer programmer's motto still sums it up best: "Garbage in, garbage out."

So it is as we plan our futures. We make plans based on the rosiest scenario we can imagine. Or sometimes the most dismal ones. And it's not that we do this consciously. The truth simply has a hard time getting past our mental and emotional filters. We can just as easily ignore what's in our favor as the harsher realities.

Because of her emotional distance, Dr. Crusher was often able to see what her patients couldn't. We can provide that same service for our friends. And we frequently need that "outside" perspective for ourselves.

Support and guidance are all around us. All we need to do is ask for it. That's what our Spiritual Network is for.

I alone am responsible for my choices, but I need not make them alone. With the help of others and my inner guidance, I see more clearly my true path.

09.17

Sometimes things between men and women can get a little complicated.

— CAPTAIN SISKO : INDISCRETION : Stardate Not Given

Let's take a quick reading: How are your relationships with members of the opposite sex?

Though you may not know it, what's being asked is nothing less than how comfortable you are with your *own* sexual identity. And whether or not you can transcend it.

Because the complications between men and women depend, first, on how we define ourselves; and only secondarily on how we regard the other sex. If we don't know what it means to be a "man," we can't expect our relationships with women (or even other men) to be as healthy and fulfilling as they could be. And vice versa.

Equally crucial is our ability to recognize what is the same in each of us, despite our sexual identities. Do we know what it means to be a "person" first? Can we see the individual behind the physical form, or are we unable to separate the "self" from the body it resides in?

Try this: Imagine what it would be like to take your core identity – what many traditions call the "soul" – and implant it within a body of the opposite sex. Can you?

No wonder things get complicated. We are not only persons, but co-workers, lovers, mothers and fathers. The challenge is finding a balance between our biology and our spirituality. The joy is that it takes a lifetime to do it.

My sexuality is one of my greatest gifts. I will use it to discover the inner self that lies beyond it.

09.18

Talk to people... ask questions... learn the truth for yourself.

— LIEUTENANT TORRES : REMEMBER : 50211.4

Accepting what others tell us, on faith, can never be a sound basis for Faith.

The "truths" we build our lives around are too important to rest on custom or convention, on what someone *says* happened two hundred years ago, or two thousand.

Not because what someone says is necessarily wrong. Or because social customs don't play a useful role. It's because we can't fully know our truths to be true until we've questioned them, even doubted them… until in some sense we "discover" them for ourselves.

The things that motivate us, that have the power to transform our lives, are the deeply felt truths whose confirmation comes from within. And even if they depend in part on the testimony of others, or on words inscribed in a book, their meaning must resonate in our hearts and minds. They must translate into attitudes and actions that make a difference to us personally.

In fact what *doesn't* resonate has no real meaning for us. What can't "translate" ultimately makes no difference.

Our quest for spiritual or religious truth is less about what's true than *what conveys the truth to us* – in a way that makes us feel it deeply, then inspires us to act.

The Universe knows what "language" I speak. It is conveying its truths to me right now, if I will listen.

09.19

Why not try a carrot instead of a stick?

— DR. McCOY : METAMORPHOSIS : 3219.4

McCoy's question recalls the medieval tale of the boy who can't get the family donkey to pull their cart. After whipping the stubborn animal with his stick, the boy finally uses his stick to dangle a succulent carrot in front of its nose. The excited donkey lunges forward, pulling the cart with him, and keeps moving as long as the carrot is held there.

The debate about what motivates us is largely settled. Negative reinforcement – the "stick" – has limited value. Pain doesn't tell us where to go; only to stop doing whatever we're doing. Positive reinforcement – the "carrot" – is not only more inspiring, it gives us direction.

What's more, we can apply positive reinforcement to ourselves. It works almost as well if we dangle the carrot in front of our own noses!

And sometimes we need to. For example, most of us can envision the kind of stronger, more loving person we'd like to become someday. But getting there can be hard work. There may be few rewards, and lots of pain.

Which is why, if we know we're headed in the right direction, we should reward ourselves for every small step we take toward our goals: A night out, perhaps; or a warm bath; or maybe a quiet evening with someone special.

Think what fun we could have rewarding each other!

I will no longer think in terms of "punishing" myself (or others) for failure. I hereby promise only to reward success.

09.20

If you're going to judge me, judge me for what I am now.

— ENSIGN SITO : LOWER DECKS : 47566

Making judgments about others often serves a useful purpose. Judgments help us "package" the experience we've gained, enabling us to form productive relationships based on what we can realistically expect.

But judgments can also be limiting and destructive. If we enter a new relationship with someone based on the negative things other people say about them, we prevent the opportunity for a positive relationship in our case. And even if our judgments are drawn from first-hand knowledge, we do damage by casting those judgments in concrete. To judge another too harshly is to deny them the possibility of change. It freezes them at one stage of development when progressive evolution is a law of the universe.

The long-discredited practice of imprisoning criminals was abandoned for exactly that reason: It confirmed negative behavior rather than allowing people to unshackle themselves from the past, in order to be transformed.

What's worse, by denying the possibility of transformation in others, we subconsciously tell ourselves that we, too, are incapable of change. Instead, we must actively look for – and celebrate – positive changes in others. Not only for their sake, but for our own.

I release others – and myself – to become the highest and best we can be. I will celebrate every change for the better, no matter how small.

09.21

Wishing for a thing does not make it so.

— CAPTAIN PICARD : SAMARITAN SNARE : 42779.1

Actually, the statement isn't as benign as it might seem at first glance. Because our "wishing" for something can often *prevent* that something from ever coming about.

The same holds true for some forms of prayer. As they are practiced on many planets, both wishing and prayer incorrectly place all the power of "fulfillment" outside of ourselves. We see ourselves at the mercy of some dictatorial Power which usually doesn't want what we want — or at least doesn't care one way or the other. According to this mode of thinking, we are impoverished. We lack. We suffer neglect unless we continually petition this power, or otherwise show how desperate our need is and how granting our wish would make us *so* happy.

But what we desperately need is to change this attitude of desperation. What we need is to stop practicing our own spiritual disempowerment.

At this very moment The Universe is ready to give us our heart's desire. Our desires will often be fulfilled even if we later come to regret it, since taking responsibility for those desires may be an important life's lesson. For most of us, realizing this — *practicing* this — is the key.

Think about it: When you raise your arm you don't wish for it. You just *do* it. "Making it so" is not that different.

The ability to make my dreams come true lies in my own attitudes. Prayer is the technology for "making it so" by aligning my Self with The Universe.

09.22

I fail to see how excrement of any kind bears relevance on our current situation.

— SPOCK : STAR TREK BEYOND : CIRCA 2263.3

Dr. Spock, like Lt. Data, was always good for a laugh whenever he mistakenly took words literally, failing to understand the subtext within ordinary human conversation. His reply to Dr. McCoy's characterization of his previous comment as the four-letter equivalent of equine road apples is one such example.

True, many of us are justly offended when such four-letter words intrude into our daily discourse. But not only are they "relevant" in some cases, they can be the *best* words to bring home a point. Not only can the occasional "swear word" convey our frustration and let off steam by merely saying it, such words often act as shorthand for much longer explanations or position statements.

Sitting at his writing desk, the sixteenth-century playwright William Shakspeare was considered Earth's leading expert at crafting incisive phrases and clever puns to deliver the same one-two punch today's abrasive expletives sometimes provide. But in certain circumstances there's simply no time for carefully crafted phrases and clever witticisms.

Sometimes we need to forcefully declare an end to our discussions. Because it's time to *act*.

I will endeavor to listen to what others are saying beneath the literal meaning of their words, not only when those words are shocking, but because *they are*.

09.23

We just have to make the best of the little time we have... we can't waste a second.

— CHIEF O'BRIEN : FASCINATION : Stardate Not Given

Even if we don't waste a second, we can't do everything. Considering all the star systems we'd like to explore, all the subjects we'd like to master, all the personal qualities we'd like to refine, transform, or just get rid of – a single lifetime simply isn't enough.

It's fortunate, therefore, that The Universe does not judge us by our individual Goal Achievement Rates. (Besides, what we consider "the goal" may only be an excuse for working on the *real* objective.) What The Universe is concerned with, instead, is whether we've used our limited time wisely, whether we've managed that resource with an understanding of how precious it is.

The coming day will be unlike any other, if we would only look for its unique treasures. Each new hour offers opportunities for growth, chances to transform our lives, to reach out in service to others. Watching for these hidden, one-time opportunities (even as we stay focused on our long-term goals) gives us a more open and spontaneous attitude toward life. It also fills our time with more spiritual riches than we could ever make plans to accumulate.

We are, after all, in the care of a Higher Power. Being ready to accept its gifts is the best use of our time.

I will embrace today like a loving friend whom I won't see again. The treasures of The Universe are right here, right now. I will relish every moment.

09.24

It doesn't matter what you're made of. What matters is who you are.

— COMMANDER CHAKOTAY : PROJECTIONS : 48892.1

A half-century earlier and seventy thousand light years across the galaxy, Captain Picard had already expressed a similar idea this way: "Let us not condemn anyone," he said, "for their bloodlines."

Not that the idea was original even then. Three thousand years before, a Romulan general wrote that he had more in common with the attacking Klingons he was trying to repel than his fellow Romulans who had fled their assault.

In other words, courage and commitment are more important than chromosomes. Standing for something is what counts. Heroism transcends heritage.

Which is as true today as ever. What distinguishes us from others – or what makes us alike – is not a question of race or planetary origin. Or whether we're composed of flesh and bone, bionic parts, or pure energy.

As a great King once said, it's "the content of our character." It's the way we relate to the natural world and to other sentient beings. It's whether we tend to think of others as competitors or compatriots; whether we treat the universe as a resource to waste and exploit, or a garden to care for and cultivate.

And thereby cultivate Who We Are.

My body is only a vehicle. In the way I live my life I define my true identity. By the way I treat others I expose – and continue to refine – who I am.

09.25

Maybe it's time to stop brooding and start talking.

— MAJOR KIRA : THE SEARCH, PART I : 47212.4

By now, most of us have begun to receive the benefits of our private meditations. In fact, whenever we skip our daily "soul-work," even for good reason, we feel like we're missing something. The truth is, we are.

But there are times when our meditative practice can turn sour. Like when we use meditation to escape our daily life rather than deepen it. We may be going through a crisis in a relationship, for instance. Or maybe our jobs aren't going well. Perhaps we've done something stupid.

Under such conditions we often find ourselves not so much meditating as brooding. We ponder our sorry state endlessly, rather than seeking inner resources to end it.

The best way to break out of this cycle, ironically, is to *stop* meditating. Instead, we need to find a sympathetic ear — someone who won't try to offer advice but simply let us "air out" our concerns. And then we need to start talking.

Vocalizing our problems is a different process entirely. As we listen to our own words, we begin to separate ourselves from our troubles in a way that breathes objectivity and new insight into our lives. Our very thought patterns refresh themselves, crawl out of their own dungeons.

Through another, we can reconnect with our Self.

I do not allow brooding to infect my meditations. I can temporarily substitute spoken words for private thoughts, thereby re-grounding myself in reality.

09.26

Given a choice between slim and none, I'll take slim any day.

— COMMANDER RIKER : DEJA Q : 43539.1

This one's about hope. And the fact that even the smallest shred of it can keep us going when nothing else will.

Our uncritical expectations that life will get better someday, or that justice will be served someday, or that we'll find our true love someday — all these "hopes" have enormous power. They are powerful precisely because they are so uncritical. Even illogical.

Because if we calculated the odds, if we only knew how slim our chances really were, we might easily give up. By *not* knowing, we allow ourselves to keep trying. And in most real-life situations, it's not our critical faculties or our logical brilliance or our "practicality" that wins out; it's our persistence. It is our dogged, never-say-die, keep-the-faith, thick-headed *persistence.*

In fact, for the really important things in life, the slimmest odds are often the best odds. Winning nine times in ten presents no challenge. Fifty-fifty odds may level the playing field, but aren't likely to change us. It's the one-in-a-hundred shot that makes us dig down deep, that forces us to commit fully, that transforms us from opportunists seeking the easiest route into disciplined explorers on The Inner Voyage. That, finally, is where our hope lies.

My success isn't based on "the odds" but on the depth of my commitment. I will hope for it; I will expect it; therefore I will achieve it.

The beginning of wisdom is... I do not know.

— DATA : WHERE SILENCE HAS LEASE : 42193.6

Look again. It's not that Data is confused about our concept of wisdom. He knows exactly where wisdom begins: By openly admitting that "I do not know."

Get it?

A similar statement can be found in a five-thousand-year-old Bajoran text. And in the ancient record of Earth's most famous gadfly, Socrates. "The truly wise man," as Socrates described him, "is he who knows how ignorant he is."

Which doesn't mean stupid. Stupidity is usually an attribute of the individual who thinks he knows everything. This person is open to very little, can be taught very little, and will consequently grow very little.

That's just stupid.

In contrast, it is our frank admission that we are ignorant of so much — compared to what there is to know — which starts us down the path of knowledge. It is our willingness to live with partial answers along the way which keeps us open to new information. It is our joyful acceptance that learning never ends which keeps us growing, improving... alive.

And that's wise.

I will cheerfully admit when I do not know something. I will ask questions, and I will open myself to the truth, wherever it may lead.

Your primitive impulses will not alter the circumstances.

— SPOCK : REQUIEM FOR METHUSELAH : 5843.7

Most of us wouldn't phrase it quite as delicately as Mr. Spock. Something more like: "You can rant and rave all you want, but it ain't gonna change anything, Charlie." Or maybe: "Once the Terulian wine has been spilled, all the tears on the planet won't put it back in the flask."

And it's true. We can't change what has already happened simply by expressing anger or disappointment or grief. On the other hand, we can't change what's already happened by *not* expressing those emotions, either.

What Vulcans don't readily comprehend is that, for emotional beings, ranting and raving and grieving can be part of our healing process. Or at least helpful in releasing the energy that builds up when life slaps us in the face.

Not that we can't go overboard on occasion. We're often blinded by our emotions. We can hurt ourselves, hurt others, and live to regret it. Or, as often happens, we use our "emotional state" to avoid responsibility, to force someone else to pick up the pieces because "We just can't face it."

But all that emotional energy is designed precisely so we *can* face it. That's why it exists: To be transformed into the strength we need to deal with "the circumstances."

Which is what Spock always tried to teach us.

My emotional reactions to situations are what it "feels like" when my body is giving me the energy to face reality. I will use it wisely.

09.29

When every logical course of action is exhausted, the only option that remains is inaction.

— LIEUTENANT TUVOK : TWISTED : Stardate Not Given

Sometimes the best thing to do is… nothing.

Which, as we've said before, isn't really "nothing." Not taking action is itself an action. Or at least a decision.

And it's not necessarily a decision we reach because we've thrown up our hands and don't know what else to do. It's because a choice we could've made earlier is now easier to accept: We can wait patiently on The Universe.

Though Vulcans might not rush to admit it, logic does have limits. It may be that we just don't have enough raw data to allow the use of logic. Or perhaps the answers can't be formulated in logical terms to begin with. We aren't able to deduce them so much as "intuit" or feel them, or receive them as if by divine revelation.

So when we run into the proverbial dead end, it may be time to turn the popular slogan on its head: Don't just *do* something – *sit* there! In other words, be still. Wait.

The Universe, after all, has its own higher logic. Often our problems will resolve themselves if we'd only give them time. New options will appear – but only because we've stopped looking so hard. Or maybe we just need to be reminded, once again, who's in control.

Inaction also plays a role in my search for solutions. I must be patient as The Universe integrates my needs with others' needs – at its own pace, not mine.

09.30

We're all vulnerable in one way or another.

— CAPTAIN KIRK : IS THERE IN TRUTH NO BEAUTY? : 5630.7

Ancient Terrans told the story of Achilles, a warrior whose body was magically protected from enemy arrows much as a Starship is shielded from phasers. In Achilles' case, however, one tiny spot on his heel was left unprotected. And that spot eventually led to his downfall.

All of us, it turns out, have some physical or emotional "Achilles heel" – or perhaps several – that can leave us vulnerable, or may even lead to our downfall. And like Achilles, most of us try to keep these "soft spots" secret, so our enemies can't take advantage of them.

The problem is, we also end up keeping them secret from ourselves. Which is why we're often surprised when certain emotions surface, or we suddenly start behaving in ways that "just aren't like us."

Instead of hiding our vulnerabilities, we need to face them. But not so we can learn how to work around them. These emotional soft spots are our psyche's way of pointing to unfinished emotional business. They are portals into the interior territory we most need to explore, not shy away from. They are the "wormholes" connecting our past hurts to our future healing.

And because others must play a role in that healing, they connect us to each other.

I acknowledge the inner work my vulnerability calls me to continue. I accept my psyche's invitation to learn more about myself, and grow even stronger.

10

CORRESPONDING TO THE MONTH OF

October

10.01

Perhaps today is a good day to die!

For Klingons, as with many of Earth's tribal societies, this pronouncement was often made just before going into battle. But it was less a "battle cry" meant to rally the troops than a warrior's personal declaration of faith. It affirmed that the warrior was prepared to do his or her duty, even if it required paying the ultimate price.

For those of us whose daily battles aren't quite so life-threatening, Worf's statement can still hold meaning. In a symbolic sense, to be ready to die is to affirm what's important in life, to have some concept of what we're living for. And when the things we value most are in danger of being lost, we must be willing to "die" for them.

Because if what we have (or are) is worth saving, it's worth risking everything to save it. And fortunately we won't face that task alone. On the other hand, if the life we're living isn't worth saving – if we've taken a terribly wrong turn without knowing it, if what we've become is a sham, if we've settled for less than we deserve – then we must also be willing to let that life expire.

In this sense, to affirm that we're prepared to die is to release the past, to recognize that it may be necessary to start over, to reconstruct our lives from the ground up. And either way, we trust the outcome to The Universe.

Each moment holds the promise of a new life. I am ready to give up this life today if it enables me to live a richer, more fulfilling one tomorrow.

10.02

It is a blessing to understand that we are special... each in his own way.

We feel joy and pain. We set goals and strive toward them. We live and love and learn, and eventually die. And hopefully along the way we find a reason for it all.

In so many ways we are alike. And yet we are different. Our lives offer unique possibilities. Each of us develops a set of traits and talents that is ours alone. In the history of the universe, no one else has ever been, or *can* be, us.

To realize we are "special" is not merely to recognize this uniqueness. It means accepting responsibility for a one-of-a-kind role only we can fulfill. Not merely for our own sake, but for others'.

After all, "special" is a relative concept. It assumes a relationship in which our uniqueness is the missing piece that helps others complete a larger whole. In fact, *all* of our pieces are essential. Finding where we "fit" energizes us, gives meaning to our struggles. It is perhaps life's greatest blessing.

But take note: To receive this blessing doesn't require that we've already found where we fit. "Finding" is an action verb. It's an ongoing process. Simply knowing that we *do* fit, somewhere, is enough for now.

I joyfully affirm the role that Universe has created especially for me. Others will help me clarify and recognize my role, as I will help them with theirs.

10.03

Recovery from a great loss involves a great deal of pain. If we try to avoid that pain, we make it harder on ourselves in the long run.

— COUNSELOR TROI : THE LOSS : 44356.9

It bears repeating: Our minds may be products of the modern world – inheritors of technology and science and the cultural gifts of an entire galaxy. But our bodies are children of the past, the biological offspring of a localized planetary environment that existed long before our species became sentient. To disregard what our bodies are telling us is to ignore who we are and what we need.

For example, the pain of loss – what some people call "grief" – is a physical message which demands an equally physical response. We can suppress that message through pain-killing drugs, or by immersing ourselves in our work, or by trying to deal with it on a purely intellectual level since, after all, we are rational beings, aren't we?

And yet we can no more dismiss our pain than we can deny the pangs of hunger that remind us to take nourishment. It's true the pangs may eventually go away. But the need that gave rise to them will remain. And if we continue to suppress our hunger – or our grief – then what was once merely a call for attention becomes a condition that can threaten our very existence.

Our bodies are *for* us, not against us, if only we will listen and learn its language.

Even in pain, my body is sharing the wisdom of the ages. I will listen for the message beneath its words.

10.04

What is necessary is never unwise.

— SAREK : STAR TREK / PREQUEL : CIRCA 2258

At the time he uttered it, Sarak's statement was a call for action. It is also what logicians call a "tautology" – a claim that's true by its own definition. Doing something one already describes as necessary is a no-brainer. The action might be risky; but if it's necessary, it simply must be done.

Like removing the cancer that dooms one's life unless it is removed. Or overcoming the ignorance, bad habits and bad attitudes that keep us from realizing our potential. Or overthrowing the political and religious oppression that keeps not only individuals but whole societies from fulfilling their destiny. All of these situations demand action. In fact it would be irresponsible to ignore them, to let them fester until doing what's necessary – or doing *any*thing – is no longer possible.

But "what is necessary" is subject to debate. What one person might consider necessary may be only "an option" for another. More importantly, we must always be careful to separate the desired "end" from the means we'll be using to achieve it. We might, for example, agree that eradicating an enemy or plague or addiction is "necessary." But *how* we do so is crucial. Our actions may have unforeseen or adverse consequences. We may eliminate one problem only to create another. We might even find ourselves taking on the qualities of the enemy we seek to destroy, to destroy *him*.

Which is where the wisdom implied by Sarek's assertion comes into play. And where what's *really* "unwise" is to think we know all the answers. Or that any single person can decide what is "necessary" for the rest of us.

To determine what's necessary, I will seek the wisdom of others in addition to the resources already within me.

10.05

Let's not indulge ourselves in speculation. Can we confine our discussion to the facts?

— CAPTAIN PICARD : THE WOUNDED : 44429.6

There's a time for imagination, for unbridled speculation. If nothing else, our flights of fancy can be useful exercises for keeping our minds "limber," for maintaining creative readiness for the real challenges that lie ahead.

But sometimes we can't afford the luxury of fantasy-for-the-fun-of-it, or envisioning "the way things ought to be." Reality occasionally dumps a problem on our doorstep that demands a concrete solution now. Speculation would only waste precious time and energy.

Worse, speculation is often our (unconscious) way of putting off the decisions and actions that might change our routines – that might change *us*. We can pretend to be dealing with the issues when what we're really doing is avoiding the work. And avoiding our responsibility.

Confining ourselves to "the facts" doesn't rule out the use of imagination. It simply reminds us to stay grounded, to remember that Truth must be our ultimate foundation. Not what we wish were true, but what *is* true.

And as much as we can use our power to "go within," to help us connect with Truth, the only way to know if we've actually connected with it is by testing our solutions in the physical world. By measuring their results… in fact.

I am thankful for my imagination. And I celebrate my ability to develop strategies that will transform and improve my physical reality.

10.06

I'll live. But I won't enjoy it!

— ENSIGN CHEKOV : THE DEADLY YEARS : 3478.2

How do we react to disappointment or failure? What do we say to ourselves, what rituals can we use, to help us deal with it and move forward with our lives?

Chekov's response is clearly a common one. What's not so clear is whether he's really serious when he says it.

Many of us, however, *are* serious. And unfortunately so. Because we thereby allow our disappointment to darken our outlook. We may "live," but in a damaged state that begs for sympathy and closes our eyes to the very opportunities that might allow us to enjoy life again.

The first step to recovery is attitude. "I'll live" is actually a positive affirmation. By saying it, we not only declare our intention to survive the current setback, but to give ourselves the time to heal, to learn, to emerge stronger and wiser than we would if we hadn't had the experience.

Still, ultimate success hinges on what we mean by "I won't enjoy it." If we are determined to let our disappointments ruin our life, that's certainly within our power. But not enjoying the feeling of disappointment can also translate into a commitment to move past it. Precisely because we don't "enjoy it," we'll try again, we'll double our efforts, we'll commit to success or growth or recovery no matter how long it takes. Which is one of life's greatest joys.

I gain from having tried. I discover new resources as I try again. The Universe promises me eventual success. I will learn all I can in the meantime.

10.07

If there is a Cosmic Plan, is it not the height of hubris to think we can – or should – interfere?

— COMMANDER RIKER : PEN PALS : 42695.3

Hubris: Classical Greek for giving ourselves more credit than we deserve; arrogance. Or, as some texts use the term, acting like gods when we are mere mortals.

Riker's question is not simply rhetorical. He's not saying we can't or shouldn't interfere in the lives of others, ever. After all, what if the Cosmic Plan calls for us to come to someone else's rescue? Hubris might also refer to our arrogance in presuming we know enough *not* to interfere in other peoples' lives when, actually, we should.

In other words, nothing is automatic. Taking responsibility for our actions means responding to each new situation with our whole being, not just reacting out of habit or impulse. To know whether we're being called by the Cosmic Plan to play some specific role, we need to ask ourselves – again – what we think that Plan *is*.

The correct response to the question has less to do with Yes or No than "What does The Universe require of me?" We are arrogant only to the extent that we consider our answer permanent. Or that we can arrive at it without receiving guidance from anyone else.

Not the least of whom are those we seek to help.

If I can *help*, I have the responsibility to consider whether I should. I will listen for the clues that come from within, and an invitation from without.

10.08

What your eyes show you is only the surface of reality.

— LIEUTENANT TUVOK : COLD FIRE : Stardate Not Given

In some ways, the primitive mind was more advanced than ours. Before the advent of "scientific law," people were much more inclined to acknowledge other, unseen levels of reality. Invisible spirits who inhabited the rocks and trees were simply a pre-modern method for conceptualizing deeper forces at work – forces with whom people could establish a life-enhancing relationship.

Contemporary science has far surpassed this animistic view, if only in terms of the control it has given us over the physical world. It has also reassured us that there are specific, verifiable actions we can take to affect reality.

But this cause-and-effect view can make us skeptical of anything we can't manipulate in some purely mechanical way. We become accustomed to changing our lives solely through physical means, based on the limited view of reality provided by our sense organs.

The unfolding discoveries linking consciousness to matter have once again opened us to the earlier, "primitive" view. Our potential for affecting reality through unseen forces – that is, through meditation and spiritual disciplines – has been validated by quantum physics.

But you'll never know for sure unless you've tried it.

I trust my eyes, but I know there is even more I cannot see. I rededicate myself to that Voyage into the deeper realities.

10.09

Courage doesn't mean you don't have fear. It means you've learned to overcome it.

— LIEUTENANT PARIS : FACES : 48784.2

The person who truly feels no fear probably feels little else, either. Because the problem with trying to suppress any undesirable emotion is that you usually numb yourself to the desirable ones, too. If anything, the fact that your fear can pump you full of adrenaline and put every nerve-ending on red alert is a healthy sign that your emotional channels are open and fully operational.

Courage is often considered an "antidote" to fear, as if it's some drug that's supposed to calm jangling nerves and pump liquid confidence right along with the adrenaline. But that analogy is as unfortunate as it is untrue, because it implies that if we feel fear, we have an excuse not to act. Worse, it implies that courage is also a "feeling."

The fact is, courage is *not* a feeling. It is an attribute of our behavior. It means taking action even when we lack calm and confidence. Ironically, we are most "courageous" when we are fearful, when we're trembling in our proverbial boots; and yet something needs to be done and we do it.

As one of Earth's pre-holographic "movies" envisioned it, our life's mission is not to accumulate knowledge, not to "save our souls," but to overcome our fears.

On our Inner Voyage, the three are really one.

My courage lies in combining these three things: My knowledge, my connection to divinity, and the emotional energy that lies even within my fear.

10.10

Uncontrolled, power will turn even saints into savages... and we can all be counted on to live down to our lowest impulses.

— PARMEN : PLATO'S STEPCHILDREN : 5784.2

Earth's best-known philosopher, Plato, was the first to conceive this test of our "nature": Suppose you had a secret ring that allowed you to move among people completely undetected. (Imagine — a cloaking device twenty-six centuries before the Klingons!) If no one could see you, Plato wondered, would you behave any differently? Could you resist the temptation to peek into other people's pri-vate lives? Maybe even do harm to your enemies?

Plato took a rather dim view. No one could resist doing evil, he claimed, if they could get away with it. Later, St. Augustine would take a similar view. So has Parmen.

And, frankly, many individuals *do* "live down to their lowest impulses" if given the chance. We'd be foolish not to guard ourselves against such people.

But to some extent those impulses are less nature than nurture. Because by being suspiciously on-guard against them, we teach one another that they are to be expected. Yet if we expect high standards of morality — and set a worthy example — people will live "up" to those higher standards.

We possess the power to be saints, not savages. It's just a different "power" than Plato was talking about.

I release the Higher Power within me that brings my "impulses" into consciousness, where I can then receive help in transforming them.

10.11

Sometimes it's the result that counts.

— ENGINEER LA FORGE : LONELY AMONG US : 41249.3

Virtually everyone fails more than once before they finally succeed at something. Our failures are never truly failures us if they serve as "practice," if they prove to us what doesn't work, if we learn something new.

But sometimes we've already learned all we need to know in order to achieve our goal. Now we simply need to perform the task successfully, to break that habit once and for all, to act out the ideals we presume to believe in.

Practice is over. It's time for results.

Because even though it's healthy to accept failure as a natural part of the learning process, we shouldn't allow ourselves to become too comfortable with it. "Failure is okay" can serve as an easy excuse for no longer trying. "Everyone fails" can become a handy slogan for people who've decided that overcoming their faults is too much work, who would rather hide from their responsibility.

During one of Earth's first spaceflights, an accident destroyed much of the primitive craft's oxygen supply. It seemed the "astronauts" would not survive their return trip. The officer in charge of finding a solution put it simply: "Failure is not an option." It would not be enough to *try* to bring them home safely. Actually *doing* it was all that mattered.

They did. And sometimes we, too, need that kind of pressure.

I accept failure only as a prelude to my success. I already know enough to achieve many of the goals I have set for myself. I am ready. I have the will.

10.12

The riskier the road, the greater the profit.

— QUARK : LITTLE GREEN MEN : Stardate Not Given

The same sentiment comes in a dozen shapes and sizes, a few of which we've already seen in this Manual. Quark could hardly be expected to keep from putting his own monetary spin on it.

Not that he's wrong. In purely economic terms, we *do* increase our "profit potential" by learning a skill others don't have, or performing a job others won't do. The more unique the skill, or the more uniquely willing we are to take on a certain task, the more economic value we have.

For Quark, "riskier roads" mean opportunities. If the risks were small, if anyone could do it, the competition would inevitably push prices down. But with higher risk decreasing the competition, prices soar. And thus profits.

Of course, this isn't a lesson in economics. What we're really talking about is the road which leads to *spiritual* rewards – inner wealth, not latinum. We're talking about valuing ourselves not by what the market would pay us, but by the refinement of our character. And by our willingness to take the risks required to further refine it.

There is another sentiment that also comes in a dozen shapes and sizes, and goes like this: "What does it profit us if we gain the whole galaxy, but lose our souls?"

The greatest risk, it turns out, is not taking that Road.

I measure my "profit" by the improvements I make in my character, not in my credit account. Taking risks is the price of transforming myself.

10.13

It's not only a matter of attitude. It's a matter of experience.

— CAPTAIN JANEWAY : LEARNING CURVE : 48846.5

Attitude is crucial, of course. A positive attitude can break through the Tholian Webs that keep us bound to our past, or that ensnare us in unproductive habits and unfulfilling lifestyles. Changing our attitude can not only open doors in the world "outside" us, it can unblock the channels to our own inner resources and energies.

Which is why attitude is called the "warp drive of transformation." But even if it can fuel our journey, attitude can't chart the course. For that we need experience.

There are two types. The first implies increasing ability. If we do something often enough we become "good at it." Eventually we'll have encountered all the variables in the process and fine-tuned our responses. It's all "familiar."

But an equally important kind of experience concerns our explorations into unfamiliar territory. Which means placing ourselves in new situations where we'll be forced to learn as we go; where our direction becomes clear only as we make real choices in the context of real life.

In the sheer act of living we learn what books and other people cannot teach us. We give The Universe an opportunity to reveal its truths directly by willingly putting ourselves at risk. And because we need to know, we learn.

With that attitude, we can't help but gain experience.

I will look for new opportunities to learn about the world, other people, and myself. I accept the risks.

10.14

Communication is a matter of patience... imagination.

— CAPTAIN PICARD : DARMOK : 45047.2

"Why don't you just say what you mean?!"

How impatient we are with others, and with their words. Yet we're just as guilty: We beat around the bush, we hold the most important things back. We make others pry the truth out of us, instead of saying it flat out.

On the other hand, these are ways of "communicating," too. If we would only use a little imagination, if we would stop insisting that all meanings be boiled down into words — which they often can't, anyway — we might find that the messages others are sending us are as obvious as the headline on an old-fashioned newspaper.

Because what is not being said can convey far more than what *is*. What someone can't seem to express, or refuses to talk about, is usually the real message.

We need to stop setting boundaries around what we'll accept as the other half of a conversation. If we've been meditating for long, chances are we've learned to recognize the volumes that are communicated in our silences. We need to practice receiving that same depth of information from others... in a feeling, a touch, a look.

Listening is far too important for us to rely on our ears alone.

What I need to know from others lies not only in, but between and around, their spoken words. When I open my mind to these other levels, I hear more clearly.

10.15

We are living beings, not playthings.

— CAPTAIN KIRK : THE SQUIRE OF GOTHOS : 2124.5

There are two equally-important themes here: The first is about our relationships with others.

Psychological studies have shown that individuals who commit serious crimes and acts of abuse usually have a diminished capacity for imagining the personal lives of other people — that others have hopes and feelings and families; that they are conscious and autonomous. That they are *real*.

We all share responsibility for this defect. For we are all guilty at times of relating to others more as "types" than individuals. Instead, we must acknowledge the feelings, the personhood, of others in every social interaction.

We must also be wary of "entertainment" that reduces people to objects; that treats life and death so casually. Especially since holosuites and the "popular media" act as substitute teachers for impressionable, growing minds. It's frightening to think that the rules for social behavior are often learned more by media modeling than by direct experience.

But Kirk's statement is about *us,* too.

It's about the fact that we shouldn't treat our own lives so casually, either. Because the time we're given is irreplaceable. This self is beyond value. We should no more consider ourselves as playthings than we should others.

In the end, the two can't be separated.

For every person I encounter, I will find some way to acknowledge their presence and affirm their worth. I will thereby reaffirm my own.

10.16

We should not fear the unknown. We should embrace it!

— LANEL : FIRST CONTACT : Stardate Not Given

This Manual understands "faith" not in terms of dogma or doctrine, or what we merely *say* we believe in. Faith is a characteristic of individuals. It's the set of personal convictions and attitudes each of us demonstrates by our behavior, both in public and in private.

And one of the most crucial parts of this personal faith is the way we face The Unknown.

For many of us, "fear" is the operative word. If we can't be absolutely sure about the outcome of some new experience, we often won't even try. And yet, ironically, what we can be sure of is that if we don't try something new, if we don't seek out new experiences and new perspectives, we can't expect to grow. After all, what we've already done is what brought us to where we are now. And the best way to insure that we stay there is simply to go on doing what we've been doing.

To embrace the unknown is to recognize that our fulfillment — our very salvation — lies in what is yet to come. We must learn to see the unknown as a repository of hidden treasures and hidden opportunities, without which learning and transformation are impossible.

And fortunately, each of us has a key.

I face the unknown with joyful expectation. I anticipate new experiences that may change my life — and the lives of those around me — for the better.

10.17

We certainly have the right to exercise control over our own bodies.

— COMMANDER RIKER : UP THE LONG LADDER : 42823.2

In recent centuries, the very same words have been used to justify all sorts of social customs. From "reproductive rights" to recreational drug use, the popular justification almost always comes down to the claim that "our own bodies" are off-limits, legislatively speaking.

And certainly, allowing outside control over our most primal possession raises grave issues. Where would it stop? If others can control our bodies, why not our minds? And then what happens to personal responsibility?

Actually, it's responsibility, not "rights," that Riker is talking about here. Because unless we have some private domain over which we, as individuals, are the sole judge and jury, we can never learn personal responsibility. The risk of harming ourselves – even irreparably – is the price we must pay for being allowed to see and feel the consequences of our actions in the most direct way possible. And therefore to become fully responsible for them.

True, life would be easier if we weren't forced to confront the personal "demons" and addictions that may already have damaged us. Society might run more smoothly if outside authorities could be allowed to "save us from ourselves." But then we'd never grow into the responsible, fully-realized selves The Universe wants us to be.

And that just wouldn't be "right."

I accept my right – and my responsibility – to exercise control over my own body.

10.18

Sooner or later you're gonna hafta choose whose side you're on. Everyone has to choose sides.

— MAJOR KIRA : NECESSARY EVIL : 47282.5

We can't remain neutral forever. At some point we must come to a decision about what's right and wrong – at least for the time being, at least for *us*. That, in fact, is how we define ourselves.

But we don't always need to choose immediately. We usually have time to consider both "sides," to objectively learn what we can about each one. *Not* doing so would close off options and deny ourselves opportunities for understanding and growth.

Yet even when we *do* choose sides, that decision need not separate us from others who take the opposite position. Political parties and religions, for example, share many of the same goals, though the tactics to reach them may differ. Choosing one method needn't suggest that others are evil, or that their members should now be looked upon as "enemies."

Neither is our choice necessarily permanent. The view from the "inside" may reveal facts that were hidden to us before. Making a careful choice can require a long, circuitous journey. Often our strongest commitments are made only after we've actively supported the opposing view.

The point is, sometimes we can't begin to decide until we take sides – any side. It's only a start. But it *is* a start.

Choosing sides is part of my decision-making process. I will give my choices adequate time to confirm themselves as I live with their consequences.

10.19

Forever is just another day. Forever is just another journey.

— LIEUTENANT UHURA : THE CONSCIENCE OF THE KING : 2817.6

It might help to know that Uhura was *singing* these lines, not speaking them. In the context of a musical composition, therefore, the words were probably less for literal meaning than for "effect." After all, no one would seriously compare the entire scope of time to another humdrum day at the office, or a Sunday cruise around one's star system… *would* they?

Maybe. Especially if the purpose of the song is to point out that "forever" isn't real; that it's only an illusion.

In fact it's an illusion we invented. Forever is simply a way of conceiving time. Like "space," it's a mental construct whereby we take a bite-sized unit of our experience and push it to its theoretical limits. And for no good reason.

Because the concept can end up squashing us. In the context of "forever," our lives can seem so meaningless, so insignificant. Compared to endless time, how can anything we do make a difference? Why act? Why care?

Uhura reminds us to keep our feet firmly planted in what we can experience. Since we live day-by-day, our individual acts have measurable significance. We can identify these acts, see their impacts on ourselves and others, and connect them into a narrative which transforms our lives into a Voyage from Point A to Point B.

And now, once again, we are in the Captain's chair.

My life is no theoretical concept. I accept the gift – and the responsibility – of living in the now.

10.20

Guidance, insight, loopholes… I'll take anything I can get.

— CAPTAIN SISKO : FAVOR THE BOLD : Stardate Not Given

It's easy to see how guidance and insight can help us along our daily Voyages. But loopholes…?

Like some attorney who gets clients off the hook by exploiting unintended omissions in our laws, are we supposed to weasel out of our problems by searching for cracks in the laws of Karma?

Hardly. Sisko isn't advocating anything dishonest here, because "loopholes" in the law – natural law, anyway – aren't unintentional. In fact, The Universe seems to put them there precisely for us to find and use them.

It's a loophole in the law of gravity that permits a satellite to orbit the planet, or allows a million tons of starship to float above its surface. What we call "loopholes" in the law are *part* of the law. So what looks like something that chains us to the earth gives us the power to escape it.

The same thing applies in our personal life. The events that appear to stop our progress actually hide clues to a new, more fulfilling path. The web of circumstances that seem to ensnare us in bad habits and limited choices may act as our springboard to greater freedom.

Once we recognize that the forces opposing us can also be used to our benefit, anything is possible.

Even if it seems otherwise, the laws of the universe are designed to assist my progress. Hidden within everything I can't do are the things I *can*.

10.21

You need to go on with your life. Don't worry about me.

— NEELIX : JETREL : 48832.1

It's an admirable thing to say… if only we meant it.

Yet how often do we tell others not to worry when we mean exactly the opposite? It's a common ploy for inducing guilt. And what we're really saying (or threatening) is, "Unless you *do* worry, you'll demonstrate to me that you don't care."

Admittedly, all of us remain connected with one another at some deeper level, even when we've "gone on" with our lives. But there are times when we must publicly sever our bonds, when we must openly acknowledge the end of certain relationships. We must do this not only for our own sakes – to make "emotional room" for new relationships and new growth – but to release others from any "baggage" that might prevent them from growing.

In fact, to release others from constricting emotional bonds is a gift we can give even to those with whom we remain close. After all, to befriend or love someone is to allow them to be themselves. It means freeing them to follow the urgings of their own hearts. It means not imposing on them any obligations they wouldn't feel naturally.

And that makes possible one of our greatest joys: To be loved by another despite their freedom; to give permission for them to leave, and know they've chosen to stay.

The price of genuine love is to release others to be who they are; I will gladly pay it.

10.22

No matter your shame, gather your strength. Find a way to help those who need you.

— SAREK : BATTLE AT BINARY STARS : Stardate 1207.5

There are times in every life when some dark secret – a selfish act or thoughtless remark, a bad business decision, a private pecadillo or hidden addiction – is finally exposed to the world, leaving us feeling ashamed and disgraced. We can try to "rationalize" our way out of it with excuses: We're only human, right? Others have failed even more miserably. Or the fall-back position most of us retreat to when nothing else works: "It was someone else's fault!"

Any of which may be true, but rarely helps our recovery because "shame" is as much a physical condition as mental. The best solution to this full-body assault on our self-respect, it turns out, is to refocus not on ourselves, but on others; to take a few deep breaths and *get back to work.*

We may still require forgiveness and ongoing counseling to fully recover. But in the meantime, if we can look around for others who are likewise hurting or in need of a helping hand – a community organization short on volunteers, perhaps, or an elderly neighbor who could use help with a household repair – we can find channels for our physical energy that might otherwise be directed in self-destructive ways.

And you know what happens? Our selfless labor for others hastens our own healing, and provides new insight into our own life. We begin to see that, despite our personal failings, we *do* have worth. We aren't the lost souls we thought. The Universe can still make use of us… if we let It.

As imperfect as I am, I can still fulfill needs in others' lives. By turning my attention to them, the Universe can attend to my own healing.

10.23

It's a miracle!

— NAVIGATION OFFICER DARWIN : STAR TREK / INTO DARKNESS : CIRCA 2259

Once again, the reason for including Darwin's joyful announcement in this Manual – no doubt repeated countless times in all sorts of situations, and all across the universe – doesn't lie in the statement itself but in Spock's rejoinder: "There are no such things."

On one level, Spock is absolutely correct. Anything that actually happens can't be "miraculous" in the sense that it doesn't conform to physics or logic or "natural law." To reply that an event is "supernatural" doesn't help, either. Even something that happens by "divine intervention" must also follow some kind of "law." It's just that we're not aware what it is. We haven't found a reliable formula, mathematical or experiential, to repeat the event.

That's not to say the word "miracle" has no meaning. It's simply to suggest that a miracle is less about physics or logic than expectations. It's about how we often prepare for the worst, and are shocked that things turn out better than we could've hoped. It's the goal that seems impossible, and we achieve it despite the odds. It's the Prodigal Son returning. It's when the walls that separate us suddenly come a'tumblin' down.

And what makes these unexpected events truly miraculous is not that they're so rare, but that they're so commonplace… if only we'd open our eyes to the beauty that surrounds us. If only we'd look for the divinity in others, and in ourselves. If only we'd realize, deep down, that what seems "super" is really completely natural.

My expectations have power. By believing in the goodness of others, and in the benevolence of The Universe, I make miracles happen.

10.24

Those that hate and fight must stop themselves. Otherwise it is not stopped.

— SPOCK : DAY OF THE DOVE : Stardate Not Given

There are two equally important ways to understand Spock's statement. The first interpretation places the emphasis on the word "stop."

Because the things all of us are doing wrong in our lives – acting selfishly, judging others, bickering, sometimes even fighting openly – must be stopped. Once we recognize how we're hurting ourselves, we must put an end to the damage. There's no magic solution, no easy way. We simply decide to stop, realizing that The Universe has empowered us to do so. And then we stop.

The second interpretation emphasizes "themselves." Or, by implication, on *our*selves.

Or by implication, *you.*

Because nobody can end your bad habits and harmful thoughts for you. Someone else may intervene and force you to stop, yes. But being prevented from acting out your lower impulses isn't the same as "stopping" them.

Only you can do that.

And only then can you – and, by implication, any of us – be transformed.

The Universe gives me the power, and the sole responsibility, to transform myself. I accept that responsibility. I accept that power.

10.25

My logic was not in error. But I was.

— LIEUTENANT TUVOK : PRIME FACTORS : 48642.5

The trouble with logic isn't the logic. It's with the people who use it.

Analyzing any set of facts to produce a logical decision does not insure that the decision is "right." For one thing, logic can only work with the data available to it. Relevant data may not yet be known. Certain factors may not be reducible to the categories logic can digest.

Worse, relevant details can be withheld by dishonest "logicians," or specifically selected to produce a desired conclusion. Dictatorships throughout human history – and throughout the Quadrant – are populated by such masters of manipulation. And despite their perfectly "logical" policies, they are no less wrong.

Tuvoc's words, however, are not about defending ourselves against dictators. They're about guarding against our own tendency to let logic alone dictate our actions. Or to pick and choose what we consider "relevant" so our own use of logic produces exactly the conclusion we happen to be looking for at the moment.

It's called "rationalizing." We've all done it. We must be vigilant in preventing it. And we must be big enough to admit, whenever we catch ourselves doing it again, that we are "in error."

My logic may be flawless. But I will remember to temper it with compassion... and with the perspective I can achieve only by looking beyond myself.

10.26

I'm really easy to get along with most of the time. But I don't like bullies and I don't like threats.

— CAPTAIN JANEWAY : STATE OF FLUX : 48658.2

We've all had experiences with "bullies" – people who use their physical size or power to take whatever they want, or to continually remind us "who's boss."

One of the first signs of our developing empathy is the fact that we can get just as angry seeing other people mistreated by bullies as when we ourselves are threatened. The playground bully, pitiful child that he is, at least serves to link others together through shared feelings. My own experience of fear, anger and injustice at the hands of a bully is what makes me all the more sympathetic to yours.

But it's our *next* response that changes things. Instead of reacting to the bullies in our lives by threatening them back, we can express our anger like Captain Janeway.

"I don't like bullies" defines the situation in a way that still allows for both reconciliation and growth. We desire harmony; do they really want to defy a Law of the Universe? We demonstrate our inner strength by not responding in the usual knee-jerk fashion; their noisy blustering, in contrast, only proves how weak and insecure they must be.

And it is that contrast which inspires growth: In the bully who finally sees his own flaws – and in us, by confirming that if bullies can change, so can we.

I no longer react in anger when I feel threatened. I will pause, look for options, and set the example.

10.27

The more they overtake the plumbing, the more they stop up the drain!

— CHIEF ENGINEER SCOTT : THE SEARCH FOR SPOCK : 8210.3

What psychologists call "the need to control" is, in most planetary cultures, a primarily male characteristic. The trait can manifest positively in the quest for knowledge, or the ongoing search for new ways of doing things. But it can also manifest in a quest for power, or the search for what *can* be done rather than what *should* be done.

And sometimes what should be done is to simply let go, to give up control, to trust nature to do its job.

Which has nothing to do with the plumbing on a Federation Starship… except this:

The universe has a kind of built-in plumbing, too. Long before our arrival it developed a finely tuned system for delivering the necessities of life and carrying off "waste." We didn't design or install this system. Nor could we have. But what we can do, instead, is simply allow it to keep flowing – to nurture the process, not "overtake" it; because if we did, we'd almost certainly clog up the drain.

"Allowing" and "nurturing," in most cultures, are seen as female characteristics. These traits are manifest in giving birth to the new rather than constructing it; in following our bliss, not chasing it; in aligning our wills with The Universe instead of demanding that it conform to ours.

Let this be a parable of The Inner Voyage.

I release the flow of Spirit within me. I allow my higher Self to be born. I nurture the Life I am given.

10.28

I wasn't programmed for any of this! It's just not acceptable!

— THE DOCTOR : PHAGE : 48532.4

The holographic Doctor has once again elegantly expressed our own feelings and frustrations. And the frustration, this time around, has to do with confronting new situations for which we have no prior experience.

These "new situations" can be potentially positive as well as harmful. Ironically, we're often just as frightened of success as we are of failure or injury. The problem is less in the outcome than not knowing how to handle it.

So we take refuge in habit. Familiar routines give us a sense of security – even when those routines stunt our growth or keep us mired in destructive relationships.

At least we know what to expect, right?

It's the *un*expected that frightens us. Or rather, that threatens our ego. Ego, after all, is our current "programming." It's a superficial "image" of Who We Are now. And like someone facing his own demise, the ego will do everything it can to preserve its "life," the Status Quo.

Submitting to this rigid ego amounts to worshipping an "idol." The Universe calls us to reject this image – first by taking responsibility for our own programming, then by changing it. And what was once "just not acceptable" becomes our greatest source of joy and fulfillment.

I am in charge of my programming now. In spite of my fears, I welcome the new situations that lead to learning, growth, and transformation.

10.29

A good joke just seems to make fear dissolve.

— NEELIX : THE THAW : Stardate Not Given

It's often true. In fact, even a bad joke (which Neelix was known for) can do the job. The question is, *Why?*

In the midst of a crisis, most of us have a tendency to focus so intently on our problem that we lose sight of everything else. And fortunately so, since this ability enables us to devote all our energies to finding a solution.

But sometimes our fears have no identifiable source; there is no specific problem to solve. We simply harbor a vague, seemingly-permanent sense of foreboding.

Fortunately, this feeling is not permanent. And that's precisely what a joke – or some other distraction – can show us.

By giving us something else to focus on, we step back from our fears for the moment. By the release of tension a good laugh (or even a forced laugh) can give us, we extract ourselves from our emotional straightjacket. In that moment, we recognize that we can control our attitude, even if we can't control the circumstances.

Better yet, we prove once again that, by controlling our attitude, we *do* control the circumstances. Detached from our fears, we regain perspective, clarity of mind. We reconnect with our inner, healing resources. We remember that, with The Universe, all things are possible.

I can use humor to break through fear. By giving myself opportunities to laugh as I would give myself medicine, I restore balance and perspective.

10.30

Tempering is taken to extremes... We'll need a fine edge that won't dull at the first touch of resistance.

— CAPTAIN PICARD : PEN PALS : 42695.3

In developing any skill or discipline, there comes a point when practice no longer helps. In fact, beyond that point, not only do we stop seeing any further gains, we may begin to lose our skills.

Because what we begin practicing is *practicing.* We end up "working out" for the sake of the workout. Or we meditate because meditation is now an end in itself. The connection of our discipline to our "real world" dissolves. Worse, practice *substitutes* for the real world.

To push the Captain's analogy, we must temper our spiritual "edge" not simply to make it glisten in the light, but to increase its ability to cut through the problems we encounter. If we get carried away by all that polishing, we end up with an edge that has no substance behind it. Or one we're afraid to use for fear it may get a few nicks.

Our spiritual discipline must integrate seamlessly with the rest of our lives. An effective meditation encourages us to immediately seek out opportunities in our daily experience to apply what we've learned.

That's why, when you've finished reading this, you'll know just what to do.

Even as I read these words my mind is searching for ways to test the skills I am developing. I accept the problems I encounter as part of my daily practice.

10.31

Every culture has its demons. They embody the darkest emotions of its peoples. Giving them physical form... is a way of exploring those feelings.

— COMMANDER CHAKOTAY : HEROES AND DEMONS : 48693.2

Satan and Shiva, witches and goblins, demons and devils and Lucifer himself... The question is not whether these scary beings are "real," but how we can use them to deal with the negative forces they represent.

We think in terms of opposites: Light and dark; good and bad; success and failure; matter and anti-matter. Dualism gives us a "handle" on reality. We can imagine forces working toward one extreme or the other. And it explains a lot to say we are "caught in the middle."

But our minds are not content with mere "forces." We need to put faces on them. We ascribe personality even where it doesn't exist – which is our way of acknowledging that we are affected *personally* by these forces. We have a personal stake. We must make a personal choice.

Our demons are no less real for being artificial embodiments of the forces we finally choose to oppose. And if we visualize our bad habits, attitude problems and character flaws as "evil entities" with a life of their own – which in a sense they are – we enable ourselves to become the very real "heroes" who learn to overcome them.

Religions do it. So it is with our dreams. Take a lesson.

I must "face" my flaws before I can overcome them. I will name my sins, and then I will be forgiven.

11

November

11.01

It's life. You can miss it if you don't open your eyes.

— CAPTAIN SISKO : THE VISITOR : Stardate Not Given

Learning how to remain "focused" despite all the distractions can take years. Or a lifetime. Still, it's well worth the effort. To know what you want to do, and then to concentrate your whole being on doing it, is one of life's greatest pleasures.

But our lives do not take place in a vacuum. (Not even when we're traveling in space!) We are connected to other people, to other life forms. And we need to remain connected.

Because as important as our own experience is, we are incomplete if we cut ourselves off from the experience of others. As trustworthy as our own insight is, we can still use someone else's perspective now and then. Especially when we're so focused on one task – or one purpose, or one phase of our life – that we forget everything else.

Or when something bad happens to us and we retreat into our shells. That's often when we need others most: To bring balance back into our lives; to remind us that goodness still surrounds us, that joy is still possible.

The opposite is also true. Because we can sometimes experience such a run of success and happiness that we forget how much tragedy, how much misery, still exists.

But misery is part of life, too. To open our eyes to it – *all* of it – keeps us linked. If nothing else, to our own feelings.

I stay in touch with my own feelings – and with my self – only as I maintain my connection to other people, and to the world around me.

11.02

Spare me the analysis. It's enough that it works!

— DR. McCOY : MIRI : 2713.5

Sometimes asking how or why is the worst thing we can do. Sometimes *not* understanding is what "works."

The rational mind is a wonderful thing. Few people would give back their intellect for the unreflective, half-conscious existence of some primordial Garden of Eden. And yet, in harvesting the fruits of the Tree of Knowledge, our minds occasionally get in our own way.

Most of our body's life-preserving functions evolved long before rational thought – and still work best without it. Healing from illness, for example, is a natural process we can short-circuit if we over-analyze or worry about it. Not that we can't use mental affirmations and medical technologies. It's our egotistical need to "control" the process that becomes a problem. If we would only *accept* our healing, we are more likely to improve our recovery.

Our emotional and spiritual lives operate in much the same way. If we learn to trust our inner resources, to celebrate and strengthen our connection to our Source, we will receive the guidance and healing we seek.

"Let go and let God" is a common mantra. It's the difference between praying for what we think we need, and attuning oneself to a Universe that already knows.

I accept my inner, subconscious resources as well as my intellect. I will seek a balance that works for me, and embrace opportunities to test it.

11.03

I find that maintaining protocol reminds us of where we came from, and hopefully where we're going.

— CAPTAIN JANEWAY : EQUINOX : Stardate Not Given

Substitute the word "tradition" for "protocol," and you have an explanation for why many religions and spiritual disciplines seem to cling to the past. And why *we* do.

What we're clinging to isn't so much "the past" as our *experience*. And our sense of direction.

There's no question that doing things the way we've always done them can hinder our growth. Not to mention that it doesn't always work – especially when we're confronting new situations we've never faced before.

But it's precisely in new situations that tradition can save us. For one thing, what we see as "new" often turns out to be the same conditions dressed in different clothing. If we're too willing to throw out what's worked for us in the past, we devalue our own hard-won experience.

We also lose the formula for self-transformation. After all, we don't automatically rebuild our principles from scratch every time we meet a challenge that requires us to change. We modify our existing theories. We make adjustments to current behavior patterns. We recalculate our course.

Protocol isn't lifeless and unchanging. It evolves and grows just as we do. But not so fast that we forget Who We Are.

In honoring the past, I remember who I am. In tracing my Voyage from past to present, I draw a line pointing toward my future.

11.04

You can't snatch people and put them into your fantasies and expect them to respond.

— COMMANDER RIKER : TRUE Q. 46192.3

Back in Earth's early days of imaging technology, there was a thriving religious subculture whose members refused to allow "photographs" to be taken of them. The Amish (as they are still known) were therefore regarded as a bit "quaint." Maybe they were just being careful.

Not because they thought the images contained some sort of magic, like the voodoo dolls that could reportedly be used to "control" the people they resembled. It's just that photographs were such superficial copies of people. They couldn't capture a person's real identity, their "truth." Nor could they speak for themselves, or defend themselves.

Which tempted whoever possessed the photograph to read any personality into the picture they might wish. That fantasy would then become attached to the visual image. And that would inevitably affect their expectations and reactions to the real person should they ever meet.

Our fantasies about other people operate in the same way. We become boxed in by our "images" and private thoughts about others, rather than letting their behavior and interactions with us define who they are.

People need freedom to be themselves, to grow toward their own vision, not ours. Only if we give them that freedom do we have a right to expect it for ourselves.

I am not bound by others' fantasies. I am who my thoughts, intentions and actions reveal me to be.

11.05

Who am I to argue with me?

— DR. BASHIR : VISIONARY : Stardate Not Given

Conflicted. It's a word that describes the psychological state when one part of us says "yes," another part "no." It's the painful condition of having an idea of where we want to be, while realizing how far we have to go before we get there.

In Bashir's statement, "I" represents the self we *can* be, and "me" is the person we *are* at the moment. Too often, who we are dominates the argument. Which effectively stops further growth. Our present identity, with all its weaknesses and self-enforced limitations, remains in control.

But the very fact of internal conflict is actually a good sign. Conflict confirms that we stand at the threshold of change, and it's only natural to experience some resistance from an ego which fears being replaced.

The Vulcan approach can help us here — first, by simply reminding us that our egos are not our selves. Who we are right now is a transitory phenomenon, a work-in-progress. And if we look at that "work" without emotion, without attachment, we can begin to decide what kind of person we'd like to be… and then make the logical choices that bring us more and more into alignment with that vision of ourselves.

Who am I to argue with me—? "Me" considers it an argument. "I" understands that it's really a healthy discussion about how best to realize our potential.

It is natural to experience inner conflict. I trust the Voyage I have embarked on to guide me through conflict to higher awareness, and to my higher Self.

11.06

It was a mistake… I have made some fine ones in my time.

— CAPTAIN PICARD : FIRST CONTACT : Stardate Not Given

Recognizing that we're not perfect isn't meant to excuse bad behavior, or to absolve us from the continuing goal of personal and communal redemption. (Or at least "self-improvement.") Indeed, redemption applies only to the ongoing refinement of that which is *im*perfect.

Actually, our imperfections are the required first steps toward improvement. It's not just that getting it wrong precedes getting it right. Getting it wrong is what helps us *make* it right.

Like Captain Picard, the most inspiring role models in Starfleet history did not breeze through The Academy — or go on to serve The Federation — with spotless records. The same applies to human history. The most beloved Holy Ones were cherished as much for their raw humanity as their "divinity." Even the paradigm Avatars and Divine Incarnations had their moments of blind rage, their dark nights of doubt, their strategic blunders… their imperfections.

And the reason we continue to draw inspiration from these models is precisely because they *were* so imperfect; because they were as fully "human" as we are; because they were subject to the same flaws and temptations of living "in the flesh" — and yet they kept going, kept trying, kept growing. And if they could, so can we.

I will not condone my mistakes simply because others make them, too. Others learn from them, transcend them. I choose to follow their example.

11.07

We're going to get through this together!

— KES : PHAGE : 48532.4

From one end of the galaxy to the other, virtually no sentient species has been discovered whose evolutionary origins designed it for a totally isolated existence. True, certain individuals within a species may become accustomed to living or being alone. A few may even come to prefer it. But their biological make-up practically shouts for companionship.

We are, in other words, hard-wired for community.

This is no more evident than during periods of turmoil or personal distress. Even our apparent instinct to withdraw at such times, to "be by ourselves," is a call to be "missed" by someone, a plea to be rescued from conditions that feel like we alone have been selected to suffer.

Except that we are never truly "alone." And we must not allow anyone else to remain alone for long, either. Because study after study has proven that social isolation destroys individuals — and eventually destroys the societies that allow those individuals' wounds to fester. Whether the wounds are real or imagined.

Our personal and communal destinies are as intertwined as the nerves in our brains. There is nothing we can't "get through" if we go through it together. And few things we can't achieve if we do it together.

My consolation, my strength, comes from reaching out to others — to give help as much as receive it.

11.08

When we do battle, it is only because we have no choice.

— CAPTAIN KIRK : THE SQUIRE OF GOTHOS : 2124.5

Almost without exception, people who go out looking for a fight are really at war with themselves. "Enemies" only reflect the inner demons they are still battling.

But even when we've overcome our aggressive tendencies, open conflict with others can sometimes seem unavoidable. Or even the *right* thing to do.

Kirk's fellow crewmembers knew better. "War is never imperative," Dr. McCoy reminds us. "There are always alternatives," Spock would add with an admonishing scowl.

And there are. So is Captain Kirk mistaken?

Not if we read between the lines. When we resort to violence, personally or communally, it's not because we have no choice. It's because we *think* we have no choice.

Maybe we feel like we're alone. Or we assume no one else can (or will) intervene. Or we're so emotionally close to the situation that we can't think straight to begin with.

But that only goes to show how much we need others to point out what we often can't see for ourselves. We need a network of people — the more diverse the better — who may have been down this path before; who can help both sides visualize the consequences. And who, together, can keep the peace long enough to let us work things out.

"I have no choice" is a statement of perspective, not fact. I can always call on others, or my own Inner Light, to help change my perspective.

11.09

There are times when it's best just to let things out.

— COUNSELOR TROI : PARALLELS : 47391.2

Much has already been said about our bodies' inherent needs – about the importance of keeping in touch with the physical/emotional legacy we've inherited from our species' evolution. And the fact is, if we don't continually work on integrating body and mind, we risk *dis*integration. Or, in the medical jargon of past centuries, schizophrenia.

Of course, there are layers of social conventions concerning the "proper" expression of physical and emotional urges, as well as sound reasons for *not* expressing them. We learn to control our anger because it might destroy crucial relationships. We restrain our sexual instincts because un-checked reproduction now works against our species' survival. We also choke back tears; we stifle our laughter; and we try to hide how frightened we are at times.

And the toll can be devastating. Because the psychic energy of all those repressed emotions doesn't just go away. It builds like water behind a dam. Finding ways to re-channel that energy – art, or gardening or athletics – is essential. But sometimes the best solution is simply to find a "safe haven" where those emotions can be expressed in their most primitive form: To cry in sorrow, pound our fists in anger, and hopefully shout for joy every now and then.

Because dams break.

It is healthy and natural to release my emotions. I will find a private place, or relationship, or group, where I can do so safely, and in mutual trust.

11.10

Curious how my failure, added to your own, should improve your feelings.

— LIEUTENANT TUVOK : STATE OF FLUX : 48568.2

It *is* curious. Most of us are so conscious of our own faults and mistakes that we find great reassur-ance in the faults and mistakes of others. That's a healthy response if it prevents us from being too harsh on ourselves, if it frees us to make the mistakes that precede genuine growth.

But there's a danger: This kind of "reassurance" can easily develop into "delight." And then we start actively *looking* for faults and weaknesses in others – especially in our competitors, or even our leaders. We begin to revel in scandal, calling out the media bloodhounds to dig up still more dirt, to spell out everything they find in lurid detail.

Why? Because it serves to excuse our own weakness. Because if we concentrate on others' defects we can ignore our own. And then we have "permission" to avoid the self-transformation that, deep down, we know is required but our egos hope to put off for as long as possible.

We need to counter this mindset. Not so much by turning a deaf ear to the latest gossip, or by deciding not to download the latest edition of Galactic Enquirer. The solution is to revel in our mutual progress toward positive change, to focus on all the good things we find in each other.

And what's even more "curious" is that we will not only improve our "feelings," we'll improve our lives.

I will look upon others' faults as a reminder to work on my own. I will find something good – something to praise – in everyone.

11.11

The more we fight each other, the weaker we'll get and the less chance we'll have.

— CAPTAIN SISKO : THE WAY OF THE WARRIOR : 49011.4

One sure indication of progress on our Inner Voyage relates to how fully we've overcome our inbred violence.

The biological roots of violence are strong in most sentient species, and usually stronger in one sex. The urge to inflict harm is literally a primitive one, connected with our emergence from the Animal Kingdom. It was the inevitable outcome of our competition for territory, for reproductive dominance, for self-preservation.

But it almost never meant death. Violence was the painful, pre-sentient, pre-verbal message to go find another valley to live in, or another mate to live with – or at least to submit to someone else's rules about where and with whom to live. Killing was rarely necessary to make the point. And still is for most non-sentient species.

Ironic that this same non-lethal violence, combined with our technological "progress," has now turned us into killers. It has also brought mass destruction of property and endless arms races, not to mention the stealing of precious resources from other, peaceful uses.

As citizens of the universe, our progress depends on fighting *this legacy,* not each other. Fortunately, the more we recognize our weakness, the more chance we'll have.

Within me are echoes of the distant past. To go on living in the present, I must transcend the past by affirming the person I wish to become in the future.

11.12

Our job is not to police the galaxy.

— COMMANDER RIKER : LOUD AS A WHISPER : 42477.2

The policies of governments begin with individuals. People tend to transfer what they believe in privately, what works in their own personal lives, to the public domain.

It's possible, therefore, to read Riker's words not so much as a statement about Federation policy as a warning to each of us personally.

Because all too often we *do* take on the role of policeman. We monitor what others are doing, who their friends are. We make judgments. And sometimes we intervene by offering advice, or helping to solve problems – or even by forcing our beliefs and lifestyle on others.

Such "help" is rarely appreciated, and may even create an atmosphere of resentment or rebellion. Especially if it's ongoing. Or if it stifles others' freedom to make mistakes, to develop their capacity to think for themselves.

Our "job" is to police our *own* lives. In fact, when we find ourselves meddling in other peoples' lives, it's probably because we haven't been policing our own properly. Often, the only way our subconscious can show us the flaws we still need to fix in ourselves is through others.

So let's concentrate on cleaning up our own house first. Then, by our example, we'll have far more influence on others than we'd ever have by flashing a badge.

I am responsible for prescribing, and living up to, my own standards. My success in that effort is what translates into a positive influence on others.

11.13

When your only reality is an illusion, then illusion is a reality.

— THE CLOWN : THE THAW : Stardate Not Given

It's remarkable how "reality" is defined by our earliest experiences. People who grow up in poverty, fear or conflict think these conditions are normal. Space travelers who have crashed on uncharted planets, who have been forced to start over without the benefits of their previous technology, have raised new generations that seem to accommodate themselves to hardship as if this is what life is about. Having experienced nothing else, that is their reality. It's also an illusion.

The truth is, all of our personal experiences of what's normal, or routine, or "what life is all about," are only a tiny bandwidth in an incomprehensibly larger spectrum.

Which is why we cannot depend on our experiences alone. However comfortable we may be with our local version of reality, we must look beyond that limited horizon to have any sense of what the greater Reality is. We must talk to other people, read books about others' lives — past and present, around the globe, across the galaxy.

The immediate benefit is not simply an expansion of our reality, but expanded possibilities, more options, a deeper, broader, more interconnected sense of Self.

And inevitably, one by one, our illusions will disappear.

I am overcoming my illusions. Each week through the end of this year I will give myself at least one new experience. And I will ask someone from a different culture about their experiences.

11.14

I have a human half you see as well as an alien half... constantly at war with each other. I survive it because my intelligence wins out, makes them live together.

— SPOCK : THE ENEMY WITHIN : 1672.1

Inner conflict is hardly a new subject on these pages. Or in our personal lives. All of us feel the occasional warring of factions within us — between our intellect and our emotions, for example, or between desire and duty.

Another subject that's not exactly new is the need for some kind of mediating force to make our conflicting factions "live together." For Spock, the mediator was his intelligence. For many of us, however, that isn't enough... unless, perhaps, we capitalize the word.

Because "Intelligence" happens to be another name for the greater power that *is* enough — to accomplish anything.

It is not necessary to worship that Intelligence the way our ancestors carried on with their gods. We have only to recognize that the Power sustaining the universe also sustains *us*. The Law which balances a star's explosive interior with its own gravitational collapse — and in the process creates a stable source of light — can also balance the thoughts and feelings that sometimes explode inside us.

Our inner conflict is actually a sign of this Intelligence. We can be sure its ultimate purpose is to create Light.

The Intelligence reflected in the universe is also at work within me. Through my inner conflict I become aware of the lessons it is trying to teach me.

11.15

Sometimes the bad memories can be the most intense of all.

— ENGINEER LA FORGE : VIOLATIONS : 45429.3

If we admit that Geordi's observation is true, *why* is it true? Why should unpleasant memories be stronger?

First, let's be clear about what *isn't* the correct explanation: The intensity of bad memories is not meant as punishment. It is not designed to induce guilt. And its purpose is not to make us feel bad about ourselves, or "unworthy" to feel joy and fulfillment.

The fact is, in the language of emotion, intensity is almost always a function of *importance*.

If we feel especially bad about something we did, our subconscious is telling us that there is an important lesson to be gained from the experience; and chances are we haven't learned it yet. If we are unusually disturbed by a past event – sometimes even if we weren't directly involved – our body/mind is sending us a signal that there is special significance in that event for us; and we still need to come to grips with some issue it has raised.

Our memories have a practical function, of course. But our feelings about them are meant to teach us, to make us wiser, and ultimately to bring us into a more productive relationship with other people and the universe.

Even my bad memories are for my own good. I will reflect on those that hurt most, and with the help of others learn the lessons hiding within them.

11.16

I saw the network... an entire universe of possibilities I never dreamed existed. It's unspeakably beautiful.

— SCIENCE OFFICER STAMETS : CHOOSE YOUR PAIN: Stardate 1408.7

The first thing to understand about this wonder-struck statement is that it represents Stamets' feelings while under the influence of mycelium. The second is that it is almost word-for-word how psychadelic adventurers from Earth's past described their "trips" on mescaline or LSD. The third thing to realize is that religious mystics all across the galaxy have spoken in similar fashion about their own visions while lost in the reveries they generated by prolonged prayer and fasting.

And it's true: The mind is capable of opening itself to deeper dimensions, when chemically or physically induced, that reveal the elegant inter-connectedness of matter and energy, of time and space, of possibility and actuality, in ways words can only inadequately express. The potential problem with these "unspeakably beautiful" visions isn't that they're delusional, or that they paint an inaccurate picture of fundamental reality. Rather, it's what happens to the person involved. It's the mental cost exacted on those who undergo the experience, and on others affected by them.

In the "Hero's Journey" outlined by author Joseph Campbell, or in the Buddhist ascetic's quest for Nirvana, the ultimate goal was never to reach some deeper dimension only to stay there. It was to find the unique treasures the "otherworld" hides from our normal consciousness, and then bring them back to *this* dimension, returning with new knowledge, new answers and insights to meet the challenges the rest of us face in our daily lives. *That's* what's unspeakably beautiful.

I do not seek visions or mystical experiences so much as a beautiful heart filled with compassion, and a commitment to be of service to others.

11.17

Adopting a siege mentality is ultimately self-defeating.

— LT. COMMANDER WORF : TO THE DEATH : 49904.2

Fortify the ramparts! Shut the gates! Batten down the hatches! Here they come again!

According to "siege mentality," life is a defensive action. It's us against everybody else. It's the sign on our perimeter fence to *KEEP OUT!* And even if it's understandable, it's bad strategy.

For one thing, building a fence practically invites trespassers. Not that jumping someone's fence is our "right." It's just that people are naturally curious… What are we hiding? Besides, people are social animals; we expect others to interact with us, not build walls of separation and isolation.

Furthermore, the walls people build to keep others out ultimately change those who build them – usually for the worse. Either they become hardened to the rest of the world ("I've got mine, now go get your own"); or they grow increasingly paranoid ("Everyone's trying to take away what I have"). Fortresses breed fear, not a sense of safety.

The best "defense," it turns out, is to get out in the world – to show others who we are, what we believe in, and how we've earned what we have; to show that we are in the world *for* something, not to stand against it.

And the best thing is, The Universe stands behind *us* when we do that. Which changes us – for the better.

My best protection is to simply be Who I Am, without fear, and with respect for Who Others Are.

11.18

You choose your enemies, you choose your friends. But family… that's in the stars.

— CHIEF O'BRIEN : THE ICARUS FACTOR : 42686.4

In one sense, O'Brien's claim seems to contradict other advice you'll find in this Manual. Haven't we implied that each of us defines "family" for ourselves? Isn't our support network, and the spiritual tradition we align ourselves with – which we choose – our family too?

Of course. But biology is still at our core. Every species has its "blood relations." Even with genetic engineering, we cannot change our heritage.

Nor should we try. The Universe does not toss us into biological units haphazardly. There is meaning and reason for this specific mother and father, that brother or sister, this uncle and that grandmother. Or sometimes the lack of them. For O'Brien, "in the stars" is shorthand for acknowledging just how important these relationships are – not merely in terms of our physical existence, but for our spiritual growth.

At some point in our lives, it's not uncommon to wish we could replace this biological unit with a different one. But these most intimate relationships, as difficult, as confrontational – and yes, even abusive – as they may sometimes be, are those we are destined to learn the most from.

By facing both their pain and their joys, we take on a heritage beyond biology, as deep as boundless Spirit.

I accept the family locked into my chromosomes. I unlock my spiritual self by learning the lessons only these relationships can teach me.

11.19

For humans, touch can connect you to an object in a very personal way... Makes it seem more real.

— CAPTAIN PICARD : FIRST CONTACT : 50893.5

And it's not just "objects" that become more real. It's other living beings, other people.

Just before the turn of the Millennium, many people on Earth began to rediscover the language of touch. Psychologists proved that babies who weren't cuddled and stroked soon became withdrawn – and sometimes died. People affixed "bumper stickers" to their personal transports promoting the frequent hugging of one's children. Or even trees.

The purpose was not only to communicate affection, but to absorb the "reality" of others at the most primitive level. The fact that we can't always translate those messages into words makes them no less meaningful.

Not that just anybody can send such a message, any time they wish. Touch, without permission, can be a violation of one's personal boundaries. In some cases, it's sexual harassment. Many of us still have trouble recognizing where those boundaries are, or what constitutes "permission."

But what's worse is when we fail to see when touch is not only permitted, but desperately needed. For example, in cases where young people feel so unloved or unnoticed that violence is the only way they can attract attention. Or when a gentle hand on the shoulder can say far more than words ever could.

Touch is our first language. It's time we learned it.

I will learn the vocabulary of touch the same way I learned the language I speak: By using it. But I must also honor the "silence" others may prefer.

11.20

This is one puppet who doesn't like her strings pulled.

— MAJOR KIRA : VISIONARY : Stardate Not Given

In a sense we are all puppets. We have so-called "heartstrings" that others can tug on to arouse our sympathies. We also have "hot buttons" – those especially sensitive places in our psyches that can trigger anger or jealousy or lust, or cause us to react in other predictable ways.

But most of us don't *like* having our strings pulled or our buttons pushed. We don't appreciate the feeling that we're being "manipulated" by someone else. Worse, we don't like the idea that we *can* be manipulated in the first place, that someone could actually bypass our rational minds and play our emotions like a musical instrument.

Which is why some of us flatly deny it. Trouble is, that only makes us more vulnerable to manipulation. By assuming that no one else can control us, we close our eyes to defenses that might prevent us from being controlled. We also fail to accept an important part of who we are.

Ironically, not liking our strings pulled is a crucial step toward transcending our "puppethood." At least we're aware of it. Only then can we learn how to counteract it, or learn how to pull our own strings in pursuit of our goals.

We might also learn when The Universe is pulling, and when to just relax and enjoy the dance.

The fact that I can sometimes be manipulated is no dishonor. I am learning what my "strings" are, and how to use that knowledge to my own advantage.

11.21

Are you doing the best thing... or are you doing what's best for you?

— DR. CRUSHER : BLOODLINES : 47829.1

It's always a fair question. At face value we're being asked whether our actions are mostly selfish, or if we're taking others' needs into account. If we *are,* are we considering the effects of our actions only on those in our own social circle? Or could there be consequences for the wider community? Or on people we may not even know?

The irony here is that "the best thing" and what's "best for you" are ultimately the same. We only presume there's a difference because our view is so narrow, or only concerned with the short term. If we would consider *all* the people we touch, if we could account for the long-term ramifications, we'd see how our own interests are virtually inseparable from the best interests of all.

The problem is, we can't do that. We're not omnipotent. Nor do we always have the time to analyze these things beforehand. Besides, taking care of our own small patch of the universe really *is* our primary responsibility.

But we can draw on other people's advice whenever it's practical. We can also "check in" with The Universe through regular meditation and other spiritual exercises.

Because it's along this Path where selfish and self*less* merge... where what's best for you is simply what's best.

I will work toward the goal of making what's "best for me" what's best for those around me. Starting with family and friends, I will continually widen my circle.

11.22

We don't have to like each other to work well together.

— COMMANDER RIKER : THE BEST OF BOTH WORLDS, PART II : 44001.4

Most of us do not work – or live – in isolation. In the course of our daily routines we will interact with dozens of other people. And chances are, at least a few of these people will reflect personal qualities we don't like.

Like... Such a misnomer. Because to "like" someone usually means to *be like* them, to recognize something you have in common. And yet much of what we see in others are the very qualities we like the least in ourselves. So we often end up disliking those who are most like us, and liking those whom we are not like (but would like to be like).

All of which is simply to point out how fickle our "likes" are, how unreliable they are as guides to interpersonal relationships. Some of our planet's greatest advances, after all, have come from partnerships between people who haven't particularly liked one another. Or worse.

But Riker's advice isn't ultimately about learning to work with people even if we don't like them. It's about learning not to make that superficial assessment in the first place. It's about giving them a chance. It's about giving ourselves a chance to seek out the goodness in others that makes us "like" them, and allowing others to discover the goodness to "like" in us.

I will think of at least one trait I have in common with each person I encounter today. I will look for the things in my co-workers that make us alike.

11.23

Why is any object we don't understand always called a "thing"?

— DR. McCOY : STAR TREK/TMP : 7412.6

Here's the harsh truth right up front: The words we use to "name" an object often convey as much about *us* as the object itself.

Other people, for instance. Whole races have been reduced to their skin colors or most prominent features. Members of a particular sex are labeled by a single "function" or physical characteristic rather than by their individual qualities or proper names. This is done (supposedly) because we don't yet know their qualities or names. Unfortunately, by sticking people into these simplistic boxes, we can prevent ourselves from ever knowing them as unique individuals. They remain mere objects to us; and *we* thereby remain simplistic and insensitive.

And if we can turn people into objects, how much less consideration do we give the natural world! Animals, plants, land – whole planets – become "things" to possess and exploit. Which defines us as tyrants and exploiters.

"Thing" is a perfectly good word, a useful word. It points. It acknowledges existence. It "stands for" objects until we get to know them better. But in doing so it points to our ignorance. It reminds us that we don't yet understand.

Ideally, it reminds us to *keep learning* until we do.

My words describe me as much as the objects they represent. I will listen for what they teach me about myself, and about what I have yet to learn.

11.24

I never fully appreciated how difficult and how rewarding it is to be human.

— COUNSELOR TROI : THE LOSS : 44356.9

Just to be in the game is an honor. To be born into this world, to be alive and conscious, is a reward in itself.

Not that life doesn't send us difficulties that can make us wonder if being alive is all that nifty. Worse, while we're having all those difficulties we end up fantasizing about how things might have been. And far from comforting us, our dreams of a better life only increase our pain. Our ability to imagine heaven makes our current problems seem all the more like hell.

But let's try imagining this: Let's say we were given a choice before entering this world. We could have been incarnated as a happy, contented piglet – or the weary, get-up-before-dawn farmer who keeps it fed. One has a secure, mud-filled pen and all the corn cobs he can eat. The other has twelve-hour workdays… and the stars at night.

In a sense, we've already made the choice. And we make it again at each day's dawning. We trade an unconscious, unknowing, unmerited contentment for the conscious fulfillment we must earn by overcoming countless obstacles and character defects.

To "be human" is to finally appreciate that having to earn it is the highest reward.

I am grateful for the challenges in my life. I will reward myself for overcoming them. The Universe will reward me for the stronger person I become.

11.25

I suggest that good spirits might make an effective weapon.

— SPOCK : DAY OF THE DOVE : Stardate Not Given

When nothing else works, when one of life's sticky problems can't seem to get unstuck, when nothing else can stop the coming storm, we still have one weapon: Our attitude. Our ability to face the storm clouds… and laugh.

It would be valuable enough if keeping a positive attitude were simply a technique for avoiding depression – a mental gimmick for minimizing the doom and gloom, for looking ahead to a time when fortune might smile on us again. After all, in the normal cycle of things, bad times do eventually give way to good. A positive attitude at least preserves us for that brighter future.

But Spock is being even bolder. He's reminding us that good spirits can effectively change reality *now.*

For one thing, the very cells of our bodies become infused with increased vitality. And because our revitalized bodies are connected to the world, external changes are now possible.

What's more, in the network of consciousness, a display of positive attitude can evoke a sympathetic reaction in other people. The resulting communal positivity not only creates an atmosphere for finding solutions where none existed before, but cancels out negative karma like the effect of two opposing wave forms.

If I can't control external events, I can control my attitude about them. I give up nothing by trying. I take back my life if I succeed.

11.26

What is the point of doing battle if you cannot enjoy the fruits of your victory?

— LT. COMMANDER WORF : FOR THE CAUSE : Stardate Not Given

According to many traditions, "spiritual maturity" is demonstrated by an increasing ability to postpone the rewards for one's efforts for longer and longer periods of time. Like the promise of "heaven," it should be enough to know that we are working steadily toward some goal, and that we'll receive the benefits someday.

And there's some truth to this. But the fruits of victory can't be delayed indefinitely. We are not only spiritual beings; our material dimension deserves respect. And like the Captain who knows the limitations of his crew, we must give our bodies their due – if only to reinforce positive effort and inspire ourselves to re-enter the battle.

The eventual goal may be to transcend our bodies. In the meantime, however, we must not pass up opportunities to "stand down" from the struggle, to consolidate recent gains and live in their afterglow; and thereby send our psyche the life-affirming message that The Path may be rocky and dangerous but the views are worth every step.

And something happens: As we become seasoned soldiers of the spirit, we find ourselves growing less and less dependent on the fruits of victory, and enjoying the struggle more and more for its own sake.

My body/mind is a gift from The Universe. I will honor its needs. I welcome new opportunities to earn the rewards that encourage my progress.

11.27

Enjoy these times... it's the time of your life that'll never come again. When it's gone... it's gone.

— CHIEF ENGINEER SCOTT : RELICS : 46125.3

If only we could learn the lesson before it's too late: How precious are our lives… and how fleeting is time!

The fact that we have physical lives makes the lesson all the more urgent. We are born, we die; and between those two events is a finite period during which we gain experience and try to live out whatever purpose we discover for ourselves. We may not know how long that period is. We only know it's limited. Our eventual death is simply the universe's reminder to pay attention.

Which is exactly what Scotty is trying to point out. The times we live in, the people we interact with, the very bodies through which we experience our lives – all of these are changing constantly. The precise combination of factors that are present in this moment will never come together again anywhere in the universe.

We are therefore advised to "enjoy" these times. Not so much in the sense of "having fun," but in an attitude of being joyful; of seeing each moment as the unique treasure it is, and being glad for it. Of being open to each new once-in-a-lifetime opportunity for learning… and in giving thanks no matter what its lesson.

Time, like energy, can be transformed into matter. By using and appreciating the time I am given, time no longer "passes." It becomes part of me.

11.28

We all work for our supper. You'll be surprised how much sweeter it tastes when you do.

— ALIXUS : PARADISE : 47573.1

We take so much for granted. We accept the ease and comfort our technology gives us with hardly a second thought.

And for the most part this is good. By not having to deal with the physical challenges our ancestors faced, we are free to concentrate on more "spiritual" matters – like self-improvement, creative expression, the Quest for Truth.

But there is a price. We can become too lazy, too dependent. We can forget how to "fend for ourselves" if our technology were ever taken away. We can lose touch with the most basic requirements of our own survival.

We can also lose touch with the "simple pleasures" of living. Like the satisfaction of growing the very food we put on our table. Or the pride that comes from helping to build the machines we use, or the homes we inhabit. Or the delight in creating something – out of words, or clay, or sound – for our own personal enjoyment.

Often, our recurring feelings of being "unfulfilled" are simply the result of having too few opportunities to practice self-reliance, to do things _for ourselves_. To "work for our supper."

Fortunately, it's a situation that's easily remedied.

I will endeavor to link what I do with the benefits I enjoy. I will find projects or hobbies that allow me to "taste" the fruits of my own labor.

11.29

Rudeness will get you nowhere.

— QUARK : FOR THE CAUSE : Stardate Not Given

A lesson in social graces… from *Quark?*

Why not? Even the ever-scheming Quark has standards for "appropriate behavior," though they're often at odds with other cultures. One area of agreement, however, is that public interactions are not the proper context for venting one's private frustrations.

Yet that is frequently just what we do. We bring our unresolved personal issues from one situation into the next. Angry over our jobs or relationships or unmet goals, we end up "taking it out" on others – including people we don't even know. Make that *especially* people we don't even know.

Those who work in the public sector, like Quark, encounter this phenomenon daily. From bartenders to sales clerks, the "anonymous" people we meet in stores and other public places make easy targets for our unhappiness. Since we have no relationship to lose, we somehow feel under no obligation to treat them with courtesy. But they, of course, are required to treat *us* with courtesy or else we report them to their superiors (which restores that sense of "power" we may have lost in some previous situation).

It's not just that these people deserve better from us. It's that practicing courtesy – *especially* on people we don't even know – is a good indicator of our spiritual growth.

The person most affected by my rudeness – or my kindness – is me. My first reaction to frustration is to be even more respectful and courteous to others.

11.30

May the sun and moon watch your comings and going, in the endless nights and days that are before you.

— CADET TILLY : CHOOSE YOUR PAIN : Stardate 1408.7

What are commonly known as "blessings" are indigenous to every society our planetary explorations have encountered, from the most primitive to the most advanced. And if the latter should come as a shock, it's only because many of us have lost touch with what they are meant to express.

Clearly, they're not expressions of scientific fact. The sun and moon, in this particular blessing, cannot possibly "watch" our daily activities, even if our ancestors imagined they could. So when we repeat them, we're acknowledging, first of all, our historic connection to a people who *did* believe this, while also affirming that our own progress was a direct outcome of their pre-scientific efforts to understand what was central to their lives, to identify what was constant amidst relentless change.

We're also affirming, as they did, that whatever this "constant" might be, it applies equally to everyone and everything, that it is a beneficial influence, a source of illumination rather than darkness; and that wishing it upon others is not only good for them, but good for us.

We might analyze the specifics of Tilly's blessing for other meanings, too: That the sun and moon symbolize male and female, the *yin-yang* whose seeming opposites are really expressions of The One; that the phrase "endless nights and days" recalls the promise of immortality, or at least of ongoing opportunities for us to "see the light," even when we stubbornly refuse to open our eyes.

All of which is hardly primitive. In fact, it's our best hope for a brighter future.

I affirm the goodness the Universe bestows on me, and on others through me.

CORRESPONDING TO THE MONTH OF

December

12.01

Make it so.

— CAPTAIN PICARD : ENCOUNTER AT FARPOINT : 41153.7

In Earth's venerable story of Genesis, the Creator says, "Let there be light." And lo, there *was* light. The rest of the universe was similarly created by divine command, from planets to plants, from humus to human beings. Words never had such power.

But words themselves don't actually do the work of creation. Even God needed a mechanism to carry out his orders. "Let there be…" is only a poetic symbol for that universal Order which must precede the verbal order.

Likewise, Picard's famous command could have no effect without a proper mechanism — in this case his highly-skilled crew, committed to their interdependent roles and to their mission; and the Starship Enterprise, with its arsenal of technology. All of these elements were necessary before "Make it so" could become anything more than wishful rhetoric. But once everything was in place, this "rhetoric" wielded the power of the universe.

That same power lies within us. We too can make our wishes "so" — but only if we have the proper mechanism in place. By acknowledging and aligning ourselves with the universal Order, by affirming our roles in the Interdependent Web of Life, by becoming conscious of the mission that infuses each of us with a unique purpose — only then do our words (and even our thoughts) become instruments of creation.

As I increasingly align my will with that of The Universe, I continue to strengthen my power to "Make it so."

12.02

That is the exploration that awaits you: Not mapping stars and studying nebulae, but charting the unknown possibilities of existence.

— Q : ALL GOOD THINGS : 47988.1

No matter how far we may go on our travels among the galaxies, we are never more than a heartbeat from the primary object of our explorations: *Us.*

Q knew what we only suspected. Stars, nebulae, and alien life-forms were never really the point. Bringing back new information about the cosmos, or new technology and artifacts from other civilizations — even forming new alliances — are only by-products of The Real Adventure.

Because in pushing the boundaries of the known universe, we are actually expanding the limits of our own minds. In journeying through space and time, we are really charting the hidden dimensions within us. By mapping stars and the routes between them, we are not only connecting with one another but to Existence itself.

Many of us remain blissfully unaware that our explorations "out there" are only symbols for this Inner Voyage. And maybe that's as it should be, because the adventure can also be enjoyed for its own sake. But someday, when we look back, we'll see that we haven't so much been on a journey through the universe, as a quest into our*selves.*

Today offers a new opportunity to explore my self. With each new task I redefine Who I Am. With every new challenge I transform my life for the better.

12.03

The lure of perfection is powerful.

Working to get things "just right" can be a healthy goal. Whether it's a new project or a new relationship, or perhaps a personal skill we'd like to develop – striving for perfection can be a useful mantra to focus our attention.

But if we expect to actually achieve it, perfection begins to enslave us. The temptation to keep tinkering until we reach some point where further improvement is impossible can distract us from other needs. We end up losing perspective – *and* the time to pursue other projects and relationships that provide balance. Perfection becomes a merciless taskmaster that can never call the task complete, if only because we can never know when something is perfect.

Aye, there's the rub. "Perfection" has no objective, universally-accepted definition. It can therefore never be achieved.

The word is useful when it describes a direction, not a destination. Its "lure" is productive when it encourages us to keep growing, yet damaging when it refuses to be satisfied.

Ultimately, it is we who must decide when we're satisfied. Part of growing, in fact, is learning how to recognize when enough is enough… when it's time to switch gears, work on something else, or simply take a break and enjoy the unique, transitory set of imperfections that is us, now.

I seek not perfection, but the wisdom to know when I've done enough. I accept the flaws that remain, as long as I am making progress.

12.04

For your information, I don't appreciate being deactivated in the middle of a sentence.

Neither do any of us. Trouble is, it happens all the time. Especially to the people we're talking to. Or *at*.

Because we often forget that the art of conversation is not so much about talking; it's about listening. And yet we're often so intent on showing off our own brilliance that we can hardly wait for the next opportunity to speak. We're so starved for attention that when someone tells a tale of sorrow or success, we can't help but go one better.

Taking care not to "deactivate" our partners in conversation, however, is a sign that we value and respect their experience – and we don't *over*-value our own. When we listen attentively to what they have to say, we affirm their worth, while acknowledging the divinity within them.

We also give that divinity a chance to reveal what may be important for us at that moment. Because every conversation holds the possibility for discovering something new, something The Universe wants us to know. And the answers to our questions – or prayers – are more likely to come through another person than "divine revelation."

If we would only *let* them come… by being open to the Spirit that moves in and through the sentences we exchange.

Today I will practice the art of listening. I will say little, prompting others to say more. By treating their words as gifts, I discover the treasures within them.

12.05

We've seen development at different rates on different planets.

— LIEUTENANT UHURA : A PRIVATE LITTLE WAR : 4211.4

A well-documented pattern of evolution can be seen throughout the galaxy: Given the proper conditions, autonomous, sentient life inevitably emerges from more primitive life forms, along with a natural inter-dependence among members of that species. This natural "community" is later overshadowed by individualism and "privatism," which are eventually brought into a more productive balance between individual and society.

So the course is virtually locked in. But the rates of progress can vary greatly. Or grind to a halt on occasion. In fact, many planetary cultures become so mired in this era of individualism – the "I/Me/Mine" stage – that one final, cathartic orgy of selfishness is the only way to break through it.

Unfortunately, if weapons of mass destruction are part of the mix, the results can be disastrous. A few planetary races have had to virtually start over after such a destructive catharsis. And the survivors don't always learn their lesson.

So it is in our personal lives. Our ultimate destinations are given. But our rates vary. Side-trips can seem endless. We can become stuck in various stages, sometimes breaking out of our patterns only at great cost – to others as well as ourselves. But if we become conscious of our own development, our journeys seem to go a bit smoother.

We might even learn our lessons "once and for all."

I celebrate the Voyage I've been on, despite its turns and stops, because I know the ultimate destination.

12.06

Our feelings are what make us all human.

— COMMANDER RIKER : THE ICARUS FACTOR : 42686.4

Naturally, the Commander doesn't mean "human" in the sense of a particular species from Earth. He's talking about the one personal quality shared by living, sentient beings everywhere: The ability to *feel.*

But it's more than a mere sensitivity to physical stimuli. All life forms can sense and respond to the external environment. "Feelings" refers to an interior sensitivity. And what's being felt is one's own state of mind.

The trouble is, many of us are so sensitive to this inner feedback that we've come to fear it – often to the point of more or less disconnecting ourselves from it. Ironically, the very people who appear to show no feelings are sometimes the ones who feel most deeply. Or at least they could in the past – before some emotional trauma hurt them so badly that their subconscious mind created a shield to prevent any further assaults.

Yet that reaction, too, is "human." So we must not only be aware of our own tendency to "raise shields," we must accept that others may also be cut off from their own feelings. In that realization, we begin to "humanize" them, which eventually leads to forgiving them. Which in turn re-humanizes *us,* and reminds us to forgive ourselves.

If my own feelings can make me defensive, so it must be with others. Today I will lower my "shields," so that someone else will feel safe in lowering theirs.

12.07

Just give up...? I don't think so!

— DR. BASHIR : DISTANT VOICES : Stardate Not Given

There's no better formula for success: In striving to achieve our goals, we should never give up. In following our dreams, we mustn't give up. In seeking to transform ourselves, we simply *cannot* give up.

The age-old wisdom about success consisting of one part inspiration and 99 parts *per*spiration is true. It's not intellectual brilliance that ultimately wins out. It's not our good looks. It's not our talent or money or "who we know" that is most likely to bring success.

It's our willingness to keep trying, to stay in the game, to embrace the ongoing struggle. Even more important is the realization that achieving our goals and dreams isn't the top priority anyway. All of these factors are just excuses to continue refining our character – to make us more committed, more courageous individuals; to force us to look within ourselves, to connect with the deeper resources each of us has, but we pretend we can get along without.

Few of us will make these life-enriching connections unless we are confronted by some extraordinary threat or challenge. Ironically, it is when we feel defeated by these events, when we are tempted to "just give up," that we are most able to discover and release our true power.

Be still. Try to feel it, to *live* it. Don't give up until you do.

I may not achieve all my goals and dreams. But I will achieve something even greater by continuing to make the effort despite the challenges... by not giving up.

12.08

I admire gall!

— LIEUTENANT WORF : THE SURVIVORS : 43152.4

The omnipedia on the Ship's Computer defines "gall" as "Rudeness or impudence; asserting oneself in a way that ignores authority, custom or convention."

Which is why gall is usually considered a negative personal trait in "polite society." But it can be decidedly positive in situations where taking risks is necessary to the achievement of one's goals. Especially spiritual ones.

Because among the traits that usually accompany gall is a healthy dose of confidence (bordering on over-confidence), as well as a readiness to take a stand for what one believes – even when doing so would invite danger. Klingons call this kind of brazen self-assertion *nuQ'nuH,* while on Earth it's known as "chutzpah."

We should all be so brazen. And the fact is, we *can* be. After all, when it comes to asserting ourselves for what we believe, we never face the danger alone. Inspired by our example, others will join us. And since the energies of the universe are drawn to efforts that complement its own redemptive purposes, we'll have all the support we need.

Try this exercise for developing your own capacity for "gall": Without putting anyone else at risk, do something that flies in the face of convention, or goes against "the odds." Savor what it feels like. Notice how you survive... win or lose. Then do it again. Because someday it will matter.

I am confident. The Universe is with me. I take risks for what I believe in, and for my spiritual growth.

12.09

We change. We have to. Or we spend the rest of our lives fighting the same battles.

— CAPTAIN KIRK : STAR TREK BEYOND : CIRCA 2263.3

One of Earth's most renowned geniuses defined "insanity" as follows: To repeat an action that has consistently resulted in a certain outcome in the past, and expect it to produce a different outcome in the future.

Sadly enough, many of us make the same mistakes again and again, expecting things to turn out better this time around, even though we've done nothing to change our behavior. Like reacting to criticism with the same explosive anger. Or continuing to "hang out" with the same crowd of people who invariably bring out the worst in us. Or falling into the same old habits and lifestyles that got us into trouble the last time, and the time before that.

But Kirk's view here isn't as pessimistic as it might first sound. Because if we _do_ find ourselves fighting the same battles all over again, we can assume The Universe is patiently sending us the same crucial message — that not only do we need to change our behavior, here's yet another opportunity to _do_ it, to test a new approach, to get past the obstacle still blocking our path, to finally learn an important lesson or life skill without which we will never achieve our spiritual destiny.

And sometimes the lesson is simply that there's no shame in admitting we need a new attitude, new tactics, new spiritual tools, a new faith. And not only can't we do it by ourselves, we _shouldn't_.

I admit the insanity of thinking that I can keep doing what I've always done and expect things to change. I will work with others to make the improvements I desire in my life, while helping them with theirs.

12.10

Patience is a lost virtue to most. To me, an ally.

— CONSTABLE ODO : NECESSARY EVIL : 47282.5

In a world of warp-drives and personal transporters, time is perceived differently. The rhythms of biology are no longer our primary reference. Our "natural" sense of time is redefined by the increasing speed of our artifical devices. Patience is a lost virtue if only because our interactions with technology rarely require it!

But our _personal_ interactions are another matter. Here, biology is still the defining factor. "Real time" must be readjusted for the slower pace of thinking and feeling; for the deliberate nurturing of relationships; and for the subtle, cumulative effects that combine to change our lives. One spiritual tradition symbolizes this "living" process in the sacred image of the lotus flower, unfolding itself petal by petal, until it is finally revealed in all its glory.

Patience is the quiet acceptance of the fact that some things must be allowed, like the lotus, to unfold at their own pace. Love is the classic example. Likewise developing a spiritual discipline, overcoming our fears, or finding our life's purpose. These things must "unfold." Rushing them can only disrupt or prevent their flowering.

In the process, it's not really patience that becomes our ally. It's The Universe.

I won't be rushed by the timetable of technology. I will take time to fully absorb the lessons I must learn. My life is unfolding at just the right pace.

12.11

Even the eagle knows when to sleep.

— COMMANDER CHAKOTAY : RESOLUTIONS : 49690.1

It's a common reaction: When at last we demonstrate some measure of mastery over our own lives, we may suddenly feel an even greater need to prove ourselves. When we finally assume command over our personal circumstances — which is what the eagle represents — we also assume the role of "spiritual example" for others.

It's as if we've taken on a new job. We are now "the strong one." We must be the role model. Others begin looking to us for advice, reassurance, inspiration. Having shown a glimmer of our divine spark, it has now become our responsibility to lead the way. If not save the world.

Part of this messianic attitude comes from the understandable desire to confirm that we really *have* seen The Light, that our newly acquired spiritual gifts are for real and not some fluke. The problem is, we are still fallible, vulnerable, imperfect creatures. We can't be round-the-clock role models. That's far too much pressure.

Besides which we still have our own personal needs… for advice and reassurance; for room to experiment, to make mistakes without feeling like we're causing others to stumble. And for simply being alone now and then.

Part of spiritual mastery is knowing when to put our overblown self-image to bed and just be ourselves.

No matter how spiritually "adept" I become, I am still the same person. Though I may soar like the eagle, I share the same basic needs as everyone else.

12.12

It's the differences that have made us strong.

— CAPTAIN PICARD : UP THE LONG LADDER : 42823.2

At its best, the Federation has been a grand experiment in learning to live and work together productively — despite a stunning variety of races and cultures. In stark contrast are the nations, past and present, where "ethnic purity" is the ideal. Or where diverse cultures have tolerated one another only because of an enforced "peace."

Not that the Federation's experiment has been altogether peaceful either. Living with differences requires work. Communities must always guard against the kinds of acts that incite division. Individuals must remind themselves (and each other) how much richer the social fabric is when the whole spectrum of colors is woven in.

A community's strength depends on differences, not sameness. What one person can't do, another can. As in the practice of teamwork, the experience and talents of each individual is multiplied by every other.

This principle is valid at every level, right down to our own personal lives. Because within each of us is a similar diversity of roles and responsibilities, needs and wants, strengths and weaknesses — some of which may seem to conflict. Our happiness depends not on repressing these inner differences, but accepting and integrating them.

I accept the diversity within me, and the diversity around me. I celebrate the many relationships and inner resources that make me strong.

12.13

All the knowledge of the universe, and all the power that it bestows, is of intrinsic value to everyone.

— JETREL : JETREL : 48832.1

As Captain Picard said more than once, "The search for knowledge is always our primary mission." Here, Jetrel is simply trying to explain why.

Why should knowledge be so all-important? After all, isn't there something to be said for the bliss of ignorance? Who among us wouldn't trade a few I.Q. points – or a few gigabytes of cerebral storage space – for a greater ability to enjoy the simple things in life? Or for a renewed sense of purpose? Or the capacity to love and feel loved? Aren't these qualities far more valuable to us than the mere accumulation of facts?

Jetrel's point is that "knowing" is the key to increasing our enjoyment of the simpler things. Knowledge is what gives us the ability to discover and act out our life's purpose. To know the universe, to know someone else, to know ourselves – as fully as we can – *is* to love and feel loved.

Knowledge doesn't only bestow power. It bestows the power for good. It also bestows the recognition that we must use that power to increase everyone's good.

Everyone's. Because if we hoard our knowledge, if we try to use it for our benefit alone, it quickly loses value. Knowledge, like love, increases its worth only as we share it.

As I make new discoveries about myself and the universe, I will look for opportunities to share my knowledge with others, and for them to share theirs.

12.14

I believe in embracing surprises.

— DR. PHLOX : FUTURE TENSE : CIRCA ECE2153

We should never be surprised at, well… being surprised.

Life isn't 100% predictable. Nor would we want it to be. Our lives melt into bland nothingness when things no longer surprise us. An unvarying routine can literally sap our strength and strangle our minds. We begin to shrivel up spiritually; we start sleepwalking through life.

In contrast, we often feel most awake when we don't know what's going to happen next. The only thing we *do* know is that challenges lie ahead; events we can't begin to imagine are bound to change our lives; and if we don't pay attention, we may learn our next lesson the hard way.

And that's precisely the point: The Universe is still in control, still teaching us its lessons. In fact, surprise can sometimes be the best way to focus our attention on the most important ones. If we weren't caught by surprise now and then, we might go on ignoring some essential piece of information, some new experience necessary for our continued growth. Surprise is the "wake-up call," the knock at the door, the bell ringing for our next class.

If we don't think we're ready yet, we're not giving ourselves enough credit.

I am thankful for the surprises in my life, pleasant or otherwise. I know The Universe is using them to point to the areas in my life that need attention.

12.15

What can I offer except myself?

— COUNSELOR TROI : SKIN OF EVIL : 41601.3

We often think about gifts in terms of "things" – the kinds of things taken off store shelves, or found in the pages of a NetSpace catalog. We might even think such gifts are meaningful. After all, whole industries exist to convince us that we all need these things. And if we are convinced, surely others should be impressed when we give them as gifts, right?

Except that it's not the thing given that makes a gift meaningful. It is, as the old cliché goes, "the thought that counts." What we're giving – assuming we've given it freely – is a message from our hearts. In the guise of a material object, we're sending our feelings of concern or commitment. (Or sometimes, even if we don't realize it, our *lack* of those feelings.) We may be laying the groundwork for a future relationship, or thanking someone for their kindness, or crying out for attention. Which is why we can receive two identical items, right down to the print on the wrapping paper, but the "gift" is different in each case.

That is, if we can see past the object. The fact that we often *don't* only reveals how materialistic we are.

One of Earth's great mystic poets wrote this: "See first that you yourself deserve to be a giver, and an instrument of giving. For in truth, it is Life that gives unto Life."

Becoming a giver is our greatest gift... to ourselves.

As I give of myself, I reflect The Universe giving Itself to me. I will strive daily to keep that cycle going.

12.16

Kind of exciting, isn't it? We just don't know!

— ENSIGN RO LAREN : CONUNDRUM : 45494.2

Most of us prefer to have things "settled." We like our problems solved, our investigations completed, our mysteries explained. It's nice to have a challenging puzzle to work on now and then. But we seem driven to put the pieces together so we can get on with our lives.

And yet there's a sense in which *not* settling everything is good for us. To think we know it all, or that we can answer all the Big Questions, is to presume we're larger than Life, to rank ourselves equal to The Universe. To recognize mystery – in fact to celebrate that Mystery – is to accept our place in the grand scheme of things.

Which isn't so bad. Just imagine how life would be if there were no riddles left to solve, no facets of ourselves left to explore. The "Hell" described by many primitive religions, in which sinners are subjected to eternal torment, is child's play compared to the condition in which the universe holds no more secrets, in which we know everything about everything.

To realize there will always be something we don't yet know – or perhaps can't ever know – keeps us energized, excited... alive!

And humble.

I celebrate the Mystery of existence. I give thanks for the challenges The Universe holds in store for me, no matter how much I've already accomplished.

12.17

I will not destroy life. Not even to save my own.

— DR. McCOY : THE EMPATH : 5121.5

The good doctor wasn't talking about the ebola virus or cancer cells, or the hordes of disease-carrying insects that plagued pre-scientific cultures throughout the Quadrant. McCoy would hardly lose sleep over irradiating an invasion of deadly microbes, or destroying a tumor.

What he was pointing to is the larger Web of Life that calls each of us to maintain the natural balance we've inherited from an Intelligence far beyond our own. It is a balance crucial not only to our physical, but our spiritual, survival. Because preserving or destroying life has effects that can't be measured in flesh and bone. And because we are linked at levels that transcend even consciousness.

Those who acknowledge this deeper "interconnectedness" share a tremendous responsibility. That responsibility is not merely to respect the natural balance in the way we live, but to openly demonstrate its vital importance to others who have yet to learn.

McCoy was following the path of those who have been willing to demonstrate the primacy of Life in the most radical way. And the most eloquent. Even if we're not as courageous, we can still make the same statement.

I will strive to develop a lifestyle that preserves and celebrates the sanctity of all Life, even as it preserves and celebrates my own.

12.18

If you eliminate the impossible, whatever remains, however improbable, must be the truth.

— SPOCK : STAR TREK / PREQUEL : CIRCA 2258

Using the words "however improbable" is certainly one way to phrase it. But Spock could just as easily have said, "...however much we may *dislike it,* must be the truth."

The fact is, we often make our quest for truth far more difficult than it needs to be — first, by having preconceived expectations about what can be considered "true." Or that truth must be logical. Or that it must conform to the laws of probability. It's often assumed that the truth must be "complicated" as well (all the more so in our personal relationships); and if discovering it seems too easy, it can't really be true.

We make our quest even more difficult by closing our eyes to answers we may not like, or whose implications make us feel "uncomfortable." Many of us, for example, prefer to think we're self-sufficient enough to overcome our problems and achieve our personal goals without ever needing anyone else's help, or without resorting to any "higher power" for guidance or reassurance. We'll exhaust every other possibility; we'll seek fulfillment by amassing material things, or pursuing pleasure or power until, finally, the real answer is all that remains.

What the ancient traditions have taught may seem more improbable than ever in this Age of Technology. But the search for Truth, ultimately, is still a spiritual one.

I clear my mind of all expectations. I will look for answers in the improbable and unpalatable as well as the logical and comfortable.

12.19

You'll learn to build for yourselves, think for yourselves. And what you create is yours. It's what we call freedom.

— CAPTAIN KIRK : THE APPLE : 3715.0

The dictionary definition is fine for political debate and historical analysis. But "freedom," in a personal sense, gets down to this: *Taking responsibility for your own life.*

It begins with the commitment not to blame anyone else for the condition you're in. Others may have contributed, yes; but what you do about it now is your decision. Whether you continue to wallow in misery, or face your challenges with a positive attitude, is up to you. To rephrase Kirk's words, what you create from your life is yours.

Of course, the struggle for freedom is not entirely an inner one. There are always external forces of the kind politicians and historians discuss. From a spiritual point of view, however, outward conditions exist precisely to help bring our inner conditions into better focus. Our material situation represents our own spiritual harmony, or lack of it — or perhaps the spiritual obstacles we need to overcome before we can achieve it.

We may not like the thought that the obstacles in our lives reflect something inside us. It's easier to place the blame elsewhere. But that's the slave mentality that keeps us where we are.

The alternative is freedom.

I accept the hard work that freedom requires. I declare my independence from old habits and restrictive beliefs. I am the architect of my own life.

12.20

I've always believed that what you get when you love someone is greater than what you risk.

— COMMANDER CHAKOTAY : TWISTED : Stardate Not Given

Chakotay tells us exactly what's "at risk" in the statement that leads up to this one. "Nothing makes us more vulnerable," he says, "than when we love someone."

Being vulnerable — that's the risk. It's also what scares us. Because to love someone is to give away some measure of control. Since we've allowed another person's welfare to become as important as our own, we're affected not only by what happens to us, but to them.

And it's not just what "happens"; it's what they do or say. Their every act, every word, has double the effect. An affectionate touch can send us into warp drive. An angry glance can jolt us like a phaser set on stun. Is the ride really worth it?

No contest. For one thing, to explore the depths of feeling we're capable of is to know ourselves better. What's more, we develop greater compassion for others, because everyone struggles with these same issues. Even Vulcans.

Vulnerability is also one of the few portals through which we can link with the larger Web of Life. In order to open ourselves to its riches we must lower our shields, let go of our insistence on "control." In order to feel its transforming Love, we must first feel love for another.

How I love others reflects the extent to which I allow The Universe to love me.
To love is to release my Higher Power and access the infinite reservoir within.

12.21

Perhaps someday we'll find that space and time are simpler than the human equation.

— CAPTAIN PICARD : HIDE AND Q : 41590.5

We may be curious about it, but we can survive without knowing precisely how the universe was created. The mysteries of space/time have their fascinations, but the ultimate questions are still about *us:* How the mind works; how to transform anger into love; what it is that makes us gape in wonder at the stars, or cry at a baby's first steps.

Not that quantum mechanics is a snap. The laws governing the world of matter are more intricate than most of us can imagine. But they are "simple" in the sense that they can in principle be known; and once science settles a question about the material world, it's pretty much settled.

Understanding ourselves, on the other hand, is a project that never ends. Spiritual knowledge is always open to revision. In fact, the operative word here isn't really "knowledge" at all. To fall back on the cliché, it's *faith.*

The controversy between knowledge and faith – what some people see as the conflict between science and religion – was rarely about two competing ways of "knowing." What past religious traditions deplored wasn't so much that science was "incompatible" with it, but that science distracts us from the issues we *should* be spending our time on. Like exploring what makes our lives meaningful. Like learning that no fact of science will ever fill the hole in our hearts… for each other.

I know what the most important "equation" is: The science of living with others – and with myself.

12.22

After a time, you may find that "having" is not so pleasing as "wanting." It is not logical, but it is often true.

— SPOCK : AMOK TIME : 3372.7

The Vulcan saying is much like another familiar adage: "Restrain your dreams, lest they become real."

Yet ironically, many of us would rather hold on to our dreams and fantasies than the realities they are designed to mold themselves into. After all, we can still control those dreams. We can eliminate whatever we don't like with a wave of our imagination. The fantasies we have about the perfect relationship or the ideal job are "perfect" and "ideal" only because we tend to gloss over the hard work they will inevitably require. "Wanting" demands little energy. "Having" comes with a whole lot of strings attached.

Then again, "wanting" *does* project energy. And the universe responds by coalescing its forces around our wants, and finally bringing us the realities they represent.

When we find those realities to be unfulfilling (or even self-destructive), The Universe is probably trying to teach us a lesson. It may be asking us to take responsibility for our thoughts as well as our actions. Or it may be encouraging us to look at our motivations for "wanting." Do we really need the things we want? Do we desire some things only because someone tells us we should?

Our dreams are mirrors of ourselves. Look hard. Be careful.

I will dream not so much to have whatever I want, but to want what I already have.

12.23

A structure cannot stand without a foundation.

— LIEUTENANT TUVOK : FLASHBACK : 50126.4

This is the bottom line. This is what we've been searching for – or trying to hang on to, patch up, or improve on: A foundation on which we can structure our lives.

There are parables in almost every tradition about the dangers of building on shifting sands, about our need for something solid to support us. Solid rock, the ideal foundation, symbolizes the things we can depend on, that don't change, that withstand the test of time. It's not surprising that a disciple of one of Earth's great Masters was given the name *Petros* (meaning "rock") when he founded what became the planet's largest spiritual institution.

Not that an institution can serve as a foundation. Our foundation must be made up of the same truths the universe itself is built on. These are the truths that institutions and traditions can only point at, only tell stories about, and thereby suggest how they might apply in our daily lives.

Our task is to get down to the original bedrock, with help from those institutions and traditions, perhaps – or by means of any other resource we may find during our search, not the least of which is that Piece-of-the-Rock *within* each of us.

And the miracle is, once we have that foundation, the structure on top practically builds itself.

I am restructuring my life, day by day, on the principles I am now learning. As I boldly go on my Inner Voyage, I anchor myself on Universal Truth.

12.24

The king who would be man!

— Q : DEJA Q : 43539.1

The sting of Q's remark depends on one's familiarity with a centuries-old story entitled, "The Man Who Would Be King." Among other things, the tale cautions us against our tendency to presume that we know what's best for everyone, and if only the world would do as we decreed, life would be so much better.

Except that we often *don't* have a clue what's best for ourselves, much less anyone else. And if everyone were to do exactly what we told them to, the world would probably be in much worse shape than it is already. In other words, let's not appoint ourselves king, when we're really cut out to be humble peasants.

Of course, it's one thing to be humble, and another to ignore (or even deny) the regal qualities we *do* possess. Too often we accept the role of peasant – "man," in Q's hierarchy – when we are capable of so much more.

One of Earth's most spiritually-gifted teachers, drawing from her celebrated course book, summed it up this way: "Your playing small doesn't serve the world. There's nothing enlightened about shrinking so that other people won't feel insecure around you. We were born to manifest the glory within us… And as we let our own light shine, we unconsciously give other people permission to do the same."

The true king shows others the inner royalty all of us possess.

I accept the awesome power within me to create and transform my own life's circumstances, and thereby demonstrate how others can do the same.

12.25

The channels are open and you are tied in.

— LIEUTENANT UHURA : THE ENTERPRISE INCIDENT : 5027.3

A more profound statement of spiritual Truth has never been uttered. Because the same Source that created the physical universe, that created all life – that created each of *us* – remains connected to us in ways we've only begun to imagine. One of Earth's ancient traditions described that Source as being "closer to us than our jugular vein." Another explains that we are sons and daughters of The Creator, each one embraced like a beloved child in a parent's arms.

Some traditions go even further: We are literally gods-in-the-making, sentient beings whose present form is like the caterpillar to the butterfly, the hatchling to the eagle. We are destined to soar ever higher. We may need help in learning how, but we certainly don't need to ask whether we *may*.

In fact, according to every one of these traditions, we have not only received divine "permission" but all the help we need. Channels to the deepest resources of The Universe are already open, or at least built into the fabric of Reality and awaiting our discovery. Better yet, discovering and using those channels requires no "outside" agency, no additional equipment. We are "tied in" by virtue of our consciousness, empowered by a Spirit that is the very incarnation of universal, creative energy.

With that energy we can transform ourselves and our world. And we begin simply by saying *Yes* to it.

I say "Yes!" to the awesome power within me; "Yes!" to my connection with The Universe and everything in it!

12.26

What the future holds no one knows. But forward we look, and forward we go.

— COMMANDER RIKER : SECOND CHANCES : 46915.2

There is no going back. We can't undo what was done, nor can we live in the past. Why would we want to?

Past glories and golden eras often seem more glorious in retrospect. We lose touch with the daily struggles and concerns that made life as much of a challenge then as it is now. The mistakes we made, the wrong decisions, were not without purpose, not without their lessons. Our present is the diploma we've received for all we've been through in the past. Do we really want to go back to kindergarten and relearn what we already know?

Armed with all that hard-won knowledge, we can now affect and transform our future for the better. But only if we can see it coming. Only if we're looking forward.

It is still full of unknowns, yes. But that's what's so exciting. The future is not predestined. Every decision, every action, shapes it. The quality of our future lives, the character of the person we will become, is in our own hands.

We cannot change the past, but we can redeem it by what we create from this moment on. This is what spiritual traditions envision (by various names) as The Messianic Age. But it is not some far distant future; it is *our* future. And the Messiah isn't coming. He is here now, in us.

I am part of the Cosmic Plan to shape the future. My first responsibility is to my own future, my own life. If I succeed there, the rest will fall into place.

So... five card stud, nothing wild... and the sky's the limit.

— CAPTAIN PICARD : ALL GOOD THINGS : 47988.1

In the Starfleet chronicles that have since come to be known as "The Next Generation," Captain Picard's closing words represent more than the rules for a friendly game of poker. They are, in a sense, the ground rules governing The Game of Life.

For example, we agree to play the cards we're dealt. We can occasionally improve our hand, yes. But there's no switching cards with other players, or getting more cards than anybody else.

Moreover, the cards are exactly what they appear to be. A low card is a low card, not a face card. We cannot wish our deuces into kings, our eights into aces. Nothing is "wild."

Which also means, thankfully, that the rules are not arbitrary or chaotic. As much as the game seems a matter of "luck," over the course of multiple hands it proves quite the opposite. Astute players can develop and use the skills they learn — mental, spiritual, and emotional. And even though one's advantage may be only a few percentage points, those few points make all the difference. So much so that, for all practical purposes, there are no limits on what we can win.

As the Captain said as he finally sat down to play, "I should've done this long ago." The good news is, there's still time for all of us to join in.

I will play the "cards" I am dealt. I am holding a good hand. I'm not playing to beat the Dealer, or my fellow players, but to improve my own skills.

Let's go home.

— CAPTAIN LORCA : INTO THE FOREST I GO: Stardate Circa 1523.5

Whether we're talking about the completion of a project, the achievement of a goal, or simply the end of a hard day at work, "going home" symbolizes our need to regularly take a break, to return to a safe, familiar environment where we can regroup, recharge, and reaffirm what our lives are about.

What makes our home *home,* of course, can be quite different for each of us. It may be an oasis for rest and relaxation, or a quiet sanctuary for reflecting on, and consolidating, the lessons we've just learned. Or maybe it's less a location than an activity — one that's just as demanding as our workaday lives, but it renews and re-energizes us because it brings out talents and traits that otherwise go unused.

What home is *not,* or at least shouldn't be, is a place where we go to disappear, expecting the world to simply leave us alone. It's while we're on our way home, in fact, when life often throws us a curve, and what we thought was an opportunity to take a breather was really The Universe inviting us to take the next step in our spiritual evolution.

Because sometimes the only way to consolidate our lessons is to put them to a test. Not later. Not after we've had some time off. *Now.*

But be assured: The Universe will not put us to the test unless it "believes" we can make the grade. And often the best way to go home is to just keep going.

"Home" is wherever I've found my place in life, whether I'm resting or moving. Being there is not as important as going there.

12.29

I can only hope that the future holds even greater challenges.

— CAPTAIN SISKO : THE ADVERSARY : 48959.5

If we pause to consider the past year, or the past five years, chances are we'll be astounded at how far we've come. We've learned, we've grown. We are changed people. And most of our changes have been for the better.

What's better about us is no accident. Because it's not from having won the Tarkassian lottery. Or because some genie granted our wish. Most of our progress was earned.

And most of *that* came from being challenged.

Despite the fact that it was hard, grueling work at the time, having to overcome obstacles and climb mountains was good for us. Even the times we slipped, even when we hurt ourselves, the lessons were worth the pain.

And even if it's a cliché, hardship *does* build character. Because the stronger our opposition, the more we must learn to be creative, the more we must learn teamwork, the more we must search our souls for inner strength. It is our Adversary that brings out the Hero in us.

Which is why Sisko could plead, in all sincerity, for a future filled with even greater challenges. For only then could he – or can *we* – continue to improve.

Our challenges are gifts to grow on. We are not given more than we, with help from The Universe, can bear.

I will list three things I've learned from my challenges over the past year. I will think about my biggest challenge today, and what I might learn from it.

12.30

Those little points of light out there... the great Unknown beckoning to us.

— DR. BASHIR : THE QUICKENING : Stardate Not Given

Today's space voyagers weren't the first to gaze at the stars and see them as worlds like our own, complete unto themselves, teeming with other living beings, other possibilities.

The writings of ancient Hindus hint at infinite worlds beyond our own, just as that tradition embraces the idea of countless lives beyond this present one – all of which are part of some grand Cosmic Plan designed to refine our souls to the point of perfection.

Points of light or points in our lives – these concepts symbolize what lies ahead for each of us. They represent a future we can only dimly imagine, yet holds such vast possibilities that any direction opens up whole new worlds to explore, and even the faintest glimmer can illumine our path.

To feel the beckoning of those lights and lives is to accept the responsibility of existence. It is to acknowledge that we are ready to continue our Inner Voyage, to experience new things; to learn, to grow… to *become*.

We have done well to come this far, through times of both happiness and sadness, joy and pain, ignorance and self-discovery. All we know for sure is that there will be more of each. And that we will be all the better for it.

I accept the challenge of the rest of my life. The strength to go bravely and boldly into my own future is all around me, and within me.

I envy you... taking these first steps into a new frontier.

— CAPTAIN PICARD : FIRST CONTACT : 50893.5

Admit it: It's tempting to wax nostalgic over the journeys we've already completed. We look back and recall the joy of discovery… our feelings of awe and excitement as we encountered new and unexpected possibilities… the thrill of our personal "firsts," of finally breaking through into new territory that would end up changing our lives forever.

It's tempting because we can easily forget the agony of learning those painful lessons getting there. All we remember is the ecstasy of arrival. Or at least our relief that we're done paying dues.

And that's as it should be. By envying others who are about to embark on their own explorations, we are sending the message that their struggles will strengthen them, too, that their pain will pay off. If our stories tend to gloss over the rough spots, at least we've affirmed that the ride is worth the price of the ticket. Others need to hear that.

But we're missing the point if we assume the message is meant only for *their* benefit. Our envy is also meant to inspire *us,* to re-invigorate our own continuing explorations. Because we haven't exactly reached the end of the line, either. Not while we're still breathing.

What we interpret as "envy" is really our own longing to keep moving. What we feel are the vibrations of our inner voice reminding us that another frontier awaits us.

I will offer encouragement to others who are just starting down the paths I have completed. And I recommit myself to the Voyages that still lie ahead of me.

Appendix

Editor's Note

Over the course of three previous softcover versions of this Manual, numerous small- and big-screen installments of Star Trek© have been added to the original TV series that premiered in 1967. Each of these has brought fascinating new characters into the mix, along with scores of new quotations to inspire still more daily meditations.

The problem is, incorporating this newly-available material into the Manual required that some of the book's previous meditations be "retired" in order to make room for new ones; and selecting which of them to delete was no easy task. After all, it wasn't as if the previous readings suddenly became irrelevant or obsolete. Neither was the wisdom drawn from them any less valid than what their replacements offer.

Fortunately, with the introduction of an eBook edition, it became possible to bring back these retired meditations without the need for – and expense of – more paper and ink. And now, with Print-On-Demand, more paper and ink becomes less of a factor in this new softcover edition.

The only remaining editorial challenge has been to reorganize the meditations in such a way that they can be easily incorporated into your reading regimen, and to revise the indices to reflect the latest entries. A solution soon appeared in the guise of a large M-Class planet discovered during one of the star-mapping voyages of the USS Odyssey. That planet, dubbed "Arroway" by the ship's Science Officer, is located less than thirty million miles from the small star at the center of its planetary system… and it so happens (*wink wink!*) that Arroway has an orbital cycle of 72 days, the very same number of meditations that had been retired over previous editions of this Manual.

The following collection, then, consists of one additional "year" of daily meditations – at least as they relate to the brave Federation pioneers who have since settled on Arroway. In place of calendar dates based on Earth's lunar/solar subdivisions, each of these readings has been assigned an "A" – which stands for both the planet's name and, coincidentally, for "Appendix" – followed by the numeral for the "day" in Arroway's rapid circuit around its sun. (And if a disproportionate number of these Arroway meditations are drawn from quotations uttered by Captain Picard or Kirk or Spock, it's simply because these figures were so quotable to begin with.)

Whether you'll want to add one or two of these readings to your daily regimen at the end of every week (to come out "even" at the end of an Earth year), or to read them all in a couple of sittings, is entirely up to you.* The more important question is whether they make a valuable addition to your spiritual toolkit – and whether we, collectively, can use all of these meditations to help create a universe where mutual understanding and personal fulfillment will become the legacy of our own ongoing Voyages.

---

* *For that matter, whether you read a single meditation per day, or the four shown on each "page spread" in this new edition—or a month's worth of mediations at one time—that's your choice, too!*

BOLDLY GOING ON YOUR INNER VOYAGE

A-01

People can be very frightened of change.

— CAPTAIN KIRK : THE UNDISCOVERED COUNTRY : 9521.6

Shake hands with your ego, crewman.

Because it's ego that is most afraid of change. It's ego that fears what it cannot foresee, that may not be thrilled with the status quo but at least knows what to expect.

The ego also epitomizes *the way we are now.* And above all, the ego wants to preserve itself. In a sense, when we change, we are asking our present ego to sacrifice itself for another. If we put ourselves in its shoes, we might even sympathize: Why should it go down without a fight?

Trouble is, we've been putting ourselves in our ego's shoes for much too long, on the mistaken assumption that *it* is *us.* But the ego is no more "us" than our reflection in the mirror. Its hold on us is no stronger than our willingness to remain in its grip. And the fear we feel when we contemplate change is only our concern that we might not recognize our own reflection the next time we look in the mirror.

We needn't worry. Our deeper self has an uncanny ability to identify itself in the looking glass of our lives. And to recognize what is *not* itself. The ego, it turns out, is a useful concept for imagining what is not a part of that deeper, truer Self within us, so we may "sacrifice" that image for another, hopefully-more-accurate reflection.

As many egos as it takes.

I look forward to change as one more opportunity to test my evolving consciousness against the higher self The Universe intends for me to become.

A-02

How can we be prepared for that which we do not know? But... I do know we are ready to encounter it.

— CAPTAIN PICARD : Q WHO : 42761.3

There's a subtle difference between being "prepared" and being "ready." One has more to do with ability, the other with attitude.

Preparation assumes we have a fair idea of what lies ahead. In other words, we know what to prepare for. We can take steps to polish specific skills. We can simulate the conditions we're likely to face, then practice our responses. Sometimes we can even predict the outcome. That's why we can't prepare for the unknown. We can't practice skills for conditions we can't foresee.

But what we *can* do is be ready. Because "readiness" is about accepting the fact that we don't know what's ahead, that we can't predict the outcome.

Which doesn't mean we stop preparing altogether. It simply means that if something unexpected happens, we won't fall apart, and we won't give up. We will deal with conditions as best we can, knowing that's all anyone has a right to expect of us.

And then we'll trust The Universe to give us the support we need to get on with our lives.

Of course, we need to prepare ourselves for *receiving* that support. That's a skill we can start developing in advance. In fact, it's a skill we can start using today.

I can't predict the future. I only know there are others who can help me face it, and to learn its lessons.

A-03

We are all part of a greater community. We cannot ignore it.

— **MIRASTA** : FIRST CONTACT : Stardate Not Given

The trouble is, we *can* ignore it. And often do.

What we can't ignore – at least for very long – are the consequences for refusing to join the greater community. Because if we attempt to maintain our isolation, we lose in the long run. *Every*body loses.

The practical benefits of joining together are obvious: New markets and new technologies; new solutions to common problems; exposure to new ideas, new art, new culture.

True, there are potential risks. But centuries of interplanetary experience, under the guidance of the Prime Directive, have shown that distant societies can link to one another productively without losing their identities and their roots. After all, it is our different perspectives and histories that make community so enriching.

So it is on the spiritual level – individually and collectively. Only as we view the One Truth from different perspectives can we fully absorb its riches. Only as we see the different words and forms in which Truth clothes itself can we recognize the deeper, richer meanings within them.

And only in relationship with others can we discover the richness within our own lives.

I celebrate my inter-relationships with, and inter-dependence on, others. I affirm who I am, and who I can become, within the greater community.

A-04

I suggest you avoid emotionalism.

— **SPOCK** : THAT WHICH SURVIVES : Stardate Not Given

Spock isn't counseling us to suppress every emotional response we might have. Nor was he suggesting we'd be better off living without our emotions entirely, as Vulcans are taught to do.

For most sentient species, in fact, emotions have their own powerful "logic." And their own power to flood our systems with raw energy. That energy is designed to be *used*. To suppress it is not only wasteful, but potentially damaging. Emotions are meant to help us.

Emotional*ism*, on the other hand, means allowing emotions to rule us, not merely "help." Our hormones and nerve-endings are back in the Captain's Chair, just as they were before our species developed consciousness.

It's not that hormones and nerves are bad. They're just not all we can be. Our emotions can't envision the future. They can't imagine consequences. They are blissfully unaware that we must go on even after they've subsided, leaving us to deal with their effects.

They are also blissfully unaware that they can be easily fooled. A half-baked simulation of reality can create emotions just as intense as the real thing. Emotionalism is therefore a religion of appearances, of the ephemeral, of the here today and gone tomorrow.

But we are beings of What Is Ultimately Real, and what is Eternal. Let us make these our Prime Directives.

I am energized by my emotions, not ruled by them. They can offer guidance, but I chart my course.

A-05

It's easy to transfer a problem to someone else. Too easy.

— CAPTAIN PICARD : HOLLOW PURSUITS : 43807.4

Question: What's your first response when something goes wrong? The answer — for many of us at least — is to figure out who else we can blame.

And what about problems that suddenly need to be solved? Just as often the top priority is determining who else is responsible. It's *their* job, we'll say. Let *them* handle it.

We've all worked out ways of shifting responsibility to others. We're too busy right now. It's not in our job description. We figured somebody else would take care of it. They're better at fixing things than we are, anyway.

Our excuses run the gamut. And most are no more sophisticated than the elementary school classic: "Homework—? My dog ate it."

The fact is, we may not be entirely responsible for the problems that happen in our family or community or society. But we're never completely free of responsibility, either. If only to emphasize that point, many religious traditions invented the concept of "sins of omission" — the mistakes we make by *not* doing something, often because we assume someone else will do it.

If we want to share in the benefits of The Interdependent Web, we must be willing to reciprocate. Because receiving help is only half of the equation. Giving is the other half.

Other people's problems are my problems, too. I will offer help whenever I can, trusting that The Universe will also provide help for me when I need it.

A-06

Our ambition to improve ourselves motivates everything we do.

— QUARK : PROPHET MOTIVE : Stardate Not Given

For many of us, "ambition" carries as many negative connotations as positive. In its neutral sense, the word simply refers to the inner drive that impels people toward their goals. But that drive is often seen as self-serving and ruthless. Ambition is the proverbial bull in a china shop, the loose cannon, the win-at-all-costs, take-no-prisoners assault that tramples anything that gets in its way.

This kind of ambition values goals over people, the "end" rather than the "means," the destination more than the voyage — or what we *learn* during the voyage.

In one of his more reflective moments, Quark puts ambition in its place. We should strive not for trophies or achievements, he implies, but for the personal development that takes place while earning them. We can easily misinterpret the ambition we feel as directed toward some external objective, toward the "thing" we're doing. But if that's so, we haven't given our subconscious minds enough credit. Because the real objective is always internal, and what we're really "doing" is improving ourselves.

The more we become conscious of this fact, the more likely we'll discover what it is we need to learn — and then make our primary goal to actually *learn* it.

Hidden within my external goals are clues to how my inner Self wants me to grow. I will focus less on "achieving," and more on learning my lessons.

A-07

We consider our families one of our strengths.

— COMMANDER RIKER : RASCALS : 46235.7

The point here, naturally, hinges on what the word "family" means. The social unit known on 20th-Century Earth as the "nuclear family," for example, was among the more artificial definitions that can be found throughout the galaxy. One father, one mother, and two-point-five children living contentedly in the land of fenced-in suburbia was not only a fantasy, it was light-years from the species' own evolutionary roots.

Studies of humankind's origins — and emerging sentient societies elsewhere — show that the natural family extends far beyond one's "birth parents." Uncles, aunts and grandparents play almost as significant a role. Mothers and fathers of neighbors' children, who can augment (or sometimes substitute for) the biological parents, are essential.

A family enhanced by the proximity of several generations and a diversity of role models literally moulds our initial concept of Self and the larger world. It's not just that our family is one of our strengths. Without it we are less than we might otherwise be. Our hard-wiring requires it.

If all of these relationships aren't there for us through biology, then we must create them ourselves. For our own sake. For our children's. And our neighbors' children.

My personal development does not happen in a vacuum. I honor and celebrate what The Universe teaches me through intimate family relationships.

A-08

Logic dictates caution in the face of a superior enemy.

— LIEUTENANT TUVOK : THROUGH THE LOOKING GLASS : Stardate Not Given

Storytellers have known this truth for thousands of years: No "hero" can exist without a worthy adversary. Tales about easy victories won by confident protagonists are undramatic, uninteresting, and uninstructive.

The best stories confront the leading character with a seemingly insurmountable obstacle or a clearly superior enemy. The first reaction to this challenge is usually fright or flight — or both. Because it's not just "the enemy" that our hero must overcome. It's the inner turmoil, the lack of confidence, the feeling of inability or unworthiness or isolation. In the end, victory is less about an external threat than the internal resources the hero discovers to meet it.

Such stories come in a million different forms. They're told from one end of the galaxy to the other because they distill the essence of what our own lives are about. And they all advise us to exercise caution, not so much as a battle tactic or because "logic dictates," but because that's the only way to fully integrate what is happening to us.

What's happening is nothing less than our own salvation. In the perceived "enemies" we face, The Universe is forcing us to realize the redemptive power we have within us. And the final, heroic deed is to embrace one's true Self.

My life's challenges are invitations to connect with the heroic Self that overcomes all opposition.

A-09

Villains who twirl their moustaches are easy to spot. Those who clothe themselves in good deeds are well camouflaged.

— CAPTAIN PICARD : THE DRUMHEAD : 44769.2

The "wolf in sheep's clothing" – or its counterpart in the fables of other planets – is an all-too-common character. The reason he's so common is because so many of us are so easily fooled by appearances. And we are *most* easily fooled by the individual who appears to have our best interests at heart. At least until he slips the blade between our ribs.

After all, most of us want to believe people are generous and decent and good. And when someone seems to reflect those qualities, we're only too willing to assume they're genuine. Unfortunately, by the time we learn otherwise, the damage has already been done.

And the "damage" is more than physical, more even than our humiliation at being deceived. The real damage lies in the fact that we lose our ability to trust. So what frightens us about the "villain" – or worse, about the rare "changeling" on some planets – isn't so much that one particular individual isn't what he appears to be. It's that, because he didn't turn out to be the genuine article, how can we know whether *anyone* is?

Maybe we can't know. But what we *do* know is that The Universe rewards positive expectations. When we ourselves project goodness, the people who coalesce around us are more likely to be good as well.

I will not look for hidden motives behind the good deeds of others. I will concern myself with my own intentions, and offer my example as a positive force.

A-10

The logical course is not always the right course.

— COMMANDER CHAKOTAY : TATTOO : Stardate Not Given

Once again: Logic has its place. But like a computer, it still needs a good operator. Most of all, it needs good data to work with.

Suppose we ask the Ship's Computer to plot the most direct course to a distant star system. Unfortunately, we fail to tell it that a massive black hole lies somewhere between here and there. Or maybe we don't even *know* about the black hole. Chances are, our Starship will end up a few light years off-course due to gravitational effects we didn't account for – assuming our logically-plotted route hasn't drilled us into the black hole already!

Our lives are much the same. There are so many variables that may affect our course, some we don't even know about. We can certainly use logic to give us direction when enough data is available. But we must also polish the skills that help us fly by the seat of our pants.

One of these, Chakotay knows, is intuition. Whether we envision this inner guidance system as Higher Self or Spirit or one's "animal guides," all of us have a course-correcting ability that is beyond logic, beyond conscious thought.

At this deeper level, the right course for us is already laid in. We have only to listen for its "still small voice." In fact, learning to listen is part of our course!

I can know what the right course is for me. As I learn to "listen" through daily meditation, I can also know when changes in direction are necessary.

A-11

I prefer to confront mortality rather than hide from it.

— DR. BASHIR : THE QUICKENING : Stardate Not Given

It's a psychological cliché to say that physicians like Dr. Bashir often seek out that profession as a way of confronting their own mortality. It's also no less true, because in their daily battles against pain and injury, physicians must come to grips with just how fragile our bodies are. In the inevitable circumstances where a patient's life is lost, they can't help but face their own inevitable death.

But these are events we too should face — if not daily (or as directly), then in such a way that we stop hiding from the issue. After all, to recognize our body's threshold for pain and injury is only prudent planning. To realize the possibility — and eventual certainty — of death is to begin deciding what we want from *life.*

Which often results in a radical reorganizing of priorities. Not that we should start living as if tomorrow we'll die. It simply means living as if we have specific goals to reach for, regardless of how much time we have left.

So, what goal would we like to achieve if we *did* have only one more day? What could we hope to achieve if all that remained was a week? A month? A year? Fifty years? What can wait? And what can't we afford to put off any longer?

How precious is each remaining day in my life! How grateful I am for each new opportunity to grow, to love, to receive, and to give back even more.

A-12

A dead man can't learn from his mistakes.

— CAPTAIN SISKO : TO THE DEATH : 49904.2

For the most part, Federation signatories have moved beyond killing people for their crimes — even if that crime happens to be murder. The idea that capital punishment deters others from killing was bad policy from the start. If anything, it teaches people that taking another's life is a viable, even routine, option. It also teaches us that if we can't really rehabilitate someone, we should simply get rid of them.

But this isn't a debate about capital punishment. We're talking about what punishment reveals about *us.*

Because the way we respond to people who commit anti-social acts, who are violent or even "evil," can tell us much about ourselves. More importantly, it says something about how we deal with our own flaws.

If we tend to punish vengefully or brutally, for instance, we're actually expressing a lack of control over our own habits and personal shortcomings. If we find ourselves blindly lashing out at perceived wrongdoers, it's probably because we're frustrated. If we punish someone to "set an example for others," we fail to treat that lawbreaker as a unique individual; and chances are we've forgotten that each of us — and we our*selves* — are incarnations of The Universe.

We must remember that every one of us possesses a divine spark, a potential for goodness that deserves to be nurtured, not negated... primed, not punished.

I will not change by continuing to punish myself for the mistakes I've made. Instead, I will find a way to reward my positive steps toward the Higher Self I hope to be.

A-13

Every choice we make allows us to manipulate the future.

— CAPTAIN PICARD : A MATTER OF TIME : 45349.1

The grand philosophical question – whether our choices really *do* affect the future, or whether it's all an illusion – remains unanswered. Or unanswerable.

On a cosmic scale, the universe seems to unfold according to its own inviolable Destiny. Assuming that the course of societal histories is as lawful and predictable as the evolution of stars, then the needs of the time – what some on Earth call "Zeitgeist" – will inevitably bring to pass whatever changes are required. Individuals play a part, certainly; but if anyone fails at some crucial task, another will surely succeed.

At the personal level, however, we certainly *can* "manipulate" our own futures. Because what we do right now – like reading this Meditation Manual – sets up a "probability field" which makes some events more likely to happen than others. If, for example, we spend our time dwelling on our anger, we increase the potential for emotional (or even violent) reactions to circumstances that seem "beyond our control." But if we start each day by opening our minds to a wider perspective, to new and more positive possibilities – to our inherent potential for growth – we choose a very different future for ourselves.

If not for our world.

The Universe will move toward its own destiny no matter what I do. But what I do still matters to me, and to others whom I can affect in a positive way.

A-14

I don't think we can start second-guessing ourselves. I think we have to proceed normally and deal with each situation as it occurs.

— COUNSELOR TROI : ALL GOOD THINGS. : 47988

There's something to be said for "hunches."

Despite the Vulcan preference for logic, the rest of us rarely make decisions by conscious thought alone. Our subconscious plays a major role – or perhaps *the* major role – processing far more data than our "aware mind" could ever gather, much less keep track of.

Unfortunately, the subconscious decisions (hunches) presented to our awareness often seem too easy. We become suspicious of the fact that we didn't have to think very hard, or do a lot of preliminary analysis. As a result, our logical mind begins reviewing the process and, naturally, can't always determine the basis for our decision. A second decision is made, which is more like a "guess" because now we've begun doubting ourselves. And that's usually a big mistake.

The exception is when we realize that our first hunch is based not on our intuitive decision-making powers, but on some knee-jerk reaction or habit. Or our hormones.

Ultimately it's a matter of looking at the *source* of our decision, not the decision itself. It's a matter of learning to trust a part of ourselves we don't consciously control.

I can feel my decisions are "right" without always knowing how I arrived at them. I will trust my inner guidance, and let my experience confirm the results.

A-15

Hollow is the sound of victory without someone to share it with. Honor gives little comfort to a man alone in his home and in his heart.

— GENERAL MURTOK : YOU ARE CORDIALLY INVITED : 51247.5

The blessings of companionship and love are only one aspect of this reflection from Worf's friend and fellow warrior. At face value, the General is pointing out that our personal triumphs in life are magnified when others can join in celebrating them. Equally important, sharing our victories yields psychic rewards that reinforce our gains and inspire us to face even greater challenges.

But there's a deeper level to Murtok's message. Because sometimes our victory and honor is bought at the expense of those we love. Sometimes we struggle so hard to win, to always be "right," that we drive away the people close to us. We prove our point but poison our relationships. We defend our ego and offend everyone else's.

In short, Murtok reminds us, winning isn't everything. Being "right" isn't always about having the facts on our side. Rather, it's about nurturing harmony in our lives, about empowering and encouraging those around us.

The true victor knows when letting others "have their way" is a small price for keeping the peace. The truly honorable are those who know that how things look on the surface is no substitute for how things *are*... in their homes, and in their hearts.

Today I will strive to get right in my relationships. Love and friendship are the honors that sustain me.

A-16

It's been my experience that the prejudices people feel about each other disappear when they get to know each other.

— CAPTAIN KIRK : ELAAN OF TROYIUS ; 4372.5

We've also heard the exact opposite, of course. Like "Familiarity breeds contempt." Which actually reveals more about the person making the statement than relationships in general.

Ideally, the more we get to know each other, the more we should like each other. Or at least, as Kirk implies, we should better *understand* one another – and thereby lose our simplistic, cardboard-cut-out images.

And it's generally true: Once we learn more, we realize that our prejudices and stereotypes weren't accurate; that others have admirable qualities along with their inevitable flaws; that, in short, they are more like us than not.

Perhaps the best advice comes from Earth's Native American culture. "Do not judge your neighbor," the saying goes, "until you've walked a mile in his moccasins."

Not that putting ourselves in their shoes requires us to excuse any negative behavior. What it does, instead, is establish common ground. It gives us enough insight into their lives to offer genuine help, not judgmental criticism. It confirms that we are all in this struggle together, all battling the same demons... and the same prejudices.

I open myself to the experiences and perspectives of others. As different as they are, they can teach me much about life, and about my self.

At least I'm consistent!

— QUARK : VISIONARY : Stardate Not Given

By itself, consistency is no virtue. Telling people that our bad behavior is simply "to be expected" doesn't make that behavior any more acceptable. Quark surely knew this even as he repeated these four words.

Actually, the value of consistency lies in helping us to measure the kind of people *we* are now. What attitudes and thoughts do we consistently reflect? What behaviors and actions can we be expected to perform? (We're not talking about thinking or doing something continuously or invariably – only enough to know that there's an established pattern.) For example, we may consider ourselves charitable, honest, and non-judgmental. But if we don't actively reflect those characteristics far more often than not, we *aren't*.

On the other hand, we may think of ourselves as morally weak or self-serving. But if we would only count how often we resist temptation or act compassionately toward others, we might realize how strong and generous we really are.

"Counting" our thoughts and actions, in fact, allows us to begin taking full responsibility for Who We Are. By documenting the regularity with which we have certain feelings or thoughts, or act in certain ways, we gain the insight we need to change ourselves. And change our destiny.

Transformation begins with understanding. For the next ten days I will write down the things I do and think consistently. Then I will know what to change.

Open your mind to the past... art, history, philosophy... Then all this may mean something.

— CAPTAIN PICARD : SAMARITAN SNARE : 42779.1

The purpose of an education never has been, never *will* be, to learn the skills necessary to "get a job." Education provides the tools by which we think, act... *live*.

A good education also traces our origins, searches for the elements that make us what we are. It provides a body of shared knowledge that can draw people together even when their present life experiences are different. From the history of one's own race or planet to an overview of life as it developed throughout the universe, we begin to see ourselves as part of something larger, as meaningful components of a Whole. Our lives have context.

Which gives us more control. Because what happens next is always connected to what has happened before. Without this perceived connection, events seem haphazard; they don't "follow." With it we have a better sense of what to expect – from the future, and from ourselves.

It's the reason many adopted children want to know who their birth parents were. It's why all children long to hear stories about their own past. Again and again.

Because it explain us to ourselves. And with this as our starting point, we begin to take responsibility for our lives.

No matter where I am in my life, I affirm the value of everything that has brought me to this point... for learning, for building on, for re-inventing my Self.

A-19

I can give you a long and boring analysis. Suffice it to say... I don't know what's going on!

— CAPTAIN JANEWAY : PARALLAX : 48439.7

Most of us are quite adept at making excuses. We can rationalize our lack of understanding and invent logical justifications for how little we know. We can even devise brilliant explanations that make our continuing ignorance seem like a special kind of knowledge – what past generations referred to as "smokescreens" or "snow-jobs."

But a much better approach to not knowing something is simply to admit it. Because when we put our energies into making excuses, there's little left for finding answers. When we try to justify why we don't know or haven't learned, we create a psychological predisposition for *not* knowing and *not* learning.

However, by fearlessly acknowledging that "we don't know," we open the door to solutions. Defending our ego is no longer an issue. Others come to our aid because it's not a matter of "me" or "you" finding the answer, but *us*.

Captain Janeway was wise to admit whenever she had no answers. And she was no less a leader for it. In fact, leadership is rarely about having answers. It's about the *search* for answers. It's about inspiring others to join us on that search.

It's about being on the search... *together*.

I am always ready to admit when I don't know. Not knowing is the prelude to growth.

A-20

There's another way to survive: Mutual trust and help.

— CAPTAIN KIRK : DAY OF THE DOVE : Stardate Not Given

It's a common assumption, but mistaken. The instinct for self-preservation does not automatically translate into the notion of "Every person for himself." If it did, our various planetary races would not have survived to this point.

Galactic archeologists point to no less than fifty planetary civilizations that no longer exist. And the reason, it's now thought, is because narrow selfishness overruled common interest. When survival was at stake, individuals sought their own safety apart from the group. The wreckage they left behind is witness to that philosophy.

Our own survival testifies to the approach Kirk recommends. Not that we deserve the credit for inventing it. Built into our very chromosomes is a biological predisposition to give help to one another. And it's almost miraculous. In times of disaster or common threat, people seem to naturally come together, to drop their presumed barriers, to forge the networks necessary to overcome virtually any challenge.

But that "predisposition" can't be taken for granted. It must be nurtured. Our spiritual disciplines keep us connected to one another by reminding us of our connection to the Source which created us all.

And the irony is, it's the most selfish thing we can do.

My personal survival is inextricably bound to the survival of my fellow beings. I help myself most when I freely and gratefully help others.

A-21

Try to maintain your emotional equanimity. You should not be concerned with success or failure.

— LIEUTENANT TUVOK : COLD FIRE : Stardate Not Given

"Equanimity" is simply Tuvok's ten-credit word for "emotional balance." It's the opposite of all those wild mood swings many of us give ourselves — from agony to ecstasy, depression to exhilaration, fear to fearlessness. And make no mistake: We *do* give them to ourselves. Because heightened emotions can sometimes become the drug we use to mask our own lack of direction. We may not feel a sense of purpose, but at least we feel *alive,* right?

The problem is, sooner or later our emotional roller-coaster rides take a toll on our bodies. Chances are even better that they'll damage our relationships.

One of the best ways to regain emotional balance is to detach ourselves from the outcome of our efforts. Not that we shouldn't have goals, or strive to achieve them. It's just that while we're "striving," worrying about whether we'll succeed or fail can distract us. By *not* being concerned with success, we free ourselves to concentrate on the job itself, and on doing the best we can.

And that frees The Universe to do the job *It* does best: Balancing our wants with what we actually need.

Which is the *spiritual* version of equanimity.

I can feel alive without using my emotions as a thrill ride. I will control my temperament and my effort, and let The Universe control the rest.

A-22

Ever feel like you're really not wanted?

— ENGINEER LA FORGE : ANGEL ONE : 41636.9

What's your threshold for rejection? At what point do you finally get the message that nothing you do will ever be enough? That it's not even what you do; it's... *you?*

Social rejection is one thing. It's a common occurrence when two people just don't "hit it off." Most of us have learned to accept that. And then we move on.

What's worse is when our ideas and our hard work aren't appreciated; when we've put our hearts and souls into some project and our efforts are ignored, or even dismissed. Our self-worth can drop right off the scale.

But only if we depend on others for our worth.

One of life's primary lessons is learning to take satisfaction from the task, not from its outcome or from what other people may think. Even where a job is assigned to us by someone else, we must find our own reasons for doing it. How can this help me grow? What can I learn from the experience, regardless of the end result?

And ironically, what often happens is that when other people see the satisfaction we're getting from a task, they begin to take greater interest in it. When others know we're doing something because we believe in it, and not simply to impress somebody, *they're* impressed.

What's also ironic is, by that time it doesn't matter.

Whether I'm "not wanted" by others is not my concern. Doing what I believe in, and leaving the outcome to The Universe, is.

A-23

There can be no justice as long as there are absolutes. Even life itself is an exercise in exceptions.

— CAPTAIN PICARD : JUSTICE : 41255.6

Let's start with the physical world: Most of us have learned that the universe is founded on certain invariable laws. In every region of space we've explored, these laws seem to hold, to the point that we now call them "absolutes." If there are occasional exceptions, it's because some higher law takes precedence – a law we may not have fully understood before, or even knew existed.

Science continually attempts to account for the interactions between all these laws and absolutes. If the result is summarized in a formula that states something like "A equals B + C, except on Tuesdays," that statement is no less an absolute for having included a so-called "exception."

So how does all this apply to the concept of justice?

For one thing, it should make us more humble, more careful. Are we really sure that our "laws," our attempts to apply the scientific model to social interactions, should never allow for exceptions? Does our "justice" try to enforce a level of certainty and inflexibility that doesn't exist even in the physical world? And are there any higher laws that might take precedence now and then?

"An eye for an eye" is one law. "Forgive those that do harm unto you" is another. Which is the higher one? In *every* case?

As I judge, so will I be judged. As I define "justice" for others, so will justice be applied to me.

A-24

Sometimes it's healthy to explore the darker side of the psyche. Jung called it "owning your own shadow."

— COUNSELOR TROI : FRAME OF MIND : 46778.1

More often than not, Who We Are and who we *think* we are don't match up. It's so easy to fool ourselves – and not just in our tendency to regard ourselves too highly. Almost as often we don't regard ourselves highly *enough*. Ironically, the same self-denial accounts for both.

Like sentient beings throughout the galaxy, our species' consciousness emerged only after an evolutionary journey that imprinted our bodies with all the earmarks of the Animal Kingdom. Within our very cells is the legacy of that journey: A physical (and psychological) urge to reproduce; a tendency toward aggressive behavior that once promoted our species' survival; and, in general, an emotional toolkit designed for a harsher, more primitive environment that no longer exists.

That ancestral "toolkit" frequently conflicts with social custom, which is why we label it our "darker side." And yet it's an irrepressible part of us. If we fail to acknowledge it, we may assume a moral "superiority" that we don't truly earn until we've faced and struggled with it. Or else we grow to distrust and dislike ourselves, not realizing that those darker tendencies are perfectly natural.

And, if only we would own them, a source of strength.

I accept the evolutionary legacy that lies within me. And in accepting it, I can begin to transcend it.

A-25

No one can guarantee the actions of another.

— SPOCK : DAY OF THE DOVE : Stardate Not Given

There's a saying common to dozens of planetary cultures: "Speak for yourself." Because as much as we may *think* we know someone else, we can never presume to express exactly what that person really feels or thinks.

The same goes for "guaranteeing" another person's actions. We can't live inside anyone else's mind. We can't feel what they feel, remember their memories, know every little detail that might affect their behavior. We have a hard enough time knowing what makes *us* tick! How many times have we surprised ourselves – positively and negatively – by doing something we never thought we could (or would) do?

When we pretend to know someone else better than we have a right, it's often an expression of our desire to know ourselves better. After all, we'd like to be able to count on *some*body. We desperately want someone to be reliable, consistent… knowable. And when we repeatedly fail our own test, we may transfer those hopes to someone else.

There's another saying that's almost universal: "Know thyself." The good news is, we *can*. By being objective about our own behavior. And by continuing to run the daily diagnostic on ourselves called "meditation."

My first priority is guaranteeing my own actions. As I become aware of my behavior, I can begin to change it for the better.

A-26

In our travels we've encountered many other creatures, perhaps even stranger than ourselves. But we try to co-exist peacefully.

— CAPTAIN PICARD : EVOLUTION : 43125.8

Close encounters with other sentient species can often lead to a valuable lesson in self-identity. That's because, when confronted by the variety of other forms consciousness can take, we are inevitably forced to re-evaluate what it is that makes us *us*.

And the variety of other forms is dazzling, even among humanoids! Skin color and texture, facial features; vocal, reproductive, and internal organs – these can seem "strange" if only because we are so unfamiliar with them.

Yet our ability to imagine a spiritual entity within these other forms, similar to the Self within us, can often remove this seeming "strangeness." It can also provide the basis for a relationship that offers not just peaceful co-existence, but a thriving, productive interchange of material goods and novel ideas.

What's equally productive is that our relationship to our Self benefits as well. Experience with other species helps us recognize which of our own personal attributes are essential to Who We Are, and which aren't; which traits, if we improved them, might make a genuine difference in our lives, and which of those would only alter "appearances."

In the face of "the other," we see our most revealing reflection.

Beneath the exterior of others, I see a fellow soul. Within my bodily clothing, I sense a deeper Spirit. As I co-exist with others, I make peace with myself.

A-27

Without trust there's no friendship, no closeness... none of the emotional bonds that make us who we are.

— COMMANDER RIKER : LEGACY : 44215.2

The concept almost seems self-contradictory: To form a bond of such closeness, such intimacy, that two people feel connected even when they're apart; yet leaves each one free and unrestricted by the other.

And it *would* be contradictory – without mutual trust.

Trying to enforce closeness is the real contradiction. Because if we insist on knowing where a friend or lover is at all times, or what they're "up to" whenever we're separated, we can only end up driving them away. If we insist on being "alike" as a sign of our affection – the same beliefs, the same interests, the same social circles – we create a relationship based on meeting requirements, not on *being ourselves.* It's still a "relationship" of sorts, but it can never be as close.

Trust is our gift of freedom for others to be who they are, to go where they may, and to return to us of their own free will. To trust others in this manner is really to value ourselves, to believe that we are worth returning to – even, ironically enough, if the other person doesn't return!

The emotions that build around these trusting, voluntary relationships invite us to grow, to accept, to *be.* They expand our feeling of connection to others, and therefore expand the boundaries of our Self.

I am truly connected to others only as I free them to be who they are, and free myself to be who I am.

A-28

What's important is what you think.

— CAPTAIN SISKO : THE WAY OF THE WARRIOR : 49011.4

No, Deep Space Nine's resident Emissary isn't giving us permission to think only of ourselves, or to disregard the opinions of others. What he *is* saying is that we, individually, are the ones who must live with our decisions. *We* are the ones most affected.

Not only our actions, but our innermost thoughts, have karma. We will inevitably reap their consequences, both positive and negative – if not immediately, then over time. In fact, it's the long-term effects of our thoughts that constitute their real power.

In recognizing that power, Sisko knew, we are also encouraged to accept responsibility for them. Because if our thoughts can affect us that much, we'd better learn to control them. Or at least come to terms with them.

Yet some of us still don't want to. We prefer to rely on what other people think since, that way, responsibility for our happiness or success is someone else's problem. And if we seek others' guidance, and make decisions based on what *they* think, we also avoid blame if things go wrong. "I was only following your advice" becomes our repeated refrain. And, repeatedly, we fail to grow.

The Universe can transform us only through the thoughts we have and the choices we make. To value what *we* think is to take our lives into our own hands.

I need the opinions of others to add perspective to my own. But I accept final responsibility for my decisions, my thoughts, and my own happiness.

A-29

"34th Rule of Acquisition: War is good for business."
"35th Rule of Acquisition: Peace is good for business. It's easy to get them confused!"

— QUARK & LT. COMMANDER DAX : DESTINY : 48543.2

Economics isn't the only domain where paradoxes are common. One of the perennial paradoxes in science, for example, concerns the nature of light. From one point of view, light is a "particle." From another, it's clearly a "wave" phenomenon, or even a "string." Yet both can't be true.

Which is an obvious clue that we still don't fully understand it. Or that our perspective alters our understanding.

The Ferengi perspective on war is such a case. Admittedly, some businesses thrive in wartime, or at least in times of potential conflict. But over an extended duration, warfare ends up sapping the economy, leaving fewer people to pay for the destruction (not to mention fewer people to fight). Ultimately, war profits are unsustainable.

The paradox here is less about reality than our mistaking short-term gain for what's best in the long run. Most of our problems, in fact, are rooted in this mistake. Too often we make choices that are blind to their long-term consequences. Or to their effects on our fellow beings.

Spirituality is about widening our perspective, about connecting not only with the larger community but the farthest future. When we acquire that connection, we're less likely to get confused.

I live in the here and now. Yet I am part of the Infinite and the Eternal. That paradox sustains me.

A-30

We are born, we grow, we live, and we die. In all the ways that matter we are alike.

— CAPTAIN PICARD : WHO WATCHES THE WATCHERS? : 43173.5

So… how fine do you want to cut it?

Admittedly, our ability to make distinctions serves a useful purpose. The tiny differences we observe in nature give us greater control over it; they increase our species' chances for survival; they enhance our own creativity and sense of personal satisfaction. Our ability matters.

But when it comes to interpersonal relationships – to getting along with other races and other species – what matters then? Should it make any difference that someone has blue eyes rather than brown? What about brown skin versus pink? Thinning grey hair or lustrous blonde? Flowing robes or tight-fitting uniforms? Should someone's praying to nature, or to a sacred icon, or to no one at all, automatically determine how we relate to them?

We can make all these obvious distinctions between people, and even finer ones. But which are necessary? Which serve a beneficial purpose? Captain Picard may oversimplify to make the point. But the truth is, noticing differences often raises artificial barriers that can only harm us.

And the deeper truth is this: If we remain divided from others, we can't be united with ourselves. But… tear down the walls outside, and the divisions within us are healed.

I can retain my critical powers without letting them dictate my relationships. Today, if I catch myself noticing a difference, I will find only the good in it.

A-31

If we're going to do it, we're going to do it by the book.

— CAPTAIN KIRK : THE FINAL FRONTIER : 8454.1

"Anything worth doing," an old proverb claims, "is worth doing well." And for everything worth doing, we might add, there's probably a dozen books telling you *how*.

Doing something "by the book" is simply another way of saying, "Let's do this assignment or project or task as well as we can — according to the most reliable, time-tested information we can find." This doesn't mean blindly following directions. It *does* mean admitting that many of the paths we walk were explored by others long before we came along. How foolish we'd be to ignore the roadmaps they've left behind, or delete any Ships' Logs that might make our own voyages safer and more productive.

And yet that is often exactly what we do. Simply because other books — or traditions, or religions — were written in another cultural setting or a previous century, we assume they can't teach us anything useful. Which is like saying that anyone who speaks a foreign language doesn't have anything meaningful to tell us.

We might think of "The Book" as the accumulated wisdom of past generations — the collective resources which can tell us not only what works, but how to find answers for ourselves if the existing ones *don't*. And that's when we become authors for the next generation.

I am grateful for the Book of Life others have left for me. I will strive to make my own contribution.

A-32

When you lie or steal, you not only dishonor yourself, but your family.

— LIEUTENANT WORF : NEW GROUND : 45376.3

It's not that the readers of this Manual need a lecture about lying and stealing. There is a deeper issue here.

At some point in our lives we finally come to accept responsibility for the choices we make. This is a healthy, necessary stage. The problem is, it often brings with it a tendency to think of ourselves as autonomous, self-made beings no longer bound to those who originally shaped us, whether through influence or genes… or both.

And the fact is, *all* of these people — parents, teachers, siblings, friends — continue to have a stake in us, if only because of the time, sweat, and emotional energy they've invested in our development. That doesn't give them the right to use their "investment" to make us feel unduly obligated, of course. Honor is also about releasing attachments, about having the freedom to leave the nest, to try our wings, to make our own mistakes.

But our actions link us to the people in our past nevertheless. When our actions demonstrate our own higher qualities, they reaffirm theirs. When our behavior falls painfully short, it recalls the anguish of occasions when they too missed the mark. "Honor" is Worf's word — an ancient, venerable, *visceral* word — for recognizing these links.

I will live and act as if the people who first cared for me and encouraged me… who believed in my potential the most… are present with me now.

A-33

You exist only inside your mind.

— LIEUTENANT TUVOK : INNOCENCE : Stardate Not Given

Just because there's a light in the window, how do we know anyone is home?

It's one of the oldest philosophical conundrums: We're certain that *we* exist. We have self-awareness. We not only feel and think, we are conscious of our feeling and thinking. But we can't get into other people's minds to verify that *they* are self-aware. Maybe they're only robots.

Then again, maybe *we* are only robots. Maybe our Self is some disembodied entity composed of pure thought, or Mind. And our body — or maybe everything that seems "material" — is a kind of virtual reality we put on like a child's playsuit.

Tuvok's statement invites us into such endless speculations. But at some point we must simply accept this reality as Reality, and get on with learning what only this playsuit can teach us.

One of those lessons is that our minds do, in fact, mediate Reality for us. In a sense, then, our lives do not depend so much on what happens "out there" but how we react "in here." We become responsible for our own happiness and fulfillment, because *that* we can control.

The riddle that we exist "only in our minds" is not meant to throw us into confusion or doubt. It is meant to affirm the power we have over our own lives… a power The Universe itself gives us.

It is logical and intuitively right to affirm the same existence for others as I claim for myself. Together we can conceive and create a reality that benefits us all.

A-34

You explore the universe. We've discovered that a single moment in time can be a universe in itself… full of powerful forces.

— ANIJ : INSURRECTION : Stardate Not Given

No matter how small or large the "world" we inhabit — from the space inside our skulls to an entire galaxy — there remain uncharted realms ripe for exploration. One of these mysterious realms is the concept of Time.

No less real than length, depth and height, time is the dimension that connects cause and effect… that links our actions to their consequences. And every moment of it, like the smallest particle of matter, contains great energy.

If we could dissect each moment like Anij's people have, we would see it reaching into every other dimension. We would also be amazed at how the energy from even the most trivial action is carried far into the future, and far beyond our immediate relationships.

But what if we didn't *like* what we saw? What if we wanted to take back the energy we already set in motion?

To a greater degree than we think, we *can.* Not by going back in time, or stopping it, but by using the powerful forces each new moment presents. Because every new action sends out energy through time and space, too; and just the *right* one can counteract the mistakes of our past.

If we are mindful of our moments, we can create new worlds, and boldly go into a future of our own choosing.

I will close my eyes and feel the power of this moment. I accept its energy as fuel for my growth.

A-35

A lifetime of building emotional barriers… they're very difficult to break down.

— CAPTAIN PICARD : UNIFICATION, PART I : 45236.4

Transformation is rarely quick, and almost never easy. We mustn't lose heart in our struggle to change ourselves — and our world — simply because the results are so long in coming. Or turn out to be less than we hoped for.

We often forget that we've fashioned ourselves over years of practice. Just think of it: If we'd consciously set out to become the person we are now — with all our imperfections and emotional defenses — it would probably have taken exactly *this* long to achieve our goal! How unrealistic we are to expect any rapid reversals.

Not to mention that some of our problems stem from childhood traumas we've repressed so completely that we're simply unaware of them. Memories of abuse, for example, often don't resurface until we're better prepared to deal with them. Or until we've given mental "permission."

The fact that we want to change is a good sign that we *are* prepared now, that we've given ourselves permission.

And there is hope. If we can find others with whom we can openly reveal ourselves, emotional barriers can crumble in surprisingly short order. And if we can surrender to the Power that is far greater than the combined emotional energy we've spent in an entire lifetime — or a *hundred* lifetimes — no barrier can stand in our way.

I cannot expect immediate results. But I know they will come if I persevere. And I will *persevere*.

A-36

It is not a lie to keep the truth to oneself.

— SPOCK : THE ENTERPRISE INCIDENT : 5027.3

One could go even further than Spock does here: Sometimes it is a "lie" to tell the truth!

The Truth, after all, is not just an accurate reporting of the facts. It's a conscious, harmonious, productive relationship between yourself and the larger Reality around you. Sometimes that Reality includes other people who have a different understanding of "the facts," or who may not be fully aware of them.

Learning when to debate the truth, or when to reveal it to others, is something of an art form. Many would call that art "Wisdom." In any case, the decision to speak or not speak should never derive from a wish to maintain some personal, selfish advantage. That would be a "lie." Keeping the truth to oneself must always serve the greater good. Will it preserve harmony without sacrificing trust? Would "the truth" be misused by others if they knew it — like some wonderful new technology that could just as easily be turned into a bomb as a blessing?

The Inner Voyage places the Quest for Truth among our highest priorities. But the real test of truth is whether it actually improves our lives. And the real test for *us* is whether we can use it responsibly.

I recognize that lying and truth-telling are more than a function of words. I honor the truth by living in an honest, harmonious relationship with others.

A-37

We believe everything in the universe has a right to exist.

— COMMANDER RIKER : SKIN OF EVIL : 41601.3

Wait just a minute, Commander. *Do* we—?

Do we really think cancer has a right to exist? Should we treat viruses that mutate into bio-logical death squads the same as endangered species that deserve our protection?

Let's try re-phrasing the statement: We believe everything in the universe exists *for a reason.*

That's better. Because it doesn't mean we should submissively accept whatever happens, or that whatever exists must therefore be "good," or worth preserving. Maybe some things exist specifically for us to get rid of them.

Or maybe they exist to tell us something.

Cancer, for example, can be a sign that our lifestyle has gotten out of balance; that we've been dumping too many chemicals and too much stress into our personal and collective environments. The deadly virus that escapes from some orbiting laboratory, then threatens to wipe out the population on the planet below, is a sign that life's genetic patterns aren't to be toyed with so blithely.

The universe itself has a "pattern," too. On Earth, the ancient Chinese called that pattern *Tao,* the Way. According to tradition, if we watch for the signs, we'll find the Way. As well as the way to make our existence "right."

The Universe gives me the right to exist. I accept the challenge to grow. I will look for the signs in both my own life and others' that teach me the Way.

A-38

We have a duty to investigate.

— COUNSELOR TROI : ANGEL ONE : 41636.9

The line is most often spoken by Starship captains or science officers. After all, to explore new worlds, to seek out new life and new knowledge despite the danger — and then to bring the trea-sures from that cosmic adventure back home — is the primary mission of Starfleet.

But the line could just as easily symbolize the mission of our individual lives, too. Because Troi's statement isn't just about explorations of the cosmic variety. It's about our duty to explore ourselves. It's a rally cry to boldly go *within;* to seek new opportunities for personal learning and growth; to be curious not only about how the universe works, but about how *we* work.

Why did I do that? What causes these feelings I'm having? How can I improve the way I reacted to this event, or that person's remark, or my own inner compulsions? What standards can I use to find out if I've improved?

Our curiosity about life is a kind of faith. It's a faith that makes our existence more interesting, certainly. But it also pays dividends in greater self-awareness and greater understanding of others. As we bring back the treasures of this adventure into our daily lives, we discover that we now have more control, more options, more satisfaction.

Investigating is more than a duty. It's our purpose.

I am on a Grand Adventure. I will cultivate my curiosity as one of my most valuable tools.

A-39

If you don't join me, don't disapprove of me. Not, at least, until you've tried it.

— DR. McCOY : THE CONSCIENCE OF THE KING : 2817.6

The problem is not just that we're too judgmental. It's what we're judgmental *about*.

We criticize others (and ourselves) for minor flaws, all the while ignoring what really matters. We find fault with other peoples' private lives, how they look, their personal likes and dislikes — even their religious practices – when our only concern should be *how we get along.*

Withholding judgment (sometimes called "tolerance") is a virtue for precisely that reason. The fact that someone else may chant a mantra, or worship the Mother Goddess, or wear a turban, or go square dancing every other night, is none of our business. What matters is the kind of *people* they prove to be in their dealings with us, and with others.

Admittedly, the practices that engender harmonious qualities in these people may not work for us. But that's just the point: We can't really say until we've "tried it."

Not that Dr. McCoy is suggesting we experiment with everyone else's lifestyle and belief system, so we can render our judgment. "Stay on your own path," is what he's really saying, "unless you truly want to join me on mine." Because the bottom line is not the particular voyage we're on, it's the kind of voyager we become.

I am not in this universe to approve or condemn others, but to improve myself... and to demonstrate the person I am through the way I live.

A-40

There's only one kind of woman or man. You either believe in yourself or you don't.

— CAPTAIN KIRK : MUDD'S WOMEN : 1329.1

It's like saying a woman is "slightly pregnant." The words don't mesh. Either she is, or she *isn't.* There is, by definition, no room for qualifiers.

In the same way, an individual can be said to "believe in herself/himself" – or not. There is no middle ground. The question is, *how* do you believe in yourself? Is it a function of self-confidence? Is it about being "right" or "successful" often enough in the past that you can safely assume you'll be right or successful in the future?

Hardly. People can believe in themselves even while feeling unsure about the "correctness" of their decisions or the outcome of their actions. In fact, it's that very belief which drives them to proceed despite all those uncertainties.

It's the belief that life is less about being right or successful than being honest and courageous. It's about your willingness to try, to make mistakes, to continually push the boundaries of your experience... to recognize your place in a larger whole and to take responsibility for it.

Finally, it's about saying *"Yes!"* to your own life.

To believe in yourself is to affirm that life has meaning. Regardless of the outcome. Despite the hardships. And even if you still haven't discovered what that meaning *is.*

I can believe this: That my life is good, even when doubt clouds my vision; that I will endure and grow, through failure as well as success.

A-41

I do believe there is more within each of us than science has yet to explain.

— LIEUTENANT TUVOK : INNOCENCE : Stardate Not Given

With a few notable exceptions, this affirmation is as close as most Vulcans will ever come to traditional theology. In the language of earlier times, Tuvok would be classified as neither an "atheist" nor a "theist," but as an *agnostic* – someone who does not assert the existence of a Divinity, but who won't deny one either.

As long as science can't explain everything, "supernatural forces" will be invoked to fill in the missing pieces. And since sentient species commonly attach the same attributes to these forces as they see in themselves, (like personality and intention) – *ta dah!* – another divinity is born.

However, believing in a divinity is not a requirement of "spirituality." Tuvok, like Spock, still managed a vibrant inner life. He practiced physical and mental disciplines designed to enhance his capabilities and his sense of personal fulfillment. And he occasionally drew on inner resources, the mechanism of which he might be unable to explain, but which had a verifiable effect on his reality.

Using such techniques is only logical, whether or not we can explain how they work. Sometimes, in fact, allowing the mystery to remain *is* the explanation of "how."

And that is a kind of theology in itself.

Knowing how something works is less important than that it works. The deeper Science is applying the principles I discover, not analyzing them.

A-42

The road from legitimate suspicion to rampant paranoia is very much shorter than we think.

— CAPTAIN PICARD : THE DRUMHEAD : 44769.2

It's always tempting to blame our problems on others – on our competition, our enemies, or the latest inter-galactic conspiracy. Our fears and insecurities become a function of the external world. We aren't responsible.

But our biggest danger isn't the external world. It's the way we *react* to it. And *we* are responsible for that.

Perception is part of it. Admittedly, we sometimes have a right to be suspicious of others based on previous experience. But if we automatically take that next step, if we begin to expect the worst, we put on blinders. Goodness can't be seen, much less experienced. The world turns into an evil place where bad things are just waiting to happen. Our paranoia poisons everything we touch. And what's sad is, we aren't even aware we've made a choice.

We could just as easily choose to perceive only the good. But it's more than perception. Positive expectations can literally bring out the kinder, more harmonious elements in other people. Our conscious projection of non-violence and goodwill – a force Hindus call *ahimsa* – sets up an energy field that can physically transform our reality.

And the wonderful thing is, the road to that reality is also very much shorter than we think.

The power to transform the world lies within me. I will consciously project goodwill to everyone I meet.

A-43

If there's nothing to lose – no sacrifice – then there is nothing to gain.

— LIEUTENANT WORF : PEAK PERFORMANCE : 42923.4

Not that gambling has much to recommend it. But putting your hard-earned Federation credits on the line at some deep-space casino *does* symbolize one important Law of the Universe: Nothing of real value can ever be gained without risking something valuable of your own.

Often the only risk is your time – the hours spent learning a new skill, or exploring a different path. But time once spent can't be recovered. We tend to forget how truly precious time is until the universe reminds us there's only so much remaining.

Sometimes the risk is more obvious or frightening. Like putting our lives on the line, or our careers, or our integrity (which all amounts to the same thing). And what's ironic is, the times when we're most afraid can be the *least* risky. In fact, it may not be a "gamble" at all. Because even our losses can teach us something. And when our very future is at stake, what do we have to lose?

Energy is never lost, only transformed. The positive efforts we make will be rewarded. Even if the reward isn't exactly what we expected. Even if it may not come according to the timetable we've established.

I will take risks for what I value most... and for the person I hope to become. No sacrifice is too great to attain that which gives my life ultimate meaning.

A-44

You have no idea what the consequences might be once you involve yourself.

— CAPTAIN JANEWAY : TIME AND AGAIN : Stardate Not Given

It's a worthy goal, as Tuvoc says, to "be prepared for anything." But as Janeway reminds us, we never *can* be. The smallest detail, overlooked, can ruin our best-laid plans. And even if everything *does* go "according to plan," the full effects of our actions may not be felt for weeks or years. Or generations.

Which doesn't mean we shouldn't act at all. Nor is Janeway simply appealing for extra caution, or still more pre-planning. For one thing, we may not have that luxury.

What she means is that we must adapt ourselves to *not knowing* – to moving forward despite limited information, despite our fears and doubts. And for that we *can* prepare.

We can prepare by actively seeking "experience," by looking for new challenges where the unexpected can be expected. Naturally, we'll want to start with assignments that can't hurt us too badly if things go wrong. But just by putting ourselves in these situations, repeatedly, we automatically learn crucial lessons: That we will survive; that there is a "knowing" below the level of consciousness that can guide us; that if we take the leap, if we do "involve ourselves" in good faith, The Universe will respond in kind.

And then we'll not only survive... the consequences may turn out better than we could ever have imagined!

I am never, ever, alone. I receive divine guidance as I open myself to the full resources of The Universe.

A-45

Creativity is necessary for the health of the body.

— SPOCK : THE RETURN OF THE ARCHONS : 3156.2

The Force which fashions our individual lives doesn't simply give birth to us and then leave us to fend for ourselves. It sustains us moment by moment. It is a continuous Presence underlying all of existence.

Science confirms that the universe is more of a process than a physical "entity." And the primary characteristic of that process is creation. From atoms to galactic super-clusters, the universe re-creates itself continually — maintaining, renewing, transforming. And what The Ancients called our "spark of divinity" is none other than the creative process moving in and through us.

Ironically, we can also "create" structures that may block this creative flow. The pipeline can constrict like clogged arteries, and the symptoms are just as physical. When we suppress our natural urges for meaningful expression, we can literally lose our vision and our voice. If we're afraid to try new things, to think new thoughts, to renew our*selves,* our very bodies can grow stiff and brittle.

Artists are those who have learned not so much to control the creative process as to let *it* control *them.* And in the flow of that energy lies healing and wholeness.

I open myself to the creative process that is my heritage as a creature of this universe. I will find ways to express what is within me, and be healed.

A-46

To become a thing is to know a thing.

— CONSTABLE ODO : BEHIND THE LINES : 51149.5

One of the indigenous peoples of Earth had a saying that captured Odo's meaning on a more personal level, a saying that has been quoted on these pages already: "Do not judge your neighbor until you've walked a mile in his moccasins."

But Odo's statement — along with his ability to transform himself into other "things" — takes in objects and beings of every kind, not merely people. What's it like to be a tree, losing its leaves in an autumn downpour, or a butterfly caught in a spider's web? Or a window pane that allows objects to be seen through it, yet remains itself unseen? Odo knows.

We too can experience these "other" states of being and more — through our imagination. By closing our eyes, by quieting our normal senses, we too can "become" the tree, the butterfly, the window… or another person.

And the effects are almost as breathtaking as Odo's description of The Link, "…merging thought and form, idea and sensation." The universe opens; boundaries fall away. We transcend our usual limitations and narrow perspectives. And then we return to our ordinary lives with more sympathy and tolerance, more appreciation, less inclined to judge, less ensnared by self-centeredness.

"Becoming the Other" is a form of meditation found all across the galaxy. Almost always where peace and understanding reign.

I am open to the viewpoints and experiences of other people and creatures. Even inanimate objects can teach me much about life, and about my self.

A-47

The way I see it, freedom is a whole lot better than slavery.

— COMMANDER SISKO : THROUGH THE LOOKING GLASS : Stardate Not Given

Sisko's observation isn't all that controversial or profound, is it? Notwithstanding the Borg, everyone prefers freedom to the kind of political, racial or economic sanctions that once enslaved billions. *Don't* they…?

You'd think so. Yet the fact remains that many of us are living in slavery right now, without even realizing it.

We are restrained from further growth by our addictions. We are chained by our own unwillingness to break out of established patterns and comfortable lifestyles that limit our options or drain our creative energies. We continue to be ensnared by the notion that life itself is somehow against us; that we are essentially evil, sinful creatures whose only hope for salvation lies in "external" answers.

Mental or spiritual slavery is a lot more powerful, and certainly more insidious, than the outward kind. Freeing ourselves from *those* chains ought to be our top priority.

Freedom implies having options and choosing between them. By acknowledging our own "slave mentality" we can choose to overcome it. By becoming aware of our own patterns of action and thought, we can decide if we wish to maintain them or transcend them.

Freedom is better. But only because we must earn it.

Today I will list all the ways I am free, and all the ways I am not. I will meditate on how I can secure freedom from my own spiritual bondage.

A-48

I've never been afraid of re-evaluating my convictions.

— CAPTAIN PICARD : A MATTER OF TIME : 45349.1

We all have convictions. If we can't articulate them in words, we *do* express them in actions. It's not what we say; it's our behavior that reveals our beliefs.

The difference between the two can be embarrassing, if not deeply distressing. And the point of this difference is not that we are therefore failures or "sinners." It's that we're still growing. We are "works in progress."

To be willing to re-evaluate our convictions is to affirm that we are always working on what we believe. What's ironic is that the people who are *un*willing to question their beliefs are usually those whose convictions are weakest. These are the same people who seek to impose their beliefs on others by force or threats because if they can't somehow convince other people, they are reminded of their own darkest fear: That they might be wrong.

It takes a strong sense of self to admit we might be wrong. It takes a strong commitment to Truth to welcome new opportunities to test our beliefs. It takes great wisdom to know when our failure is the result of a mistaken conviction, or our own inability to carry out what we say we believe. Because in the end, the real test isn't about convictions anyway.

It's about our character.

Applying my convictions allows me to re-evaluate them. I am open to what these opportunities teach me about my beliefs, and about my character.

A-49

If there are self-made purgatories and we all have to live in them, mine can be no worse than someone else's.

— SPOCK : THIS SIDE OF PARADISE : 3417.3

According to one of Earth's spiritual traditions, "purgatory" was the place all human souls were sent after death – when they hadn't yet qualified for entrance to Heaven, but neither were they doomed to Hell.

A common spin on this tradition is that our present lives are purgatory. We are all, symbolically, living along the spectrum between paradise and personal annihilation. Where we are right now is exactly where we belong. And what we do next is part of a grand scheme to explore and test our character, and ultimately to "perfect" it.

The problem is, the tests we face often appear so different from others, even unfair. Our lives seem so easy compared to other individuals – or whole planetary cultures – who are struggling merely to survive. Still others' lives seem like they're in Heaven already, filled with continual comforts and pleasures and nothing to further "test" them.

But we cannot judge those lives. Nor can we say we're better or worse than those who lead them. Character is fashioned in many crucibles, each for a different purpose. We must accept the crucible given by the Universe for *us*… and then transcend it if and when we're able.

The circumstances in my life are for my own self-improvement. I will start from where I am, and not measure my progress against the lives of others.

A-50

A ship is only as good as the engineer who takes care of her.

— CHIEF ENGINEER SCOTT : RELICS : 46125.3

There's a phase in the evolution of all technological societies, (usually when computers are first coming into use), during which expectations leap far ahead of effects. A kind of disaffection sets in… followed by questions.

Like: With all this new number-crunching power, why hasn't the Federation's annual budget been balanced? Or: With graphics programs that can simulate practically anything, why isn't art thriving? Or: With access to limitless information only a voice command away, why haven't we solved all of our problems by now?

The answer is simple. Improving our tools does not necessarily improve *us*. The person behind the hardware remains unchanged. The computer – or the ship – still relies on someone to operate it, to use it purposefully, to keep it functioning at all.

And all the hardware in the Quadrant can't replace the roles only we can play. All our upgrading of technology won't change a thing until we upgrade our*selves*.

We are the engineers of our own lives. The vehicles that carry us along – our bodies, our possessions, our present circumstances – are "only as good" as Who We Are, and who we will become. Let us make taking care of *that* our top priority.

I can wait for the latest model computer or personal shuttlecraft. I can no longer wait to begin remodeling myself into the person I want to be.

A-51

Being an outsider isn't so bad. It gives one a unique perspective.

— CONSTABLE ODO : THE SEARCH, PART II : Stardate Not Given

Most societies on M-type planets have a complementary expression. Each one talks about our tendency to become so embroiled in a given situation that we "can't see the forest for the trees."

In other words our personal, emotional involvement in some mission or relationship often causes us to lose our perspective – and our balance. Our focus on the details blurs The Bigger Picture. Our increasing investment of time and resources subtly shifts our needs and goals. We become disconnected from the reasons that motivated us to become involved in the first place.

This isn't necessarily wrong. Sometimes, in getting a closer look at the individual "trees," we're forced to re-evaluate our original view of the entire "forest." But even when this happens it's wise to get a second opinion. An objective opinion. An *outside* opinion.

By acting as one another's "outsiders" we can offer much-needed balance to our lives. What's more, we can learn to remove ourselves from an emotional situation when necessary, to stand outside the turmoil, to remember Who We Are.

And hopefully, to remember who we can yet become.

I will watch for those times in life when I may be too close to a situation to remain objective. I am always open to the advice of others who care for me.

A-52

You proceed from a false assumption. I have no ego to bruise.

— SPOCK : THE WRATH OF KHAN : 8130.3

Unlike Spock, many of us still seem to organize our entire emotional lives around the protection of our egos: What will people think? How will I look? What if someone else is better? How can I save face?

It's as if we carry around a mental scorecard, giving ourselves points when we do something that impresses other people, and subtracting points when we don't – or worse, when someone else succeeds where we've failed and now everybody knows it. Especially our ego.

Problem is, our "ego" is an artificial identity given to us by others. To have an ego is to allow ourselves to be defined by how others see us. It means giving control of our very feelings to some-one else: Now I can be proud; now I feel hurt. The ego is a marionette; pull my strings.

Not that the ego serves no purpose. In childhood, we must take on the standards of others – our parents, our peers, our culture – as a kind of "preliminary operating system." It's as necessary as baby food and diapers.

But adulthood is the process of taking responsibility, of discovering a core self that is beyond being proud or being "bruised," that's less concerned with how others see us than how The Universe "sees" us. Because, ultimately, *its* standards are the ones that truly count.

I will not seek so much to "protect" my ego as to dismantle it, and meet my true Self in the process.03.30

A-53

Man stagnates if he has no ambition, no desire to be more than he is.

— CAPTAIN KIRK : THIS SIDE OF PARADISE : 3417.3

It's one thing to enjoy the fruit of one's labors, to rest on one's laurels. Or, as the ancient ballad says, to "stop and smell the roses."

But to call a halt to one's aspirations, to say that "I've achieved enough," is to commit spiritual suicide.

The Inner Voyage, after all, is a journey of continual self-improvement. The Voyage may have its way-stations, but it does not come to an end. Not in this life, anyway.

Someone's ambition to "be more than he is" begins with his first glimmerings that there are deeper dimensions to existence. We perceive, dimly at first, that we are not defined by our physical limitations, not confined to the conditions in which we originally find ourselves. We may translate that realization of "more" into a desire for material things or achievements – pleasure, possessions, power or honor. But what The Universe is trying to teach us, even in our mistaken pursuit of these trinkets, is that we *do* deserve more; that we are mirrors of what the Ancients called "the divine image"; that we can continually expand our limited notions of Who We Are until we reflect the goodness, creativity, and limitless bounty of The Universe itself.

Certainly more than we do now.

Even my materialistic ambitions hide spiritual truth: If I can have more, I can also be more. I choose "being" over "having," character over possessions.

A-54

Without the darkness, how would we recognize the light?

— LIEUTENANT TUVOK : COLD FIRE : Stardate Not Given

The debate has raged on a thousand planets: Why is there good and evil? Why can't we have beauty without ugliness? Why must darkness co-exist with the light?

It's true one can't exist without the other. But that truth is less a description of the universe than about how we think. Opposites are simply a necessary part of our mental framework. We bring our values into focus by visualizing how things might be *without* those values, or by imagining a "force" which seems to actively work against them. Even if that force is, well, imaginary.

Like darkness.

Darkness is not a real "thing" – material or otherwise. It is simply the absence of light. It is a linguistic construct, a verbal convenience.

Having a word for it does not confer existence. What it *does* do, unfortunately, is give us the illusion that darkness is some "thing" we can fight and destroy. So we end up boxing shadows and chasing phantoms when the real solution is to step over to the window, raise the blinds, and expose those corners of our lives that could use a little illumination.

"Darkness" is still a useful term for talking about our inability to see. But in developing strategies to improve our vision, let's remember what's real… and what isn't.

I can try to fight the darkness, or I can embrace the light and shine it on others. I choose the latter.

A-55

We're a part of our environment... We cannot separate ourselves from it without irrevocably altering who and what we are.

— AARON CONOR : THE MASTERPIECE SOCIETY : 45470.1

In the words of an old Bajoran proverb, "The land and the people are one." Earth's Native American tradition put it this way: We do not own the land; the land owns *us*.

Just because we are mobile – we walk, we run, we traverse time and space – we are no less the outgrowths of our home planet as the root-bound tree. Our very chemistry mirrors our species' planetary origins, as uniquely and accurately as fingerprints identify an individual.

Many people now consider it odd that the ideal single-family domicile on Twentieth Century Earth required its own front and back lawns and private vegetable garden. And yet urban dwellers were only responding to an innate need to remain connected to the earth. Mowing the lawn was an excuse to walk on something other than concrete. Tending one's garden was a way to feel the dirt beneath one's fingernails, as had countless generations before.

The call of our chromosomes is real. We are poorer if we too cannot dig the soil now and then, if we forget what grass feels like between our toes. To remain connected to our original environment, even if symbolically, is what grounds us. And only then can we "boldly go."

Every atom in my body was once part of the environment around me. To live in harmony with it is to create harmony within myself, and with others.

A-56

You want me to see past my programming. Then you must try to see past your doubts.

— THE DOCTOR : WARHEAD : Stardate Not Given

Speaking on behalf of the cybernetic entity inhabiting him at the time, The Doctor teaches us a lesson about changing our lives. And allowing others to change theirs.

The lesson begins by recognizing the flaws in the behavioral "programs" we've all inherited from our childhood and past experiences. That's hard enough. But what's *really* hard is giving each other permission to re-program ourselves, to break through the current images we have of one another so we can feel free to act differently... to continue evolving.

It's hard because we so often put people in mental "boxes" based on past disappointments. We label others as untrustworthy or sloppy, lazy or rigid, careless or selfish.

And we assume they place similar labels on us.

Those expectations not only become constricting, but self-fulfilling. We may even reward others, unconsciously, for staying in the little boxes we've put them in. Which reduces the chances for change to just about zilch.

Instead, let's agree to give each other permission to change... to see past our doubts. Even if we know it will take many more tries before a change becomes permanent.

After all, we could use a little slack ourselves.

I celebrate the ability of others to transform themselves. I will find a community of spirit where I, too, can feel free to become the person I intend to be.

A-57

Remembrances and regrets... They, too, are part of friendships.

— CAPTAIN PICARD : PEN PALS : 42695.3

Sometimes "the ties that bind" have as much to do with the bad things that happen in relationships as the good.

So often we think of a friend as someone with whom we enjoy only positive, happy, mutually-beneficial experiences. Or at least someone with whom we can "get along." In fact, if we *haven't* been getting along for a while, we figure it's time to start looking for another friend.

What it's really time for is to not give up so easily. Because the strongest relationships not only weather the inevitable disagreements and seasons of sadness, they survive periods of outright conflict.

In friendships, too, we can lose perspective in the heat of the moment. We may say harsh words, act in anger, or inappropriate passion. Later, we may regret our behavior – or at least recognize that any continuing problems needn't outweigh the mutual benefits.

Remembering – even regretting – what we've done to each other can sometimes forge even closer bonds. In retrospect, we realize that these are the moments that have forced us to grow, to mellow, to redefine ourselves.

Vinegar and oil get along so well not because they dissolve into one another, but because they don't.

"Good" memories don't necessarily mean "happy" ones. If I grow through my relationships – even those that have hurt me – I transcend regret.

A-58

What I've done, I had to do. If I hadn't tried, the cost would've been my soul.

— ADMIRAL KIRK : THE SEARCH FOR SPOCK : 8310.3

Few of our actions are significant enough in themselves to radically alter our lives. Most have a cumulative effect, like small steps, one following the other, down a path we've already chosen.

Then again, there are those occasional crossroads that can literally re-engineer Who We Are. They may be opportunities to show a new side of ourselves, to bring out our dormant divinity, or simply to decide to take responsibility for our lives instead of blaming the world.

Perhaps the toughest decision involves the so-called "lost cause," the no-win situation where it appears that nothing we do will make any lasting difference. Or where doing the right thing may even bring us pain and grief. These are the moments when we ask, Why even try?

And the answer is, because *not* trying would cost us far more than trying and losing. Because turning away – ignoring the cries for help, or the seemingly endless tide of desperate, needy people, or the injustices in the world (even if they're somewhere else) – would rob us of something so essential that it would feel like "losing our soul."

Sometimes, our highest achievement lies not in the end results, but in having tried.

As important as the outward effects of my actions are the inward effects of having acted with integrity, of striving continually to be the best I can be.

A-59

But will you respect me in the morning?

— COMMANDER RIKER : ANGEL ONE : 41636.9

Riker's half-serious question reflects the social insecurity common in cultures where one sex dominates the other. The fact that females held most positions of power on Angel One may be a rarity, but it's hardly unheard of. (For those keeping a galactic scorecard, males are the dominant sex in 83% of known planetary cultures. Of those cultures, 92% would be regarded by Federation standards as "primitive.")

But Riker's question also reflects a larger issue. The truth is, all of us occasionally do things that may seem appropriate or necessary at the time, but which we come to regret later. The dawn of another day, symbolically speaking, often brings a new light to the acts we committed in the preceding "darkness" – when we allowed ourselves to be guided primarily by emotion or physical need; when we acted out of fear rather than strength; when we didn't know what we know now.

And the question we ask of others – "Will you still respect me?" – really means "Can I still respect myself?"

To ask the question ahead of time is to already know the answer. Whatever you're thinking of doing, *don't.*

The problem is, what if we already did it?

Hint: Look up "forgiveness" in the Index.

To forgive myself today for what I did yesterday, is to respect the person I can become tomorrow.

A-60

Trust is earned, not given away.

— LIEUTENANT WORF : THE WOUNDED : 44429.6

Most of us are already aware that relationships are especially susceptible to the self-fulfilling prophecy. If we treat someone with kindness and respect, that individual is more likely to become kind and respectful. If we forgive others, they in turn become more forgiving.

Likewise, if we regard others with suspicion when we first meet, we may not only poison any future relationship, we can end up encouraging the very behavior that fuels our suspicion. In short, we can literally create the attitudes and actions in others that we expect of them.

And yet it would be foolish to simply assume that other individuals possess certain qualities until we have sufficient reason to believe that they do, in fact, possess them. Trustworthiness is one such quality. Learning whether we can rely on someone else's abilities, or their level-headedness during a crisis, or their loyalty to a certain cause, requires repeated demonstrations.

Neither can *we* expect to be fully trusted by someone else until we repeatedly prove our own trustworthiness. We shouldn't regard this as an affront to our integrity. Rather, we can look upon it as a "refresher course," as another opportunity to polish our skills – if not to reassure others, then to reaffirm Who We Are to our*selves.*

It is as important for me to know I am trustworthy – and to learn to trust myself – as it is for others. I welcome opportunities to demonstrate it.

A-61

This isn't about rules and regulations. It's about right and wrong. I won't let you cross that line again.

Rules and regulations, ideally, are formulas for preserving and living out our understanding of right and wrong.

The trouble is, we can sometimes lose sight of that connection. We make "the rules" our final authority, when it's *what the rules represent* that is the real Authority.

It's easy to get them confused. We write down our rules, put them into law books, and make them difficult to change (even if for good reason). Then we build institutions around them, create Federations to enforce them, and otherwise focus on the "letter of the law" and not the spirit. Or the Spirit behind them.

It's at this point that we often need someone else to remind us of the difference. For one thing, our laws are only rough approximations of the universal Order they try to emulate. Worse, because they reflect our own flaws, we may end up using them to pursue our own narrow agendas. Or even our personal vendettas.

Chakotay's warning calls us to a higher standard. We can try to justify our behavior by appealing to "regulations," or even by changing the rules to suit us. But we are truly justified only when we act in conformity with the higher Law. And *that* we cannot change.

I seek to embody the "spirit" of the law rather than the "letter." I focus on the spiritual beneath the material.

A-62

In critical moments men sometimes see exactly what they wish to see.

Commitment is good. The ability to focus on a task, to pursue one's objective with single-minded intensity, is a prerequisite for personal achievement.

But sometimes we can want something so much, so desperately, that it's not good for us. Because we can lose sight of our other priorities. We can lose our perspective. What we desire ends up ensnaring us just as surely as the Tholian Web.

And it's not just that we no longer see what's happening around us. It's that we start seeing things that aren't even there. Our expectations not only filter out evidence contrary to our wishes, they interpret all evidence as support for them. Our leaps of illogic can be mind-boggling.

Schizophrenia, though rare, is the most extreme manifestation of this condition. But none of us is immune, because even "normal" personalities can fragment if we don't actively pursue balance in our lives.

We may have concrete goals, but we must still pay attention to feelings and relationships. We may be willing to work around the clock, but we must still take time out for play and spiritual retreat. We may want to change the world, but the most important changes must start within.

My first wish is to see the world, and to see myself, as they really are. As I tap into the spiritual resources within me, I begin to clarify my vision.

A-63

Maybe it's better to look those feelings in the eye than to keep them locked up.

— CAPTAIN JANEWAY : PERSISTENCE OF VISION : Stardate Not Given

In purely physiological terms, "feelings" are the conscious sensations of our own energy coursing through our bodies. Each type – fear, anger, grief, or joy – represents a purposeful galvanizing of inner forces designed to support a physical response to external conditions.

Considering our obsession with appearing "in control," however, it's not surprising that we should regard these sensations as unwanted intruders. So we barely acknowledge them. Or even try to suppress them completely. And there are perfectly valid reasons for doing so. We have jobs to do, decisions to make, other people's needs to consider. We can't let emotions distract us right now.

But once the "crisis" is over, we must unlock our temporary holding cells. We must find a safe haven or a sounding-board where we can release and fully experience our feelings. And then we must stop… and "look those feelings in the eye."

Which means stepping back to analyze what may have caused them, and especially to consider what we can do with all that emotional energy. Because if we can connect our sensations to some future response – a *thoughtful* response – we turn our feelings into wellsprings of positive action. We make them whole. We make them our friends.

I will better understand my feelings, and learn to use their energy more wisely, as I regularly share and discuss them with an "emotional partner."

A-64

The acquisition of wealth is no longer the driving force in our lives. We work to better ourselves and the rest of humanity.

— CAPTAIN PICARD : FIRST CONTACT : 50893.5

Easy for Picard to say. Because when society has evolved to the point that the average citizen is better off than the kings and queens of centuries past, it's easy for people to turn their attentions to other things than "making a living," or making more money.

Then again, bettering ourselves isn't something we should focus on only after we've "made it," only when we finally achieve some predetermined level of wealth. Not that Picard meant to imply this. He understood that bettering ourselves *is* acquiring "wealth." Serving our fellow beings *is* the way to grow richer.

In fact, spiritual traditions throughout the galaxy have always advised us not to "lay up" material possessions, but to concentrate on the kind of treasures no one can ever take away. An appreciation for the simple things, for instance. Or the satisfaction of having helped someone, just when help was needed. Or having a faith in the goodness of the universe that's so powerful, so radiant, that you literally "make it so."

To develop personal – or rather *spiritual* – qualities like this should be our first priority. And the good news is, once this spiritual quest becomes the driving force in our lives, material wealth tends to take care of itself.

I seek the spiritual riches The Universe has placed within me, and in my relationships with others.

A-65

You can handle defeat in two ways: You can lose confidence, or you can learn from your mistakes.

— COUNSELOR TROI : PEAK PERFORMANCE : 42923.

Watching an infant learn to walk is an instructive, even inspirational, experience. The child gets up, stumbles, falls – cries, perhaps – then gets right back up and tries again. Confidence has nothing to do with it. Worrying about "how it looks" doesn't enter the child's mind. Nor do self-defeating thoughts about not being "allowed" or "able" or "deserving."

There is only an innate knowing that making an effort to walk leads to walking… along with the simple acceptance that falling down is a necessary part of the process.

We can look at our own failures or mistakes in life as "falling down." Unfortunately, as self-conscious adults we may become overly concerned about what others think, or whether our failures point to some deeper flaw in us. Or whether we'll ever, *ever* learn.

But learning is precisely the point. Our mistakes are among the best teaching tools The Universe has at its disposal. And it just so happens that the most resounding victories often occur after the most abysmal defeats. Breakthroughs – revelations – are more likely to arise from failure than a steady string of successes.

The Spiritual Path knows this strange irony as Grace.

Failure will not stop me. Defeat is my opportunity to reassess and to learn. Success is sweeter, and more permanent, if it comes from raw experience.

A-66

Is that not the nature of man and woman? That the pleasure is in the learning of each other?

— NATIRA : FOR THE WORLD IS HOLLOW AND I HAVE TOUCHED THE SKY : 5476.4

There are phases in every culture when the sexual identities developed by social custom no longer reflect biological reality. The fact that females in most species bear its offspring hardly justifies the division of roles – or the outright subjugation – some societies have enforced on them.

Inevitably a flashpoint is reached. And either the pendulum swings to the other side, or social regulations are redesigned to enforce an "equality" which ignores *all* sexual differences. Between these two conditions, the latter is vastly preferable. In fact, our spiritual progress depends on the realization that our ultimate identity – the soul within each of us – is neither male nor female.

And yet, we are *incarnated* souls. Our bodies are gifts from The Universe. And our full appreciation for that gift lies in recognizing the biological differences we inherit, and accepting the unique pleasures we can enjoy precisely because we are this gender and not that.

The benefits are not only physical, but deeply spiritual. Because the underlying message is that we are made whole only as we link ourselves to others, as we use our differences to achieve unity rather than create division. Or, as some humans prefer to put it, *Vive la différence!*

I am equal to others not by being identical, but by identifying and valuing what makes me different.

A-67

Friendship must dare to risk, or it's not friendship.

— CAPTAIN PICARD : CONSPIRACY : 41780.2

In an age defined by micro-genetic technology and distances measured in parsecs, genuine friendship is a rare commodity. Having a "relationship" doesn't require it: We can be Starfleet crewmen, co-workers, fellow members of organizations and races and political alliances – even partners in marriage! – without ever being "friends."

To be a friend means recognizing another person as a fellow voyager on a journey you have decided to undertake together. The journey is not so much a common path to a common destination; rather, it's a mode of travel during which you pause regularly to share experiences, reflect on the obstacles and lessons, and encourage one another along the path each is taking. Even if they diverge.

But it's more than tea and sympathy. There are risks. Because when a friend falls down, *we* hurt too. What's more, we may see obstacles our friend can't, or we'll interpret the roadsigns differently. Our friendship comes to a crossroads: Should we intervene to prevent our friend from stumbling? Or should we simply "be there" to help after they've fallen? Either choice is risky.

To take that risk is the price of preserving friendship. To make no choice is a roadsign that says, "Dead end."

I will take risks to turn "relationships" into friendships, and keep existing friendships from turning into mere relationships. My friends are worth it.

A-68

I'm sure I could be more productive if I didn't have to regenerate every day.

— CONSTABLE ODO : FOR THE CAUSE : Stardate Not Given

If only we didn't need sleep! If only we could use that extra seven or eight hours a day (Humans/Bajorans), or three hours (Vulcans/Klingons); then we might get so much more accomplished!

Or would we? Because even though Odo is restating a complaint we all have – using his own terms, of course – his characteristic sarcasm betrays a recognition that regenerating (i.e. sleeping) isn't just an annoying necessity. It's actually the best use of those precious hours.

After all, it's not as if nothing is going on. Like the Ship's Computer shutting down to optimize its data-banks and to run systems checks, our own "down time" enables us to process our experiences and consolidate learning. No artificial version of this procedure is half as effective.

And not only do we need daily "regeneration," our productivity is enhanced still more by weekly breaks and regularly-scheduled shore leave.

It's so easy to get caught up in our duties. And it helps our ego to think no one else could do what we do, so we'd better stay on the job. But if "observing the Sabbath" weren't already carved in sacred stone, we'd be forced to invent the practice for our own good. It's *that* important.

Today I will begin meditating on my next scheduled holiday. I will open myself to entirely new places and possibilities my inner wisdom will suggest to me.

A-69

Like the man said, "The only thing we have to fear is fear itself."

— ENSIGN KIM : THE THAW : Stardate Not Given

There is some debate whether "the man" Kim refers to was Franklin Roosevelt, the pre-Federation leader who presided over one of Earth's most serious economic depressions – or whether he meant Ru'agh KoHbar, an even earlier Klingon leader who inspired his fellow warriors to repel a vastly superior Romulan invasion force.

It hardly matters. Thousands of leaders from hundreds of planets have made virtually the same statement, many of them recorded millennia before either Earth or Qo'noS had any written records. Because the fact is, fear is an almost universal experience. And although it is as irrational as it is universal, it follows certain identifiable "rules."

One of those rules is that fear feeds on itself. Our original fear is rarely the culprit. How easily we let it grow, how often we seek out other people with the same fear so we can "justify" our own; and then how our combined fears end up doubling and re-doubling until a kind of mass hysteria sets in – *those* are the real culprits.

Another rule is that this hysteria is almost unstoppable until it runs its course. Which simply means that the best counter-measure is not to let it happen in the first place.

That which creates our fear is not the enemy. *Fear* is.

I will confront my fears as soon as I sense them. While accepting their role in signaling potential problems, I will make sure that "fear itself" isn't one of them.

A-70

One of these days I'm going to surprise you... But not today.

— CAPTAIN JANEWAY : PHAGE : 48532.4

It's a healthy attitude: To know that we're not straight-jacketed by our past; that we're free to do something radically new and unexpected now and then; that we can always break out of our shells, climb out of our ruts, throw off our previous limitations. Putting people "on notice" with a line like this is a way of preparing our*selves* for these changes as much as others. Not to mention that it helps keep our options open, and options are essential for growth.

On the other hand, it's also essential to take a vacation from unrelenting growth now and then. We need to periodically consolidate what we know, to live out the lessons we've just learned, to practice being Who We Are Now.

The Universe is written everywhere with the message that there's a time and season for everything. Rest and stability are no less a part of the natural order than chaos and uncertainty. To say "Not today" is to accept and enjoy these seasons of rest, while acknowledging the times of instability and change that lie ahead. Taking full advantage of rest, in fact, is what readies us for change.

Chances are we'll know when the next season is arriving. And we'll be all the more prepared to embrace it.

I deserve the periods of contentment and peace in my life. I can be comfortable with who I am today, and still be ready for change tomorrow.

There is no perfect solution.

— CAPTAIN KIRK : PLATO'S STEPCHILDREN : 5784.2

The problem isn't so much that we're unwilling to face challenges. Or that we're not willing to work. The problem is, we expect too much from our efforts. We want to be done with it. We want our problems solved. We want things perfect already.

And yet the testimony of the universe tells us that nothing is ever "perfect." There is no finished state. All is in flux, evolving, ever changing.

If we're mindful – or sometimes just lucky – we can affect the natural course of change in a way that benefits ourselves and others. But we must guard against the notion that we can solve all our problems forever, or answer our questions with any final certainty. Instead, we should try looking at life like a Science Officer, who builds steadily on previous knowledge, confident that there *are* final answers – at least in theory – but who is satisfied simply to discover one more piece of the puzzle… and then go on with his work despite incomplete information and imperfect solutions while the search continues.

The perfectionist's impossibly high standards are often a convenient excuse to remain uninvolved, to avoid the hard work. And therefore to avoid growing. On the other hand, doing the best we can with the limited knowledge we have – that's as close to "perfection" as we can get.

I'm not perfect, nor do I have all the answers. But I will continue to learn and grow every day by facing life's challenges with an open, experimental attitude.

The expulsion from Paradise… it is a reminder to me that all things end.

— SPOCK : THE UNDISCOVERED COUNTRY : 9521.6

The legend Spock refers to is not unlike creation stories found all across the galaxy. In Spock's own spiritual tradition, *Sha Ka Ree* is the mythical planet from which creation spread throughout the universe – and from which Vulcans were banished just as humans were expelled from Paradise. Stories about the Klingon equivalent, *Qui'Tu*, and the Romulan *Vorta Vor,* are embellished with similar themes.

All of these are meant to tell us that we were not designed for stasis. It's in our natures that we cannot live in an ideal world, where nothing changes because everyone and everything has already achieved perfection. If anything, our sense of *im*perfection is what drives us – to build, to grow, to improve ourselves and our world … and to *keep* growing and improving, or else we cease to exist.

Of course there are periods in our lives when we enter what seems like Paradise, where we can finally enjoy the fruits of success, and we'd be happy if nothing ever changed.

The Expulsion represents the fact that, even when things seem perfect, we still need to keep moving along our Path. Our salvation depends on it. And what sometimes feels like punishment is really the gift of new life.

I celebrate that inner Spirit which calls me onward, even if it means leaving behind what's familiar and comfortable. This day is a new beginning!

Indices

Characters / Quotations Index

A two-letter abbreviation for each Star Trek® character whose words are quoted on these pages is provided below (for use in the Topics/Characters Index), followed by the Earth date(s) and/or Arroway date on which that character's quotations appear.

Continued on next page

GK   Garak : 03.03, 08.24
GR   Captain Georgiou : 03.30, 08.07, 09.07
GN   Guinan : 02.12, 05.17

HZ   Captain Hernandez : 03.15

JK   Jake Sisko : 09.10
JT   Jetrel : 12.13
JW   Captain Janeway : 01.06, 01.27, 02.18, 02.29, 03.18, 03.29, 04.17, 05.05, 05.14,
     06.06, 07.03; 08.10, 10.13, 10.26, 11.03, A-19, A-44, A-63, A-70

KA   Krall : 04.07, 07.29
KK   Ensign / Captain / Adm. Kirk : 01.02, 01.12, 02.13, 02.27, 03.12, 03.27, 04.09,
     04.16, 04.19, 05.12, 05.20, 05.27, 06.07, 06.15, 06.23, 06.30, 07.04, 07.09, 07.15,
     07.20, 07.26, 08.02, 08.06, 08.13, 08.20, 08.25, 09.05, 09.15, 09.30, 10.15, 11.08,
     12.09, 12.19, A-01, A-16, A-20, A-31, A-40, A-53, A-58, A-71
KL   Edith Keeler : 08.01
KM   Ensign Kim : 06.04, A-69
KR   Lieutenant Kira : 03.26, 05.09, 07.18, 09.25, 10.18, 11.20
KS   Kes : 01.18, 05.04, 06.19, 08.11, 11.07

LC   Captain Lorca : 08.18, 12.28
LF   Engineer La Forge : 01.22, 03.06, 04.30, 06.12, 07.30, 09.14, 10.11, 11.15, A-22
LN   Lanel : 10.16
LX   Lwaxana Troi : 02.28, 05.11

MA   Gul Macet : 08.27
MC   Dr. McCoy : 01.07, 01.24, 02.02, 04.06, 04.21, 05.26, 07.10, 08.28, 09.01, 09.19,
     11.02, 11.23, 12.17, A-39
MR   Mirasta : A-03
MT   General Murtok : A-15

NT   Natira : 02.14, 04.27, A-66
NX   Neelix : 02.26, 04.28, 06.18, 08.21, 10.21, 10.29

OB   Chief O'Brien : 03.08, 09.23, 11.18
OD   Constable Odo : 02.11, 06.08, 07.14, 12.10, A-46, A-51, A-68

PC   Captain Picard : 01.01, 01.28, 02.10, 02.24, 03.16, 04.03, 04.14, 04.26, 05.01,
     05.06, 05.13, 05.21, 06.02, 06.17, 06.26, 07.05, 07.12, 07.22, 08.04, 08.14, 08.23,
     08.30, 09.21, 10.05, 10.14, 10.30, 11.06, 11.19, 12.01, 12.12, 12.21, 12.27, 12.31,
     A-02, A-05, A-09, A-13, A-18, A-23, A-26, A-30, A-35, A-42, A-48, A-57, A-64, A-67
PH   Dr. Phlox : 01.26, 12.14
PK   Captain Pike : 01.20

PM   Parmen : 10.10
PR   Lieutenant Paris : 03.04, 10.09
PS   Commodore Paris : 05.31

Q   Q : 02.09, 03.11, 04.23, 05.02, 07.02, 07.31, 08.12, 12.02, 12.24
QK   Quark : 01.08, 04.15, 10.12, 11.29, A-06, A-17, A-29

RD   Lieutenant Reed : 09.11
RK   Commander Riker : 01.05, 02.05, 03.13, 03.28, 06.22, 07.08, 08.16, 09.04, 09.09,
     09.26, 10.07, 10.17, 11.04, 11.12, 11.22, 12.06, 12.26, A-07, A-27, A-37, A-59
RL   Ensign Ro Laren : 12.16
RV   Riva : 01.11, 04.04, 10.02

SA   Ensign Sato : 07.16
SC   Chief Engineer Scott : 02.19, 03.17, 03.31, 10.27, 11.27, A-50
SK   Captain/Commander Sisko : 01.23, 02.06, 04.11, 04.20, 06.21, 08.08, 08.19, 09.17,
     10.20, 11.01, 11.11, 12.29, A-12, A-28, A-47
SL   Lieutenant/Commander Sulu : 02.25, 03.07, 05.23
SM   Science Officer Stamets : 06.14, 11.16
SN   Seven of Nine : 02.17, 03.22, 09.03, 12.03
SP   Spock : 01.03, 01.13, 02.01, 02.23, 03.09, 03.14, 03.21, 04.08, 04.25, 05.10,
     05.16, 05.22, 05.29, 06.01, 06.16, 06.29, 07.01, 07.07, 07.25, 08.26, 09.13, 09.22,
     09.28, 10.24, 11.14, 11.25, 12.18, 12.22, A-04, A-25, A-36, A-45, A-49, A-52, A-62,
     A-72
SR   Sarek : 04.01, 04.29, 10.04, 10.22
ST   Ensign Sito : 09.20
SU   First Officer Saru : 01.19

TL   Cadet Tilly : 04.22, 05.15, 11.30
TP   Subcommander T'Pol : 03.02, 07.17
TR   Counselor Troi : 01.09, 02.22, 05.28, 06.03, 06.13, 06.20, 07.28, 08.15, 10.03,
     11.09, 11.24, 12.15, A-14, A-24, A-38, A-65
TS   Lieutenant Torres : 01.25, 03.24, 05.03, 08.05, 09.18
TV   Lieutenant Tuvok : 01.21, 03.05, 05.18, 06.05, 07.11, 09.08, 09.29, 10.08, 10.25,
     11.10, 12.23, A-08, A-21, A-33, A-41, A-54
TY   Lieutenant Tyler : 07.19

UH   Lieutenant Uhura : 01.30, 07.13, 10.19, 12.05, 12.25

WF   Lieutenant/Cmdr. Worf : 01.15, 03.10, 04.18, 05.07, 06.27, 08.22, 09.06, 10.01,
     11.17, 11.26, 12.08, A-32, A-43, A-60
WR   The Wraith : 05.24

Topics / Characters Index

For each topic listed below in alphabetical order (in italics), the dates of all the daily meditations related to that topic are provided. Most meditations reference more than one topic.

The number for each meditation is followed by the abbreviation for the character whose quotation inspired it. (Character abbreviations may be found in the preceding Index.) After reading the selected meditation, simply return to this page for additional meditations on the same topic, or for other topics.

A

Acceptance

07.22/PC; 08.13/KK; 09.06/WF; 11.02/MC; A-49/SP

Accepting Reality

02.13/KK; 02.27/KK; 06.23/KK; 08.24/GK; 09.13/SP; 09.28/SP; 11.18/OB; 12.18/SP; A-33/TV

Achievement(s)

01.18/KS; 01.20/PK; 07.17/TP; A-06/QK; A-58/KK

Actions

01.06/JW; 02.02/MC; 02.28/LX; 03.15/HZ; 04.21/MC; 05.07/WF; 07.07/SP; 08.03DG; 08.08/SK; 08.25/KK; 09.15/KK; 09.22/SP; 09.29/TV; 10.04/SR; 11.21/CR; A-25/SP; A-48/PC; A-58/KK

Addictions

04.16/KK; 04.24/CP; 06.06/JW; 06.20/TR; 07.01/SP; 09.09/RK; A-47/SK

Admitting Ignorance

07.22/PC; 08.29/DT; 09.27/DT; 11.23/MC; A-19/JW

Ambition

08.02/KK; A-53/KK; A-06/QK

Appearance vs. Substance

02.26/NX; 04.20/SK; 07.17/TP; 10.08/TV; 11.13/CL; A-09/PC; A-54/TV

Attitude

01.11/RV; 03.22/SN; 03.24/TS; 05.09/KR; 05.24/WR; 06.06JW; 07.26/KK; 09.08/TV; 10.06/CK; 10.13/JW; 10.29/NX; 11.25/SP; A-02/PC; A-13/PC

B

Balance

07.20/KK; 08.05/TS; 08.23/PC; 11.01/SK; 11.29/QK; 12.11/CH

Beginnings

05.02/Q; 08.01/KL; 09.10/JK; 12.27/PC; 12.31/PC; A-72/SP

Believing in Yourself

01.29/BN; 03.23/DX; 05.20/KK; 06.24/CK; 08.30/PC; 12.08/WF; A-40/KK; A-62/SP

Blessing

03.14/SP; 05.23/SL; 06.25/CH; 11.30/TL

Brooding

06.19/KS; 09.25/KR; A-63/JW

C

Changing Ourselves

01.31/AL; 02.27/KK; 03.15/HZ; 07.02/Q; 10.26/JW; 10.28/DR; 12.09/KK; A-01/KK; A-12/SK; A-17/QK; A-34/AN; A-56/DR

Challenges

01.05/RK; 01.11/RV; 05.03/TS; 05.16/SP; 07.03/JW; 07.29KA; 08.02/KK; 09.26/RK; 10.20/SK; 11.24/TR; 12.29/SK

Character

04.02/CH; 07.09/KK; 07.17/TP; 09.24/CH; 10.26/JW; A-48/PC; A-53/KK

Choices

01.01/PC; 02.20/DT; 04.01/SR; 05.10/SP; 05.31/PS; 09.03/SN; 09.05/KK; 09.16/CR; A-13/PC; A-42/PC

Choosing Sides

10.18/KR; 10.31/CH

Commitment

02.18/JW; 03.23/DX; 05.24/WR; 08.22/WF; 12.07/BR

Communication

04.04/RV; 04.06/MC; 08.26/SP; 11.19/PC; 12.04/DR

Community

02.04/CB; 02.08/BR; 03.17/SC; 05.11/LX; A-03/MR; 06.01/SP; 06.02/PC; 06.30/KK; 08.07/GR; 10.02/RV; 11.07/KS

Competition

04.03/PC; 08.05/TS; 08.06/KK

Compromise

04.13/AR; 08.26/SP; 08.30/PC

Confidence

01.09/TR; 01.25./TS; 07.16/SA

Consciousness

01.26/PH; 05.05/JW; 05.17/GN; 05.11/LX; 06.05/TV; 10.08/TV; 11.16/SM

Consequences

01.26/PH; 01.30/UH; 05.19/DX; 10.04/SR; 11.16/SM; 11.21/CR; A-04/SP; A-29/QK-DX; A-44/JW

Constants

06.15/KK; 07.02/Q; 08.20/KK; A-17/QK

Controlling

07.28/TR; 08.13/KK; 09.03/SN; 09.06/WF; 10.17/RK; 10.27/SC; 11.02/MC; 12.20/CH; A-18/PC

Cooperation

04.16/KK; 04.19/KK; 06.17/PC; A-19/PC; A-20/KK

Cosmic Plan

05.28/TR; 10.07/RK; 12.26/RK

Courage

01.02/KK; 04.02/CH; 05.14/JW; 07.26/KK; 10.09/PR; A-40/KK; 12.07/BR

Courtesy

12.04/DR; A-21/TV

Creativity

05.09/KR; 12.29/SK; A-45/SP

Criticism

02.19/SC; 04.08/SP; 11.10/TV; A-16/KK; A-39/MC; A-52/SP

Curiosity

12.21/PC; 12.31/PC; A-38/TR

D

Death

04.17/JW; 07.19/TY; 11.11/SK; 11.27/SC; A-11/BR

Defeat

01.05/RK; A-65/TR; 03.16/PC; 05.24/WR; 08.06/KK

Deeper Meanings

02.29/JW; 03.28/RK; 04.04/RV; 09.22/SP; 10.20/SK; A-18/PC; A-21/TV; A-65/TR

Direction

02.06/SK; 02.25/SL; 03.09/SP; 03.26/KR; 03.31/SC; 05.12/KK; 05.31/PS

Differences / Diversity

02.17/SN; 03.21/SP; 04.07/KA; 04.13/AR; 06.13/TR; 09.07/GR; 12.12/PC; A-16/KK; A-26/PC; A-30/PC; A-66/NT

Doing

01.12/KK; 01.20/PK; 01.22/LF; 01.31/AL; 02.28/LX; 03.12/KK; 03.22/SN; 04.12/DT; 04.26/PC; 06.04/KM; 06.21/SK; 07.01/SP; 08.08/SK; 08.11/KS; 09.10/JK; 09.21/PC; 10.11/LF; A-31/KK

Double Standard

04.27/NT; A-23/PC

E

Effort

01.10/CK; 02.27/KK; 03.16/PC; 03.22/SN; 04.12/DT; 09.06/WF; 10.06/CK; 11.29/QK; 12.07/BR; A-58/KK

Ego vs. Self

11.05/BR; A-01/KK; A-52/SP

Emotional Energy

01.02/KK; 06.16/SP; 07.25/SP; 09.28/SP; 10.09/PR; 11.09/TR; A-35/PC; A-63/JW

Emotions

01.18/KS; 02.24/PC; 03.05/TV; 05.18/TV; 06.03/TR; 06.18/NX; 06.26/PC; 07.13/UH; 07.27/DT; 11.29/QK; A-04/SP; A-24/TR

Empowerment

01.12/KK; 01.23/SK; 03.31/SC; 04.25/SP; 05.17/GN; 05.22/SP; 09.21/PC; 12.01/PC; 12.25/UH; A-28/SK

Enemies

02.15/AR; 03.14/SP; 04.09/KK; 04.19/KK; 05.03/TS; 06.02/PC; 09.06/WF; 10.18/KR; 11.08/KK; A-08/TV

Exercise

03.07/SL; 07.20/KK; 10.05/PC; 11.21/CR

Expectations

01.06/JW; 01.19/SU; 01.22/LF; 02.26/NX; 03.15/HZ; 06.07/KK; 08.31/BN; 10.10/PM; 10.23/DW; 11.22/RK; 12.18/SP; A-09/PC; A-42/PC; A-56/DR

Evil

01.31/AL; 04.09/KK; 07.07/SP; 09.11/RD; 10.10/PM; A-23/PC; A-54/TV; A-69/KM

F

Failure

02.03/EZ; 03.09/SP; 03.16/PC; 04.26/PC; 05.24/WR; 08.06/KK; 10.06/CK; 10.11/LF; 11.10/TV; 11.29/QK; A-21/TV; A-65/TR

Faith (see also Attitudes)

01.09/TR; 03.11/Q; 03.26/KR; 03.29/JW; 05.13/PC; 05.16/SP; 05.22/SP; 07.28/TR; 09.18/TS; 10.16/LN; 12.21/PC; A-38/TR; A-64/PC

Family

06.01/SP; 08.03/DG; 11.20/KR; A-07/RK; A-27/RK; A-32/WF

Fantasies

01.30/UH; 03.03/GK; 08.15/TR; 10.05/PC; 11.04/RK; 12.22/SP

Fear

01.02/KK; 01.15/WF; 03.13/RK; 05.14/JW; 07.03/JW; 10.16/LN; 10.29/NX; A-01/KK; A-69/KM

Feelings

01.07/MC; 02.14/NT; 02.22/TR; 02.24/PC; 03.05/TV; 04.06/MC; 05.19/DX; 08.18/LC; 10.15/KK; 10.31/CH; 11.01/SK; 11.10/TV; 12.06/RK; A-63/JW

Feeling Useful

05.06/PC; 11.28/AL; A-22/LF

Firsts

02.01/SP; 09.07/GR; 09.10/JK

Forgiveness

02.03/EZ; 05.21/PC; 05.27/KK; 07.20/KK; 08.16/RK; 09.15/KK; 12.06/RK; A-59/RK; A-69/KM

Freedom

07.04/KK; 07.05/PC; 07.16/SA; 12.19/KK

Freeing Others

10.21/NX; 11.04/RK

Friendship

03.06/LF; 04.19/KK; 06.01/SP; 08.10/JW; 08.21/NX; 09.16/CR; A-20/KK; A-57/PC; A-67/PC

Fulfillment

01.11/RV; 01.27/JW; 02.27/KK; 03.12/KK; 04.17/JW; 04.25/SP; 06.09/DT; 08.03/DG; 10.16/LN; 11.28/AL

Future

01.01/PC; 01.04/CH; 03.11/Q; 08.12/Q; 09.16/CR; 12.14/PH; 12.26/RK; 12.29/SK; A-02/PC; A-13/PC

G

Gender Issues

06.13/TR; 07.16/SA; 09.17/SK; A-66/NT

Giving

02.10/PC; 03.01/DT; 04.28/NX; 08.03/DG; 10.07/RK; 12.15/TR; A-05/PC

Goals

01.04/CH; 01.20/PK; 01.24/MC; 02.06/SK; 03.09/SP; 04.12/DT; 04.19/KK; 05.08/DT; 05.24/WR; 06.27/WF; 08.22/WF; 12.07/BR; A-06/QK; A-11/BR

Grounding Ourselves

02.18/JW; 02.22/TR; 03.18/JW; 06.15/KK; 06.23/KK; 08.02/KK; 08.20/KK; 09.12/BN; 09.25/KR; 10.05/PC; 11.03/JW; A-55/CN

Grief

04.24/CP; 08.18/LC; 09.25/KR

Growth

01.11/RV; 01.31/AL; 02.01/SP; 02.05/RK; 03.13/RK; 03.16/PC; 05.22/SP; 06.01/SP; 06.04/KM; 06.26/PC; 07.10/MC; 08.04/PC; 08.06/KK; 08.17/DR; 09.14/LF; 10.16/LN; 12.14/PH; A-06/QK; A-19/JW; A-38/TR; A-53/KK; A-70/JW; A-72/SP

H

Habit

01.31/AL; 02.11/OD; 03.15/HZ; 04.10/DR; 06.20/TR; 10.31/CH; 09.03/SN; 10.24/SP; 10.28/DR

Happiness

02.24/PC; 03.02/TP; 04.10/DR; 06.20/TR; 09.03/SN; 10.24/SP; 10.28/DR

Hate

08.16/RK; 10.24/SP

Healing

03.28/RK; 04.24/CP; 04.29/SR; 05.04/KS; 05.15/TL; 05.27/KK; 08.18/LC; 08.31/BN; 09.30/KK; 10.03/TR; 11.02/MC; A-45/SP

Higher Power / Intelligence / The Universe / God

01.06/JW; 03.06/LF; 03.08/OB; 03.20/CK; 05.23/SL; 05.30/DK; 06.11/DR; 07.28/TR; 09.23/OB; 11.02/MC; 11.14/SP; 11.30/TL; 12.01/PC; 12.25/UH; A-45/SP

Honesty

04.21/MC; 07.24/BR; A-36/SP

Honor

03.18/JW; 04.18/WF; A-15/MT; A-32/WF; A-58/KK

Hope

05.16/SP; 08.01/KL; 09.26/RK; 11.30/TL

Humility

03.16/PC; 04.16/KK; 05.25/CR; 06.23/KK; 09.13/SP; 10.07/RK

I

Illusion

06.29/SP; 10.19/UH; 11.13/CL; A-54/TV

Imagination

01.21/TV; 03.11/Q; 05.14/JW; 05.30/DK; 06.12/LF; 10.14/PC; A-46/OD

Individuality

02.08/BR; 03.19/DT; 03.25/DR; 04.14/PC; 06.17/PC; 07.13/UH; 12.05/UH

Inner Conflict

01.31/AL; 05.26/MC; 06.02/PC; 08.05/TS; 08.22/WF; 11.05/BR; 11.14/SP

Inner Guidance

01.06/JW; 01.09/TR; 01.25./TS; 02.12/GN; 03.02/TP; 09.16/CR; A-10/CH; A-14/TR; A-44/JW

Inner Resources

01.06/JW; 01.26/PH; 02.07/CR; 03.08/OB; 05.09/KR; 05.31/PS; 07.03/JW; 09.08/TV; 11.02/MC; A-08/TV

Integrity

04.13/AR; 07.12/PC; 08.14/PC; A-43/WF; A-58/KK; A-60/WF

Interdependence

01.16/DT ; 02.08/BR; 04.28/NX; 04.29/SR; 06.01/SP; 09.04/RK; 11.07/KS; 11.13/CL; 11.30/TL; A-20/KK; A-26/PC

J

Joy

02.24/PC; 03.11/Q; 03.12/KK; 07.27/DT; 11.27/SC

Judging Others

02.26/NX; 04.27/NT; 05.21/PC; 09.20/ST; 11.12/RK; 11.22/RK; A-16/KK; A-39/MC

Justice

09.04/RK; 10.26/JW; A-23/PC; A-61/CH

K

Karma

02.10/PC; 06.25/CH; 07.05/PC; 08.30/PC; A-28/SK

Knowledge

02.23/SP; 05.25/CR; 06.07/KK; 09.13/SP; 11.16/SM; 12.13/JT; A-18/PC; A-19/JW; A-38/TR

L

Laughter

07.27/DT; 10.29/NX; 11.09/TR; 11.25/SP

Learning by Doing

01.12/KK; 03.31/SC; 04.12/DT; 06.04/KM; 08.11/KS; A-06/QK

Lessons

01.28/PC; 02.02/MC; 02.16/DS; 02.27/KK; 03.12/KK; 03.16/PC; 03.29/JW; 03.30/GR; 04.26/PC; 05.14/JW; 05.23/SL; 06.10/DU; 07.11/TV; 08.09/DT; 11.15/LF; 12.05/UH; 12.09/KK; 12.11/CH; 12.14/PH; 12.22/SP; 12.28/LC

Letting Go

01.06/JW; 01.24/MC; 03.16/PC; 04.26/PC; 06.05/TV; 06.11/DR; 06.21/SK; 06.13/TR; 07.11/TV; 08.06/KK; 09.06/WF; 10.01/WF; 10.27/SC; 11.09/TR; 11.27/SC

Lies

07.12/PC; 07.10/MC; 07.24/BR; 08.16/RK

Life as Business

04.11/SK; 04.15/QK

Life's Mission

01.02/KK; 01.22/LF; 03.02/TP; 03.27/KK; 03.29/JW; 06.09/DT; 07.26/KK; 08.03/DG; 09.05/KK; 10.09/PR; 12.13/JT; A-38/TR

Linking to Source

01.06/JW; 01.14/CR; 01.23/SK; 02.07/CR; 05.11/LX; 06.07/KK; 06.08/OD; 06.15/KK; 09.12/BN; 10.08/TV; 12.24/Q; 12.25/UH

Listening

02.12/GN; 04.04/RV; 05.04/KS; 07.14/OD; 10.03/TR; 10.14/PC; 12.04/DR

Living in the Present

01.04/CH; 01.17/DR; 06.08/OD; 06.19/KS; 08.01/KL; 08.23/PC; 09.23/OB; 10.19/UH; 11.27/SC; A-34/AN

Logic

05.29/SP; 09.13/SP; 09.29/TV; 10.25/TV; A-10/CH; A-14/TR; A-41/TV

Losing Touch

03.04/PR; 03.11/Q; 03.18/JW; 05.10/SP; 06.18/NX; 07.13/UH; 11.28/AL

Loss

02.22/TR; 08.01/KL; 10.03/TR; A-43/WF

Love

02.14/NT; 04.30/LF; 05.26/MC; 06.16/SP; 06.18/NX; 06.22/RK; 06.29/SP; 08.16/RK; 10.21/NX; 12.13/JT; 12.20/CH; A-15/MT

M

Making Excuses (Rationalizing)

02.02/MC; 02.10/PC; 05.10/SP; 06.20/TR; 09.03/SN; 10.25/TV; A-05/PC; A-19/JW

Making a Difference

01.03/SP; 02.08/BR; 03.01/DT; 08.03DG; 10.02/RV; A-13/PC

Manipulation

10.08/TV; 10.25/TV; 11.18/OB; A-13/PC

Material vs. Spiritual

01.20/PK; 03.10/ WF; 04.01/SR; 04.30/LF; 09.11/RD; 11.26/WF; A-53/KK; A-64/PC

Meditation

01.17/DR; 01.31/AL; 03.04/PR; 03.03/GK; 04.05/CR; 05.05/JW; 06.05/TV; 07.14/OD; 08.12/Q; 09.25/KR; 10.30/PC; A-10/CH; A-46/OD

Memories

02.22/TR; 05.27/KK; 08.09/DT; 11.15/LF; A-35/PC; A-57/PC

Mirroring

01.28/PC; 04.08/SP; 08.16/RK; 08.22/WF; 11.12/RK

Mindfulness

06.19/KS; 06.27/WF; A-34/AN; A-71/KK

Miracle(s)

01.26/PH; 05.04/KS; 08.31/BN; 10.23/DW; 12.23/TV

Mistakes

01.12/KK; 02.03/EZ; 02.16/DS; 03.16/PC; 06.04/KM; 07.11/TV; 11.06/PC; 11.10/TV; A-12/SK; A-21/TV; A-65/TR

Morality

01.21/TV; 02.15/AR; 04.08/SP; 07.07/SP; 07.12/PC; 10.10/PM; A-61/CH

Motivation

03.26/KR; 05.08/DT; 07.06/SU; 06.10/DU; 09.19/MC; 11.26/WF; A-06/QK

Moving Forward

02.03/EZ; 05.02/Q; 08.16/RK; 08.18/LC; 10.06/CK; 12.26/RK; 12.30/BR; 12.31/PC; A-21/TV; A-44/JW; A-65/TR; A-72/SP

Mutual Support

01.27/JW; 03.08/OB; 09.16/CR; 11.07/KS: A-02/PC; A-20/KK

Mystery

> 04.17/JW; 05.30/DK; 06.11/DR; 11.16/SM; 12.16/RL; 12.21/PC; A-41/TV

N

Needs

> 01.13/SP; 02.27/KK; 04.05/CR; 04.18/WF; 04.28/NX; 06.01/SP; 07.01/SP; 07.13/UH; 07.30/LF; 08.21/NX; 11.19/PC; 12.11/CH

Negative Thoughts

> 01.21/TV; 02.01/SP; 07.25/SP; 10.31/CH; A-69/KM

New Experiences

> 03.11/Q; 08.17/DR; 09.14/LF; 12.30/BR

Non-Attachment

> 02.11/OD; 03.10/WF; 11.29/QK

O

Objectivity

> 04.05/CR; 09.25/KR; A-25/SP; A-51/OD

Opportunities for Growth

> 01.10/CK; 01.20/PK; 02.01/SP; 05.12/KK; 05.27/KK; 05.28/TR; 07.11/TV; 07.28/TR; 08.17/DR; 08.18/LC ; 09.03/SN; 09.23/OB; 10.13/JW; 10.20/SK; 12.09/KK; A-21/TV; A-22/LF; A-38/TR; A-65/TR

Opposites

> 02.24/PC; 10.18/KR; 10.31/CH; A-54/TV

Options

> 02.15/AR; 03.09/SP; 04.15/QK; 08.25/KK; 09.02/BR; 09.03/SN; 10.18/KR; 09.29/TV; 10.31/CH; 11.13/CL; A-47/SK; A-70/JW

Others' Opinions

> 01.25./TS; A-28/SK; A-51/OD

P

Pain

> 02.24/PC; 03.28/RK; 05.27/KK; 08.19/SK; 10.03/TR; 12.31/PC; A-11/BR

Past Lives

> 07.21/DX; 08.16/RK

Patience

> 01.10/CK; 03.29/JW; 05.07/WF; 05.21/PC; 06.22/RK; 09.29/TV; 12.10/OD; 12.11/CH; A-71/KK

Peace / Peace-making / Inner Peace

02.21/BN; 02.20,/DT; 05.26/MC; 06.25/CH; 06.28/BN; 07.06/SU; 07.15/KK; 08.27/MA; 09.07/GR; 09.12/BN; 11.08/KK; A-15/MT; A-26/PC; A-42/PC

Perfectionism

12.03/SN; A-71/KK

Personal Demons

01.31/AL; 04.09/KK; 06.03/TR; 10.17/RK; 10.31/CH; 11.08/KK

Personhood

01.31/AL; 02.08/BR; 04.03/PC; 04.14/PC; 06.24/SL; 07.13/UH; 08.16/RK; 09.01/MC; 09.17/SK; 10.15/KK; 11.04/RK; 11.05/BR

Perspective

06.08/OD; 07.19/TY; 07.22/PC; 07.30/LF; 08.12/Q; 09.02/BR; 09.16/CR; 11.01/SK; 11.08/KK; A-51/OD

Planning

01.14/CR; 01.29/BN; 02.06/SK; 08.08/SK; 09.16/CR; A-02/PC

Play

02.09/Q; 03.11/Q; 04.23/Q; 06.03/TR; 07.14/OD; 12.27/PC

Practice

01.12/KK; 03.03/GK; 04.11/SK; 05.13/PC; 07.20/KK; 08.21/NX; 08.23/PC; 10.30/PC

Presence

02.14/NT; 03.06/LF; 04.24/CP; 05.04/KS

Prime Directive

02.25/SL; 06.26/PC; 08.04/PC; A-03/MR; A-04/SP

Purpose

01.07/MC; 01.20/PK; 03.02/TP; 03.24/TS; 04.18/WF; 04.28/NX; 07.11/TV; 08.11/KS; 12.10/OD; A-37/RK; A-38/TR; A-43/WF

Q

Questions

01.04/CH; 01.20/PK; 02.15/AR; 03.24/TS; 04.01/SR; 06.07/KK; 06.09/DT; 08.11/KS; 09.18/TS; 09.27/DT; 12.16/RL; 12.21/PC

R

Readiness

01.01/PC; 05.23/SL; 05.27/KK; 09.08/TV; 09.23/OB; 10.01/WF; 10.11/LF; 12.30/BR; A-02/PC; A-70/JW

Recovery

03.15/HZ; 03.29/JW; 04.24/CP; 06.20/TR; 08.01/KL; 08.09/DT; 10.03/TR; 10.06/CK; 10.22/SR; 11.02/MC

Re-Creation

01.01/PC; 01.28/PC; 07.31/Q; 08.16/RK; A-34/AN

Rejection

04.11/SK; A-22/LF

Relationships

01.16/DT; 02.18/JW; 02.21/BN; 04.20/SK; 04.24/CP; 06.14/SM; 06.22/RK; 06.28/BN; 06.29/SP; 07.10/MC; 07.19/TY; 09.07/GR; 10.15/KK; 11.09/TR; 11.22/RK; 12.12/PC; 12.15/TR; A-03/MR; A-07/RK; A-15/MT; A-26/PC; A-27/RK; A-57/PC; A-67/PC

Remembering

03.18/JW; 07.21/DX; 08.09/DT; 11.03/JW

Respect / Self-Respect

02.07/CR; 04.28/NX; 06.10/DU; 07.25/SP; 08.30/PC; 12.04/DR; A-59/RK

Responsibility / Taking Responsibility

02.10/PC; 02.20/DT; 04.22/TL; 05.10/SP; 05.17/GN ; 05.19/DX; 08.07/GR; 08.14/PC; 08.24/GK; 09.21/PC; 09.28/SP; 10.07/RK; 10.17/RK; 10.25/TV; 10.28/DR; 12.19/KK; A-05/PC; A-17/QK; A-28/SK; A-40/KK

Rest

07.31/Q; 09.09/RK; 12.28.LC; A-68/OD; A-70/JW

Results

04.26/PC; 10.05/PC; 10.11/LF; A-35/PC

Rewards

01.05/RK; 01.18/KS; 02.18/JW; 02.27/KK; 04.12/DT; 07.04/KK; 09.19/MC; 10.12/QK; 11.24/TR; 11.26/WF; A-21/TV; A-43/WF; A-65/TR

Rights

02.10/PC; 07.05/PC; 08.14/PC; 11.17/WF; A-37/RK

Risking / Taking Risks

01.24/MC; 02.05/RK; 05.01/PC; 08.25/KK; 10.12/QK; 12.08/WF; A-32/WF; A-43/WF; A-44/JW

Role Models

04.03/PC; 05.13/PC; 07.16/SA; 08.27/MA; 11.06/PC; 11.12/RK; 12.11/CH; 12.24/Q; A-07/RK

Rules

01.16/DT; 01.26/PH; 02.09/Q; 02.13/KK; 02.15/AR; 06.11/DR; 07.16/SA; 08.25/KK; 12.27/PC; A-31/KK

Running Away

01.28/PC; 04.23/Q; 08.19/SK

S

Sanctity of Life

02.28/LX; 02.29/JW; 04.14/PC; 06.16/SP; 11.27/SC; 12.17/MC; A-11/BR

Science vs. Religion

07.23/DJ; 12.21/PC

Security

07.26/KK; 09.11/RD; 10.28/DR; 11.17/WF

Self-Acceptance

02.03/EZ; 02.19/SC; 03.20/CK; 04.25/SP; 05.09/KR; 06.03/TR; 06.24/CK; 09.01/MC; 11.20/OB; 12.03/SN

Self-Deception

01.19/SU; 02.26/NX; 08.28/MC; 07.12/PC; A-62/SP

Self-Discipline

01.01/PC; 02.20/DT; 03.05/TV; 03.07/SL; 05.18/TV; 06.20/TR; 07.20/KK; 08.22/WF; 10.24/SP

Self-Discovery

01.16/DT; 04.12/DT; 08.04/PC; 08.31/BN; 09.17/SK; 12.02/Q; 12.13/JT; 12.30/BR; A-01/KK; A-08/TV; A-52/SP

Self-Improvement

01.20/PK; 03.13/RK; 04.12/DT; 07.02/Q; 10.12/QK; 11.06/PC; 12.03/SN; 12.09/KK; A-06/QK; A-49/SP; A-50/SC; A-53/KK; A-64/PC

Self-Inventory

01.19/SU; 03.04/PR; 04.10/DR; 05.15/TL; A-25/SP

Self-Knowledge

03.30/GR; 04.23/Q; 08.28/MC; 09.05/KK; 12.20/CH; 12.21/PC; A-25/SP; A-33/TV

Self-Limitation

03.23/DX; 05.01/PC; 06.07/KK; 09.14/LF; 11.05/BR; 12.24/Q; A-47/SK

Self-Transformation

01.15/WF ; 01.28/PC; 01.31/AL; 03.31/SC; 04.12/DT; 07.09/KK; 09.03/SN; 09.20/ST; 10.16/LN; 10.28/DR; 11.10/TV; 12.02/Q; 12.25/UH; A-35/PC

Self-Worth

02.04/CB; 04.11/SK; 04.14/PC; 04.23/Q; 05.06/PC; 08.01/KL; 10.01/WF; 10.15/KK; A-22/LF

Selfishness / Selflessness

03.01/DT; 04.18/WF; 06.30/KK; 07.04/IKK; 11.21/CR; A-20/KK

Serving Others

02.10/PC; 03.01/DT; 04.18/WF; 04.22/TL; 04.28/NX; 08.07/GR; 08.21/NX; 09.23/OB; 12.15/TR; A-64/PC

Technology

01.26/PH; 02.18/JW; 03.25/DR; 07.28/TR; 07.23/DJ; 08.15/TR; 11.28/AL; A-50/SC

Threats

10.26/JW; A-48/PC

Time / Taking Time

01.24/MC; 04.05/CR; 06.03/TR; 06.19/KS; 07.14/OD; 07.31/Q; 08.12/Q; 08.18/LC; 08.23/PC; 09.10/JK; 09.23/OB; 10.18/KR; 10.19/UH; 11.27/SC; 12.03/SN; 12.10/OD; 12.11/CH; A-11/BR; A-35/PC; A-34/AN; A-68/OD; A-70/JW

Tolerance

04.07/KA; 04.13/AR; 12.12/PC; A-39/MC

Touching

02.14/NT; 06.29/SP; 11.19/PC

Transcending Differences

02.17/SN; 03.19/DT; 03.21/SP; 04.13/AR; 08.29/DT; 12.12/PC; A-30/PC; A-46/OD; A-66/NT

Transformation

01.12/KK; 01.31/AL; 05.22/SP; 07.08/RK; 08.31/BN; A-35/PC; A-32/WF; A-42/PC; A-45/SP; A-56/DR

Trust

02.07/CR; 03.16/PC; 05.20/KK; 06.25/CH; 07.28/TR; 10.27/SC; 11.02/MC; A-09/PC; A-10/CH; A-20/KK; A-27/RK; A-60/WF

Truth

03.21/SP; 03.26/KR; 04.27/NT; 06.12/LF; 07.08/KR; 07.24/BR; 07.23/DJ; 09.16/CR; 09.18/TS; 10.05/PC; 12.18/SP; 12.23/TV; A-03/MR; A-36/SP; A-48/PC

u

Uniqueness

01.29/BN; 02.08/BR; 02.17/SN; 03.19/DT; 04.25/SP; 09.01/MC; 10.02/RV

Unity

03.17/SC; 04.07/KA; 09.07/GR

The Unknown

01.02/KK; 03.13/RK; 10.16/LN; 12.02/Q; 12.26/RK; 12.30/BR; A-02/PC

V

Values

01.08/QK; 01.16/DT; 04.13/AR; 05.06/PC; A-32/WF; A-54/TV

Violence

04.09/KK; 05.03/TS; 07.15/KK; 09.11/RD; 11.11/SK

Vocation

01.08/QK; 03.27/KK; 06.09/DT; 09.05/KK

Vulnerability

08.27/MA; 09.30/KK; 11.18/OB; 12.20/CH

W

Wanting

01.13/SP; 01.26/PH; 02.13/KK; 04.30/LF; 05.10/SP; 06.19/KS; 12.22/SP; A-62/SP

Wealth

10.12/QK; A-64/PC

Web of Life

04.28/NX; 06.01/SP; 08.03/DG; 08.10/JW; 09.04/RK; 12.01/PC; 12.17/MC; 12.20/CH; A-05/PC

Wholeness

02.21/BN; 06.28/BN

Who We Are

01.01/PC; 02.15/AR; 03.18/JW; 04.02/CH; 04.25/SP; 05.31/PS; 06.09/DT; 06.14/SM; 07.02/Q; 07.15/KK; 07.16/SA; 07.17/TP; 07.29/KA; 08.11/KS; 08.19/SK; 09.24/CH; A-26/PC; A-24/TR

Winning

01.10/CK; 08.06/KK; 09.26/RK; A-15/MT

Wisdom

01.06/JW; 02.12/GN; 02.23/SP; 05.29/SP; 07.18/KR; 09.27/DT; 10.04/SR; A-36/SP; A-31/KK

Wishing / Well-Wishing

01.26/PH; 01.30/UH; 03.14/SP; 06.19/KS; 06.25/CH; 08.07/SP; 09.19/PC; 11.30/TL

Words

03.14/SP; 04.04/RV; 04.21/MC; 07.18/KR; 09.22/SP; 10.14/PC; 11.23/MC; 12.01/PC

Extras

About the Author

MARK HASKETT is a working artist, writer and musician, and has been a student of philosophy and religion for most of his adult life. He has authored articles, novels and non-fiction books, each of which invites his readers to explore the deeper dimensions of everyday life that provide meaning and enhance mutual understanding. (For brief summaries of his other books, turn to the next page.)

Active in his local interfaith community, Mark is a frequent guest speaker and moderator on matters of practical faith and spirituality. He occasionally tours with his "Song of The Prophet" concert/service drawn from Kahlil Gibran's poetic masterwork, *The Prophet.*

Mark resides with his wife Nancy in California's Central Valley, and may be contacted directly by going to:

www.IFMedia.org/Feedback.

Other Books by the Author

In Mark's latest novel, **GREATER MIRACLES**, Gabriel Woods is once again on the run because of the miraculous power he wields but doesn't want. When he meets Lane D'Arcy, an enigmatic beauty who appears immune to his "gift," Gabriel dreams of having his life back. A looming strike at the munitions plant in Lane's half-Anglo, half-Native American town soon gets in the way, as does a police chief determined to uncover Gabriel's secret.

The timeless wisdom of Kahlil Gibran's poetic masterwork, The Prophet, is showcased in these insightful reflections on 101 of its most compelling passages. Divided into nine deeper themes that underlie Gibran's 26 "counsels," **A DEEPER SONG** infuses his observations on what it means to be human with fresh meaning and significance.

This book will change the way you think about "faith" and "religion" …and about the loaded words we too often use without knowing what they really mean. While masquerading as a down-to-earth lexicon of inter-religious terminology, **FAITHSPEAK** is an adventure in comparative religions, as well as a handy resource for the reader's ongoing spiritual journeys.

When evangelist Jimmy Talbot opens a Gospel-themed casino in downtown Las Vegas, estranged half-brother Levi is assigned to lead an investigation into the bomb threat and the string of grisly murders connected to it. Both crime novel and social commentary, **CALVARY CASINO** is ultimately a page-turning parable on the subject of reconciliation and redemption.

For more detailed synopses of Mark's books, as well as author interviews about them all, please visit our website at www.IFMedia.org/IFBooks.

Author Interview

IF Media: *I know the preface in* Boldly Going on Your Inner Voyage *addresses this issue. But tell us again why a book with "Starfleet Daily Meditation Manual" in its subtitle isn't really a Star Trek book.*

Mark: Well, it is and it isn't. Like other "meditationals" – that's what the publishing industry calls this format – each daily reading begins with a thought-provoking quotation, followed by a reflection or short essay based on that quote, and then ends with an "affirmation" where the reader vows to perform some action or make some new commitment. But instead of a well-known quotation from, say, Thomas Jefferson or Martin Luther King, or maybe a verse from a sacred text, all of the quotes in my book come from the mouths of Star Trek's cast of characters.

IFM: *So it* is *a Star Trek book.*

Mark: I'd rather call it a year's worth of personal reflections using the fictional world of Star Trek for its inspiration. Many of the very same lines have no doubt been spoken by other literary characters and historical people. And the same universal wisdom and spiritual insights in my meditations can probably be gleaned from any number of other sources, both secular and religious. Star Trek's sci-fi setting simply offers an extremely rich environment for talking about moral issues and life's most important questions – and about our future as human beings – in a dramatic way that's not clouded by religious or political agendas. Just like the original Star Trek series attempted to do back in The Sixties.

IFM: *So it's kind of a self-help book, then…*

Mark: That's one of the genres where bookstores like Barnes & Noble would stock the early print editions – in their Self-Help section.

IFM: *I'm guessing "Spirituality" was the other…?*

Mark: As well as "Recovery." Hazelden is a major publisher of Twelve-Step books that feature the identical format: Quotation, meditation, affirmation. People in recovery from various addictions, or prison inmates – some of my most loyal readers, actually – or those of us who just want some fresh inspiration and new direction in our lives… all of these readers have found this format especially helpful. It's a good way to start the day, to remember that each new dawn presents us with one more chance to improve ourselves. It's also a good excuse for taking a moment to stop and reflect when some personal problem or temptation comes up, maybe read a meditation or two about a specific topic that might shed some new light, or suggest a possible solution.

IFM: *Speaking of which, your book's new index makes that process a little easier.*

Mark: Actually, you'll find two indices now. The first allows the reader to locate all the meditations inspired by any one of the seventy-plus characters I've quoted in the book. The second, much longer index allows readers to find meditations related to specific topics — Accepting Reality, for instance, or Emotions, Inner Guidance, Pain, or Self-Worth. There are now over a thousand entries here, not only because multiple characters might've had something to say about the same topic, but because the same meditation may speak to more than one issue, or several related issues. And if you've bought the eBook version, it's even easier. Rather than thumbing through physical pages to find a particular meditation, you simply tap on the link and *boom!* – you're there!

IFM: *So, moving on… The second edition of the Manual had a pretty good run back in the 90s, rising to third place on your distributor's best-seller list for several months in a row. Aside from the added convenience of the cross-referenced indices, what's different in the newest edition as compared to the original paperback?*

Mark: Well, you're probably aware the book went through two updates as new Star Trek series came on board. When *Deep Space Nine* and then *Voyager* followed *The Next Generation*, I was forced to take out some of the earlier meditations to make room for new ones. The print editions still featured 366 meditations — including an extra day for leap years — but a few dozen new meditations would replace the same number of previous ones. Captain Kirk, Picard and Spock had the most lines, so their quotations were the ones I often sacrificed so Janeway, Seven of Nine, Captain Archer — and now *Star Trek: Discovery*'s Michael Burnham — could get a word in.

IFM: *But now you've brought back all those previous meditations in the appendix.*

Mark: Almost all. A few just felt repetitive or "dated," frankly. But yes, one of the great things about both the eBook and Print-on-Demand versions is that extra pages don't cost the publisher that much extra! So in addition to the usual 366 daily meditations, there's another year's worth.

IFM: *A year, that is, on the planet "Arroway," which happens to circle its sun—*

Mark: —in seventy-two days, right. I don't want anyone to think they're getting a total of seven-hundred-plus meditations in the new edition! Not that I couldn't find that many quotable lines to use for inspiration. Especially with the three movies and two new TV series released since the last paperback.

IFM: *But you* do *have quite a few new entries from those more recent releases?*

Mark: That's another reason the Manual was due – maybe *over*due – for an update. The "prequel" Kirk and Spock, along with Captain Archer and his crew, the characters of *Star Trek: Discovery*, even a new villain or two, all provide inspiration for over fifty new meditations in the book.

IFM: *And when the next Trek sequal comes out, it'll be that much easier to find a place for the latest characters and their quotations.*

Mark: That's the plan. Which means the "year" on planet Arroway will get that much longer.

IFM: *I guess we'll all just have to wait for your scientific – or maybe spiritual – explanation for how that happens!*

Made in the USA
Middletown, DE
15 December 2021

55934029R00152